THE POWER OF FUTURE MACHINES

Essays on Artificial Intelligence

THE POWER OF FUTURE MACHINES

Essays on Artificial Intelligence

Edited by

Rajiv Malhotra | T.N. Sudarshan | Manogna Sastry

OCCAM | An Imprint of **BluOne Ink**

Published by BluOne Ink LLP
306, Tower-I, Assotech Business Cresterra,
Plot No. 22, Sector 135, Noida, U.P. India
Website: www.bluone.ink
Email: publisher@bluone.ink

Title: *The Power of Future Machines: Essays on Artificial Intelligence*
Editors: Rajiv Malhotra, T.N. Sudarshan and Manogna Sastry

ISBN: 978-93-92209-33-8

First Impression: 2023

Printed in India

OCCAM | An Imprint of **BluOne Ink**

Contents

Preface

One of the themes of research at Infinity Foundation has been the investigation of global phenomena, socio-political mechanisms, structures in polity, media influences, academic theories and modern technologies in contemporary *dharma* contexts, which is driven by understandings of the Universe that the *Vedas* have revealed. Interpreting and using our work, both for self-understanding and for influencing the wider narratives, is best achieved with a grounding in this perspective of global dharma.

My recent book, *Artificial Intelligence and the Future of Power: 5 Battlegrounds*, examined the basic assumptions driving today's march of Artificial Intelligence (AI) in multiple contexts, or 'battlegrounds'. The themes in the book can also be understood as a future-aware analysis of the evolution and transformation of power structures driven by the consolidation of AI in the mainstream. The deeper aspects of the materialist and hedonistic trajectory of modern AI, as is being conceptualized within the overarching rubric of Western Universalism, is also addressed from the perspective of its effects on humanity at large.

At Infinity Foundation, the perspectives emanating from AI influence almost all our research and content output. Our most recent book, *Snakes in the Ganga: Breaking India 2.0* is in many ways, an AI-aware analysis and presents an updated discursive narrative of the *Breaking India* phenomenon in its contemporary avatars. Much needs to be analyzed, articulated, and communicated to our wider audience: the ramifications of AI especially from dharma and *sanatana* perspectives. The traditional knowledge keepers of sanatana and the wider dharma-aware audience need to be provided with a critical analysis of the fundamental threats as well as positive influences to dharma that mainstream AI's conceptions and implementations can potentially cause. As part of our larger commitment to creating, curating, and communicating these perspectives, this selection of solicited essays by authors from varied backgrounds examines a wide range of topics that my book has initiated.

Western Universalism is the overarching threat as recently exemplified by the encoding of the dominant narratives of Western Indology and anti-Hindu bias into ChatGPT's (an AI-based chatbot) knowledge base, thereby amplifying centuries of bias in modern formats and contexts. For example, queries and discussions on Ayurveda and Yoga continue to portray these as 'myths' or as 'Hindu faith artifacts', never as a 'truth' or as a 'logical science'. Funding of Indian institutions like the Indian Institutes of Technology by Google *Devata,* Microsoft *Devata*, Facebook *Devata* and others are, in our view, aiming to sabotage dharma-driven responses from grounded Indian technologists. The secular branding of technology conceals the larger overall biases and data collection 'needs' (diversity of learning samples) of BigTech, especially in an Indian context. The goal of this anthology is to encourage serious *manthan* or churning on the ramifications of Artificial Intelligence, driven by a basis in dharma. Infinity Foundation is planning conferences and research-driven curated content in the form of videos, discussions, and books to amplify these perspectives.

We hope that this collection of essays provides our audience with some serious thought-provoking analyses and perspectives.

Rajiv Malhotra
Princeton, USA
January 2023

To the Reader

This anthology of essays by experts explores the future impact of Artificial Intelligence in various fields of human endeavor. Building upon the dialectical and analytical framework provided in the book *Artificial Intelligence and the Future of Power,* experts from various fields (military, geopolitics, strategic affairs, physics, policy and others) engage and describe for a wider audience the potential impact of AI. Given their specific vantage points and deriving from their areas of expertise, this anthology makes for a fascinating read. The essays discuss how AI will affect policy-making, both in narrow areas of expertise as well as its effect on humanity at large. Aimed at policy makers, experts and also for a broader audience, these varied perspectives on AI, add something vital to the current skewed AI discourse.

The book puts to print discussions of Rajiv Malhotra on the battlegrounds as outlined in his book, as also his discussion with the Indian military. Velina Tchakarova provides a balanced geo-political analysis of what she calls the Fourth Industrial Revolution. Ruchir Sharma provides an impactful analysis of the potential trajectories of Imperialism and Colonialism given the mainstreaming of AI. Lt. Gen. P.J.S. Pannu provides a detailed analysis of the ramifications of AI and the military theater in the larger context of national security.

Ishwara Bhat A. gives an under-the-hood analysis of data bias and its implications to the very notion of freedom of speech, especially so, in the era of bot-driven monitoring of conversations, and automated content validation and verification. Mrittunjoy Majumdar takes a broad look at how the 'doing' of physics is getting affected by AI, and its ramifications to the process of discovery in science, as is currently understood. Ravi Khanna provides a kaleidoscopic perspective on the goals and implications of AI, grounded in the consciousness perspectives that the Vedas provide. Subhodeep Mukhopadhyay and Divya Reddy round out this compilation by focussing on the deeper problem of Western Universalism (especially the amplification that AI is providing) and its ever present influence, as something that we need to be conscious of at every step, while being actively engaged in the larger inter-civilizational discourse.

Since the authors and readers are from diverse backgrounds, we have retained elements which indicate the authors' preferences and have not used diacritical marks in this anthology.

Editors
Infinity Foundation
January 2023

ONE

Analyzing the Battlegrounds of Artificial Intelligence: Conversations with Rajiv Malhotra

Editorial Note: The following conversations are curated from interviews and discussions following the release of the book[1] *Artificial Intelligence and the Future of Power: 5 Battlegrounds*[2] by Rajiv Malhotra. The book argues that this Artificial Intelligence-driven revolution will have an unequal impact on different segments of humanity. There will be new winners and losers, new haves and have-nots, resulting in an unprecedented concentration of wealth and power. After analyzing society's vulnerabilities to the impending tsunami, the book raises troubling questions that provoke immediate debate: Is the world headed toward digital colonization by the United States of America and China? Will depopulation become eventually unavoidable? *Artificial Intelligence and the Future of Power* is a wakeup call to action, compelling public intellectuals to be better informed and more engaged. It educates the social segments most at risk and wants them to demand a seat at the table where policies on AI are being formulated. The five battlegrounds the book discusses are

1. economy, industry, education and jobs;
2. geopolitics and military – US, China and India;

1. The YouTube playlist of all the interviews and discussions around the book are available here: https://www.youtube.com/playlist?list=PLGQElwzyJxtzVSAEKt-3PIrEgU_kYKSEo

2. The book's webpage is https://www.aiandpower.com/

3. moronization of the masses – bowing down to the digital deities;
4. loss of selfhood to artificial emotions and gratifications; and
5. stress-testing the Indian *rashtra* (state).

Participants: Madhu Kishwar, Usha Chaudhary, Prachi Mishra[3]

Battleground India

Madhu Kishwar (MK): *Is Artificial Intelligence primarily an instrument of surveillance, a very intrusive instrument of surveillance, and how is it going to impact Indian society?*

Rajiv Malhotra (RM): Surveillance is one of the various uses of Artificial Intelligence because when you do surveillance with a lot of sensors, you have what is called Big Data. You are gathering Big Data from which you can understand people's behavior; you can model their behavior like a psychologist. The more the psychologist knows about you, the more he can understand your behavior, and the more he can predict what your behavior will be like under different circumstances. So, this is watching your behavior, watching what messages you send, what kind of pictures you post, where you are traveling, who your friends are, what you are buying, where you click, where you don't click. Every single click on social media platforms enhances the machine learning knowledge about you. You are leaving footprints and signatures every single time. If somebody is listening to this, he will know at what points in time you nod, when you approve something, when you don't approve, what happens to the tone and inflection of your voice. The AI system is able to very minutely do surveillance, capturing information about you.

---

3. **Madhu Kishwar** is founder of the critically acclaimed journal *Manushi*. She was a professor and a senior fellow at the Centre for the Study of Developing Societies (CSDS), until retiring in 2016. She is currently chaired as professor in the Indian Council of Social Science Research. She has been awarded the Chameli Devi Jain Award for Outstanding Women Mediaperson in 1985.

 Usha Chaudhary is presently chief operations officer at *Internews*. Usha has extensive multi-disciplinary experience in the public, private, and not-for-profit sectors. She is the former senior vice president, corporate operations and chief transformation officer at MITRE. Previously, she was the president and chief operating officer of Kettler, a leading national real estate developer. She has also held executive positions at The Pew Charitable Trusts, *The Washington Post*, United Way of America, and Freddie Mac.

 Prachi Mishra is a Young Leaders in Tech Policy Fellow at the University of Chicago, presently working at CSST for their quantum meta-ethics project.

MK: *Is the Indian defense establishment aware of this challenge? Are they doing anything to meet up to it?*

RM: I have been talking a lot to the defense people and the answer is Yes, but it's too little and too late. There are some fundamental technologies that India doesn't have. China has a ten-year lead or some huge lead on quantum computing, semiconductors, avionics and so on. It is the world's largest producer of robotics and drones. They placed some good bets. They placed some good bets long ago. We are into *jugaad*, short term. And right now, we have a lot of talk, not as much action. The AI policy is coming just now. It's being discussed and debated. And I must say, I am very disappointed with NITI Aayog, (National Institution for Transforming India, the Government of India's public policy think tank). NITI Aayog should have done this long ago. But even now, they are relying a lot on secondary sources. Often the AI strategy is quoting McKinsey or some foreign (corporation), its impact on AI and so on. Actually, Indian society is very different. A bottom-up study of Indian society needs to be done in order to figure out what will be the right, the optimum way of using AI in India. So, I think, in a sense the answer is, Yes, the Indian military is aware of it. And the Indian military is very keen to do the best we can to catch up. Having said that, catching up will not be easy. (It) will not be easy because the resources needed are huge. India has lost this race, at least the first segment of the race. And now the question is: Can India catch up?

MK: *But you also link it to your thesis in this book that AI is going to be Breaking India 2.0. How does it link with the earlier Breaking India forces?*

RM: For my previous book (published a decade ago—*Breaking India: Western Interventions in Dravidian and Dalit Fault Lines)* I went into many organizations, the foreign nexuses. Some of it I was able to access myself, for some I hired people to go in because they wouldn't let me in. This kind of ability to go in, spend a few years understanding what they are up to. What are they funding in India, what is their game plan? I was able to do that and hence my book was providing evidence-based theory ahead of its time. And then for the last ten years everybody is sort of copying that idea and giving new examples. But the basic framework was there. Same way (for) my book on Artificial Intelligence.

Over the last few years, I have gone into organizations which are very deeply involved in using Artificial Intelligence to undermine India socially.

Socially, (and) politically. So, the Breaking India forces will become Breaking India 2.0. Because they'll be able to use all these technologies to create chaos in India, to create political upheaval, to create violence, to create riots. Now, when there was an anti-Citizenship (Amendment) Act, 2019 and anti-Article 370 (giving special status to Jammu & Kashmir) riots in Delhi, a lot of people started talking about, you know, that the American billionaire George Soros is (behind) it. Okay? But these are superficial views. Some of the things I haven't even put in the (current) book because I am writing a sequel. Also, I want people to understand what I have written in this book and then I'll go further.

To tell you a little bit, there are certain nexuses. There is a whole thing called Artificial Intelligence and Christianity. They are talking about the future of evangelism, the future of missionaries. There is Artificial Intelligence the Global Left has adopted for what they call social justice. This whole idea of social justice is being put into these algorithms. So, your algorithm will be tagged, and ranked, based on whether it promotes their idea of social justice. My post will be tagged, and if you are complying with them more, they'll morph you, they'll morph your thinking, modulate your thinking, the way you say something, what you should say, what you should not say, in order to become more popular on social media. This is social media moronizing the people, brainwashing them, taking over their agency, as a way of furthering their idea of social justice. But this social justice is not some Vedic idea of social justice, nor is it a *dharmic* idea of social justice. It's a Left idea of social justice. The social justice movement has now been turbocharged with a force multiplier called Artificial Intelligence. Artificial Intelligence is a huge weapon. They have a big lead on this. I won't disclose names, but I'll tell you about some well-known international wealthy guys, George Soros being only one of them. I mention his name, as they have invested in India. They have got ventures in India. One of them has more than ten start-ups with very benign names, some of them are tech start-ups, some of them are human rights start-ups, some of them are…in fact, called AI ethics.

There are a lot of AI ethics and AI watchdogs in the United States that are actually funded by companies like Google. They are funding organizations to be the watchdogs. Imagine that! There is something called responsible AI, open AI, AI for democracy, AI for minorities. But when you look into the details, a lot of the people behind the scene supporting it are the Facebook, Google, Microsoft, kinds of people because they want to be self-regulating. They want to know what the opponents will think. A guy like me who is completely independent of them is bad news for them. I am seen as a whistleblower because I know the technology. I don't care about getting anything out of them and I'm going to talk about what they are up to.

Recently there was a scandal when Google hired a woman, minority woman, very brilliant, on AI and bias. Because there is a whole movement saying that AI is biased because it's biased against Blacks, it's biased against the Lesbian, Gay, Bisexual, Transgender, and Queer+ (LGBTQ+) community. Because the kind of data and examples you use to train the machine are biased examples. If you look at crime, and you look at facial recognition and what not, then a huge number of Blacks will show up as criminals. A Black face is correlated to that of being a criminal. Artificial Intelligence has this bias. And when people are being screened for jobs, they are screening résumés and so on. Artificial Intelligence is screening for jobs, and is kind of biased against certain groups. There is a whole movement now. Thanks to the Blacks and feminists and so on. They have started these movements called AI and bias. And there is, of course, no Hindu voice. I am the only person who is talking right there, in these forums. Artificial Intelligence and bias became such an important thing that Facebook and Google hired a head of AI and bias. All these companies hired somebody to show that they are concerned about AI and bias. And this woman's job in Google was to look at the company's policies and behavior and keep flagging if there was bias. It sounded like a very nice thing. But, you know, she was fired. They got rid of her because she wrote an article pointing out, and she thought this is her job, that some of Google's practices are actually very biased. And so, she got fired. This is happening in the United States.

There is a big battleground going on. India knows nothing about it. Indian people don't want to know about it. They invite me to talk about some Hinduphobia and some old Breaking India topics. When I say I want to talk about Artificial Intelligence, they suddenly become silent. People ask, why do you want to talk about Artificial Intelligence? That's something esoteric, maybe it's science fiction. We don't even know. Our people are so dumb and so ignorant. I'll tell you, this is the whole literature, all these celebrities with their YouTube channels and Twitter handles and they are doing their *manthan* (churning) and Jaipur literary festival and all kinds of literary festivals. They have no clue about AI, a huge AI movement is happening. And that's why India's in trouble.

MK: *Forget social science guys being* buddhus (fools), *Rajiv, what it tells me, the big warning is that even our existing intelligence agencies that are supposed to gather intelligence by actually moving among people, having sources, even they do such a bad job. They've never been able to project where the wind is blowing. Whether it's Shaheen Bagh* (a protest led mainly by Muslim women against the Citizenship [Amendment] Act, 2019) *or the farmer's protests, you can see how ham-handed the government has been in handling these, say, propped up agitations. And on the other side, the agitationists are obviously using what you described. They seem to have access to AI models of mind manipulation.*

RM: Yes, so, I will tell you one thing. Suppose, magically, the owners and top people in Twitter and Facebook and so on were to say we are going to support the Hindu cause anytime we see all this whispering, this chatter, all this conspiracy, and mobilization coming together, meetings are going to happen, rallies are going to happen. We have the brains, the intelligence, and the surveillance to anticipate what's going to happen. We are actually going to shut it down. We are actually going to advice the Indian police or Indian authorities. If they wanted to, they could do that. And, of course, this is part of the negotiation. India is always looking for surveillance data and then, in exchange, India gives them the right to operate. When India says, we will shut you down unless you do this, they will say, okay, we won't interfere with (Prime Minister) Modi. Give us fifty or one hundred or two hundred handles and those will be given total freedom. We will not interfere with them, but in exchange we want some freedom to operate in your country. Now, they're very smart people. They are like the East India Company (EIC).

I'll tell you what has happened. China has pretty much colonized Pakistan already. China has got a few lakh, a few lakh surveillance cameras connected with facial recognition and image recognition. All this Big Data is Chinese property, (on) Chinese servers. They are keeping track of what this general is doing, is he having an affair, whom he is meeting, what this terrorist is doing, who is he meeting, where is he going… so, all this surveillance that previously the Intelligence Bureau would do or Research & Analysis Wing would do for India and similarly the Inter-Services Intelligence would do for Pakistan, is all being done through AI because this technology is so much more powerful. The people who own it are the Chinese in the case of Pakistan, and in the case of India it is the American private companies.

China has also pretty much colonized Africa. They have a deal with some countries in Africa. I have seen those contracts, the agreements, where they guard. The pretext is that we are giving you surveillance for national security. We will protect you. You are the king or you are the dictator and we will protect you. We will tell you by keeping track of who is doing what and keep you protected. But in the process, they are also able to blackmail their own client. It's like the East India Company protecting raja A, and making sure that raja B and C don't harm him. But in the process of protecting raja B their spies are also giving them information on how to compromise raja A. So, while he is a client today, tomorrow if he turns against you and you need to blackmail him, you have all the data. Therefore, the ability of foreign surveillance, foreign Big Data companies and AI companies to blackmail India is huge and to blackmail Pakistan is huge. So, we are heading towards recolonization.

MK: *But in India even the top half is not productive. I'm sorry. They are a liability and causing the so-called bottom half to sink deeper than ever before. So, I don't think in India the problem is of the bottom half. The bottom half will somehow still escape through because they are at least hard working, some of them. But the top half is parasitic.*

RM: That is correct, but AI brings an interesting problem. If we don't have enough AI, we have a problem. If we have too much AI, we have a problem. Let me explain. If we don't have enough Artificial Intelligence, China will eat our lunch. China, Pakistan will finish us off. We will not be competitive in weaponry. We will not be competitive in intellectual warfare, psychological warfare. All the things we talked about in the previous section, the Breaking India 2.0 forces, will get the better of us. On the one hand, we need a lot of Artificial Intelligence. We need it to be on par with the rest of the world. If they have cannons, we need to have cannons. That's the case for having a lot of AI. We need to catch up and I agree with that.

But then, (on the other hand), if we have a lot of AI, we also create obsolescence of jobs. A lot of things that require human beings to do. In the United States, Amazon has taken over small shops. People who used to work in retail shops are now working in Amazon warehouses; packing things or driving Amazon trucks, delivery trucks. I have some people who work for Amazon in AI and robotics and they tell me that there is huge investment to automate the warehouse so you don't need people there. So, the people who were in retailing are out of work and a subset of them get jobs in warehouses. Now, the jobs in warehouses will be done by robots. Similarly, Amazon is already experimenting with a delivery system where the delivery will be through drones and through various other means that you won't need human drivers. There will be driverless cars, driverless trucks.

What is happening with the advent of AI is that it is creating an economy of not only haves and have nots but less need for labor. The people who respond to this say that well, you know, we'll create service jobs. There will be more people providing massage services and more who would be emotional companions and so on. That is fine. But that's more like turning human beings into pets. You have these people and you need to feed them, so let's have them do some (work), let's have these soft skills then we can justify giving them some work. This may last for a while. But in the long run, the effect of tremendous amount of scale of efficiency is going to disempower human labor. You won't even need so much labor.

MK: *But see, we expected the same from computers. And that's why unions everywhere, especially in India in the bank sector, for example, went on strike after strike opposing computerization. Right? The fact is that computers have not taken away jobs. They created many more new jobs. We all thought that by the coming of Amazon and Flipkart and all these malls, the neighborhood* kirana (grocery) *store would just vanish. That hasn't happened. In fact, they are doing better business than ever before. The local markets are still flooded with customers. It's not as if they have become deserted. At least not in India. Go to Chandni Chowk, go to Karol Bagh* (local markets in Delhi). *Even during the pandemic* (COVID-19), *the moment restrictions were freed somewhat, there were stampedes in the markets. It's not as if people were just happy purchasing everything online.*

RM: Some of these trends are delayed coming to India. You have raised this issue, so let me give you a concrete example of the impact of automation. Let's take the automobile industry, which employs around four million, five million people in India. India is not only making cars but making auto parts which are exported. India is one of the largest exporters of automobile parts. All the big auto manufacturers, GM, Chrysler, all the European ones, Japanese ones, they buy parts from India. It employs a large number of people. Now the automobile is going to be replaced with electric cars. Electric cars are not industrial. You don't need an engine; it runs on battery. The spark plug, you don't need. The carburetor, you don't need. Some little knob here, some little screw there. A car engine has a lot of parts, little parts and many small scale, and medium scale people are manufacturing these parts. As the world shifts to electric vehicles, India will also shift to electric vehicles. Of course, companies like Mahindra will make money because they will be in the electric vehicle business. But all these small ancillary *walas* (ones) will be out of work. I have even talked to the automobile people to see if they want to address it. They are afraid to deal with this issue. They are hiding from this issue. What will happen to the few million workers that are involved in the automobile sector when the industry shifts to electric cars?

Let me explain what the electric car is. The engine of the electric car is a lithium-ion battery. China has fifty percent of the world's supply of lithium. And China made this bet long ago, like one of its many bets, that this is the future. They started investing in Research & Development (R&D). They own most of the patents, most of the technology for making this battery. The battery has to become more and more efficient, weigh less and less, and have a charge for lasting more and more miles. That is the race: to make the battery better and better. India will be dismantling an industry which is one hundred percent indigenized. Nobody needs to import (the knowledge) how to build a carburetor or a spark plug or any of that. Indians know how to do that because this technology is very old. Yes, of course, it's polluting and there is an argument of replacing this car with an electric car. That's a good argument.

What I am trying to tell you is the side effect which hasn't been considered. The side effect is that we are dismantling an old technology, and employs hundreds (millions) of people. We are replacing it with a new technology which is going to be made in China. In effect, you're going to dismantle jobs in India and create them in China. And China will make money two ways. First, it will give you the raw materials to lithium because they have fifty percent of the world market. Second, you have to buy it under license from them. I know (a) lot of people are saying we are manufacturing lithium batteries in India. But (the truth is) we are manufacturing with Chinese technology. In five years, in two years, this technology will be obsolete. You may say, under the terms we owe them royalty for a little while then it's ours. But the point is that this technology is galloping. The rate at which lithium technology is advancing has a lot to do with the use of AI. The faster it can advance, the more rapidly, the better it gets at replacing the internal combustion engine.

The example I'm giving you is that as technologies are replaced by newer technologies, it is not necessarily the case that those new technologies are indigenous to India. The new technologies may be from foreign sources. Even where computerization is concerned, it took several years for India to indigenize computers because in the beginning all computers were foreign. Even now, the heart of the computer which is silicon, the semiconductor, the processor, is imported. India does not have any worthwhile semiconductor industry. While we say, these are Made in India computers, they are assembled in India, the body is Indian, the keyboard and so on are made in India, the actual electronic engine, the semiconductor is largely imported. We have become dependent on this. Industry makes money by improving its efficiency. And if you are capital intensive ... let's talk about the economics here. This is a matter of fact. I have documented the source in my book. For every ten percent increase in Gross Domestic Product (GDP) of India, however long it takes over many years, results in only one percent increase in employment. What this growth in GDP is doing is, it is top-heavy. It is Foreign Direct Investment (FDI), people are championing FDI. Foreign Direct Investment doesn't help the small industry, the small, street vendor; it goes to the sensex people, the big corporations, they get the FDI, they get the GDP growth and that does not necessarily help everyone.

MK: *But, Rajiv, India has gone through many crashes of civilization. Would you not agree? Invasions, the Islamic invasions. Then British colonization, all these phases lasted one thousand years, won't you say this will be yet one more?*

RM: India is shrinking. It has lost territory. It has lost, at least the *bharatiya* (Indian) share, the *bharatiya* civilization has shrunk. Maybe at one time you would have Central Asia and Tibet and all the way down to Sri Lanka, and from Afghanistan all the way to Bali. The combination of external Pakistan, China with all this technology, wants to grab land and grab rivers, and Pakistan wants to do all the things they've always wanted to against India. This alliance is a very solid alliance. China has thought this out long and hard. Pakistan has mortgaged its future financially. It has no choice and is now in debt to China.

The Chinese don't understand South Asia culturally—people from India, Pakistan, Bangladesh, Sri Lanka. And they are not comfortable bossing over them in a direct man-to-man contact. So, they'll outsource that part to the Pakistanis. The Pakistanis have sold the idea to the Chinese that they know how to look after the Indians, how to manage them, how to be their boss. After all, the Mughals did it. And they can return to that era and be like the return of the Mughals, in a sense. They are looking for China to give them the hard power and Pakistan can do the dirty work, boots on the ground. This is a very serious issue India faces and AI exacerbates it, along with Breaking India forces on the internal side. Pakistan and China are the external threat. The two in combination, I don't think India can survive.

MK: *That's right. That's another phrase you use. You are stress-testing India. What does that mean?*

RM: When you visit a doctor, a stress test determines your tolerance limits; how much work you can do before the heart cannot do any further. These parameters, this data helps the doctor figure out where you need to improve, the diet you need, how much exercise is safe, not safe. The stress test gives you the parameters of the system. We need to stress test India like a system and say, what happens if AI hits at this time, in this way, these applications, these technologies, a scenario where China does this, a scenario where China does that, or a scenario under Breaking India forces.

I am working out these likely scenarios as to what are the plausible and likely things AI could trigger and the effect on India. I have divided my stress test into three levels: *sthula shareer, sukshma shareer,* and *karan shareer.* The impact of AI on each of these... the relationship of AI on each of these, one can look at. This is the physical body. The impact on the economy, the impact on jobs, the impact on inequalities, and haves and have nots. Maybe certain regions like Bengaluru will do very well. New industries will be created and they will thrive. But maybe the old industries and labor force in Bihar and Uttar Pradesh or some other places will not do so well. Maybe some industrial economy will do very well and the people dependent on farms will be worse off. That needs to be sorted; that's at the level of *sthula shareer.* The military is also an issue at the *sthula shareer* level.

The *sukshma shareer* is the mental thing we were talking about. The loss of agency, becoming colonized mentally, becoming more dependent on AI and digital media with somebody else at the controls. Somebody else decides am I a winner or a loser, who is more popular, all of this is in external hands and we are loving these *devatas*, these foreign *devatas.* That stress test shows that at the *sukshma shareer* level we are highly vulnerable. We are not very autonomous. We do not have our own sovereignty. We did not develop these platforms.

When Jio sold out so much to these foreign (companies), there were no safeguards in place. They didn't want to take my article which forms a section of my book titled *India is for Sale.* Another one is titled *Return of the East India Company.* At the very least, they could have allowed my discussion, my point so maybe they could have included something in their negotiation. But they are not interested. So, the *sukshma shareer* of India is vulnerable. Right from the top to the bottom because I don't see leadership. I don't see the leadership understanding these things; they represent, their mind represents the *sukshma shareer* of India. The average person is becoming moronized. That is the *sukshma shareer.*

As far as the *karan shareer* is concerned, that has to do with our character. Karmically, are we really fit, are we opportunistic, are we given in to corruption, are we too much into me, mine? I see a problem there too. My stress test on India shows that during this decade, India is quite vulnerable. And I am not talking about fifty years from now. I am not saying, oh, in the next century something could happen. I am saying before 2030, cracks in India's sovereignty will become undeniable.

MK: *One of the recent policies that seriously harmed India and I think you were referring to (is) the Jio sale. Right?*

RM: That's one example. That's a good example. Another one is that several years ago I exposed the fact that Harvard and several other universities are doing surveillance on the Kumbh Mela. I wrote a book; I wrote lot of articles. I went on YouTube. They (Harvard) had a project called *Mapping the Kumbh Mela* which is actually surveillance and gathering Big Data. They are plotting, where do these hundred million people come from, which villages, what *jati*, what caste, what's the power structure, what's the religion. They are mapping all this data when they interview these people along with facial recognition and figuring out stuff at the village and district level. What is the social, political demographics, who is at war with whom. They want to come up with human rights cases based on this. Maybe there is exploitation going on. Or maybe in this Kumbh Mela males have more…

MK: *What do you have to say about the young people doing cutting-edge research in AI? Whether in American universities or even in Indian Institutes of Technology (IITs) in India. How do you rate them? Are they anywhere?*

RM: There are two kinds. That's a very good question. Indians are among the cutting-edge of AI brains in the world. That is, a certain percentage of AI people in the world are brilliant people, but they are working either in the United States or Europe. And they are doing Make in America, not Make in India. The Intellectual Property they produce is not Indian. It belongs to somebody else. The ones in India doing cutting-edge work are working for Microsoft India, Google India, Facebook India. While in India they are working for westerners. They are AI coolies. The large majority are not doing this kind of cutting-edge work. The large majority of Indians learning data sciences and machine learning are going to do coolie work, which will be temporary work. Just like outsourcing and call centers.

Artificial Intelligence needs the next five to ten years to scale; it needs a lot of coolie work, which will then be dismantled and folded. Just like call centers. Many of them have. During this transition phase, you need humans to train machines. For instance, on a conveyer belt in Amazon, some packets are moving and there are pictures. Now you have to train the camera (to check movement), when the packet is upright, when it has fallen. A human being will tag that this picture is correct, the package was correct or here it has fallen. In other words, what the human is doing is called tagging, labeling. This is labor intensive, the human brain labels images so that the machine can indicate, this is the image of one kind of an item, this is (the) image of another kind of item. That kind of thing. It's like if you wanted to take all the academic people in India and have their image recognition. Then somebody would have to manually, human beings would be needed to say, okay, this is Madhu Kishwar. This one is Madhu Kishwar. This one is so and so. You have to tag them and then the machines can take over and you don't need human beings anymore because machines can do all this recognition. We are at this stage. Artificial Intelligence in Western countries needs human beings to do labeling and tagging. That is the kind of work being exported to India and we think we have trained a lot of AI people. But they are doing rudimentary, low-level coolie work. This is not going to produce technology.

MK: *Is Make in India at all addressing AI?*

RM: A few venture capital people are in it. I congratulate them. But, very little, very late. Too little, too late. The total size of the Indian venture capital is a tiny portion of US, China, Europe and so on. It's not like we're going to produce a huge amount, but we will produce something. It's better than before.

A large amount of the venture capital money and ownership comes from venture capitalists. What is happening is even when an Indian launches a start-up, his dream is for someone to buy him out and if it is worth a few hundred thousand dollars, he'll sell out to this American venture capitalist, or Google will buy him out. What is happening is, we are making some people very rich as individuals; the Intellectual Property does not belong to the country. It belongs to somebody elsewhere.

Make in India is manufacturing, but not R&D. There is a difference. The viewers should understand the difference between R&D and manufacturing. Manufacturing you can do, but you are getting imported knowhow and you are always dependent on them. And, when the world standard goes to the next generation, you have to go back, beg your way and get some more knowhow. So, we are not investing in R&D. The corporate people are not investing in R&D. The Defence Research and Development Organisation (DRDO) is investing in R&D, but not enough. The academic people are more into politics. In the United States when you are graduate students or you are working for professors who have research grants, they make you do research; here it is just teaching and not research. Besides teaching, it's politics. So, we are not a research-oriented society. When we say we are knowledge-oriented, this knowledge of the past five thousand years ago, *usne ye kiya tha, wahan par wo viman tha, ye tha, wo tha,* (he did this, he did that) is not what it takes. You have to keep up with the times.

Prachi Mishra (PM): *There is a general question I want to ask. Since its advent, AI has been seen as the savior which will rescue people, societies, governments, economies out of all their miseries. But in your book, you have provided a contrary view. Could you please share your thoughts on why, if AI is adopted in the present state of India, it will bring more problems than benefits?*

RM: Well, I am not saying it will bring more problems necessarily, but it will disrupt society. I want to say that whenever there is an equilibrium, many forces are balanced. There is a dynamic equilibrium. Something new comes, (a new technology) it disrupts the equilibrium. Because some people will use it better than others. Some have more access to it than others. It may create some jobs for some, lose jobs for others. So, the disruption of Indian society or any country's society is going to happen. It's not a case that everything goes on hunky-dory like before and problems get solved, but there is no disruption. That's not the case.

The foundations of Indian society, politics, economics, education, industry, defense, all of these will be disrupted by AI. It may be that good stuff will happen, and it may be some not-so-good stuff will happen. But to deal with the disruption is a challenge. You have to understand it. It's the new game. It's like the old game of chess has been replaced with a new game. Now you need to learn thre new rules. That's the wake-up call. Our leaders and all sections of society have to be re-educated. This is the new game and we have to learn how to play it.

Usha Chaudhary (UC): *Let's turn to battleground five. You brought up India several times in the context of some other battleground discussions we were just having. You mentioned that you have put in battleground five using India as a case study. In describing the threats that India is facing, I believe you mentioned the metaphor of the Titanic hitting the iceberg. Would you mind elaborating that for our viewers?*

RM: I don't want people to get scared and really start hitting at me because this metaphor is powerful and it's meant to shake you up. The Titanic, over one hundred years ago, was considered to be the greatest ship, so solid that nothing could happen to it. And then, it sank on its maiden voyage from England to the US, hitting an iceberg. An iceberg is something where only a small part of it is visible above the surface, most of it is beneath the water. What is above the surface maybe some miles away, but actually beneath the surface is a huge mountain and you can hit it.

The only way you know if you are reaching an iceberg is radar, underground sonar. The Titanic was equipped with a sonar, but it hit the iceberg. From the time it hit the iceberg, it took two hours and forty minutes to sink. The metaphor is, if AI is the iceberg, which means we are only seeing a part of it, we don't have that sonar. I am the sonar. I am trying to wake them up. I am saying, hey, captain, please wake up. I am detecting. This is going on and you are going to hit it. The actual Titanic, there are theories about what was going on. Either the captain was sleeping, which means the captains of India are sleeping or the captain was drunk, he was dancing on the deck, there was a party going on or the captain had turned off his radar. Whatever the reasons, there is a controversy over it, but the fact is that the captains of the ship did not take action to watch out and do something about it.

If India is a Titanic, then India is just moving ahead. The question is, have you already hit the iceberg? In which case, nothing can be done. Or, are we about to hit the iceberg, in which case if the captains were to wake up, something can be done. I believe it's the latter. I believe it's my job to really shake them up and that's why the book is a tough read. It's not a nice, we are this great civilization and we are doing well, goody-goody type of book. It's a tough book. We don't have much time left.

Now, it's very interesting, when the Titanic hit and in two hours forty minutes it sank, there were lifeboats. Some people did jump and save themselves, but a large number were dancing on the deck and a band was playing. When the ship sank, the band sank and the dancers also sank. There is a controversy: were the band players heroic because, you know, they sacrificed their lives? Well if they sacrificed their lives, it didn't help anybody. Or were they fools, were they ignorant, were they self-deluded? India is a Titanic, and its people are busy rejoicing. We have cricket matches. We are winning this/that trophy. This Bollywood thing happened. There is a latest scandal. Somebody got an FIR. Somebody got bail or did not get bail. Or in this state we won this election and we overthrew that (party), or consortium of companies. India is enjoying the *tamasha*. They are enjoying this great pop culture. They are doing very well on social media. They think their time has come. They have got rid of mainstream media and now they think they own social media, which they don't. It's the social media that owns them. This is life on the deck. We are a great nation, we are going so ahead, we are becoming *vishwa guru* (teacher to the world) and all that.

(What) I am saying is actually another model; that India is a Titanic. Its captains are sleeping as far as AI is concerned. Maybe they've just woken up this year, which is good. And the people on the deck are playing the band and enjoying life. This is a very negative, dramatic dramatization of what can go wrong with India. And the purpose of saying this…the publisher said, don't say this and I said, I have to say it. All the people who read this book said, this is very powerful. You have to say it. I am prepared to discuss whether it's a valid analogy.

My motive is, I am a lover of India. I have put all my life into India. I don't want India to hit this iceberg. I want India to be okay and I'll do whatever it takes. Right now, my job is to go find where the captains are, shake them up and say, wake up guys. Time to stop this party and do something about what is going on. So, there is a sense of urgency in the metaphor of the Titanic. There is a sense of danger. But there is also the chance that we will be saved, and we will enjoy the ride. Then we will truly be the vishwa guru. That is what I want to achieve.

PM: *If India brings out an AI law in the future, say, two, three, or five years from now, will that mean that the state gets supreme power over people's personal data?*

RM: No, I don't think that's a good idea. I don't think that the Indian government having supreme ownership of people's personal data, the way China has, is a good idea. I have better proposals than that and I am prepared to get into serious discussions on that. These are elaborate topics that will take time to explain. But I don't think that the way to protect your data is to make it nationalized data. Nationalization of data would be a bad idea.

I am also not happy with non-personal or non-private data belonging to a community. What will happen is, let's say there is a terrorist group and they are a community, and they are of a certain caste or something. They will say, it's nobody's business to understand us, to pry into our lives. All that we're doing is our private data. So, the data privacy belonging to a collective entity can backfire because it could ruin (endanger) national security. It could also encourage communities to become a little cocoon and separatist. Data owned collectively by a community, a *jati* which has a separatist tendency could actually be dangerous.

The issues are more complex than just private data and non-private data. And non-private data can be claimed by some community. I think the issues are far, far more complex. And I really wish well. The people who are doing it, they are smart people, but a lot of work has to be done. I do not think that the laws, as they presently exist, are sufficient.

PM: *Given all of this, given that we are already partially enslaved by AI, what is your message for the youth of India specifically?*

RM: The youth of India should become psychologically strong. My problem is that they are too weak. They don't want to know the truth, the facts, if it is uncomfortable. They want to just feel good and go into escapism. So many people say to me, Rajiv sir, why are you spoiling my 'feel good'. The crisis we face as humanity, not just India but as humanity, is multifaceted. We have so many other problems. Artificial Intelligence is actually helping solve some of those problems while also helping make some of those problems worse.

Artificial Intelligence is a mind amplifier. Like (a) car amplifies the physical body. Like a machine amplifies the physical body and so, whatever you could do, now with that machine, you can do better. Similarly, AI amplifies the mind. It gives you more memory, it gives you more capability. You can track much more; you can figure out more algorithms. Artificial Intelligence can be used by a good mind for good things and used by a bad mind to do bad things. This is true. And so, the balance between good and bad people is going to be disrupted because here comes a weapon, somebody will know how to use it, somebody will not know how to use it.

Each time we have a new device, the equilibrium between opposing forces gets disrupted because they do not have equal use. Some people have more use, some people have less. I want the youth of India to become very knowledgeable, not only for the technical job of writing programs in AI and doing low level work which a lot of people are doing, but become very conscious of the social implications. What are the social implications? How does it affect your culture? How does it affect the politics? How does it affect conflicts? Will somebody else be deciding that I am going to fight with you because they will put in a message that will make me angry at you, make me suspicious about you? Who is going to do the divide and rule of the future like the British did divide and rule between the rajas to fight each other?

The young people of India are very smart, but they are sleeping. They need to wake up. And they need to become more aware of all this, take charge. And I would love to have more people like you who want to be interns. I would love to have regular Zoom hangouts, Google hangouts. Once COVID-19 is gone and we are vaccinated, I would love to come to India and have hundreds of gatherings. I want to do all that for the youth of India. My book is dedicated to young scientists and technocrats. Because they are the future. This is your future. It is not my future because I'll be gone. Nothing's going to affect me. But it is your future. And therefore, you have to take control of that future.

Battleground Agency: Moronization

MK: *Rajiv, in this book you talked about the moronization of the masses. Coming on top of Macaulayization of Indian youth through the formal* *education system. What we are producing, as you well know even better than me, is unemployable young people. The British at least produced (an) intelligent class. Right? We are not even producing competent peons. That's the level to which Indian education, school education, college education has sunk. On top of which you are saying, there is Artificial Intelligence, which is going to further moronize masses. Could you please elaborate on this? And does the government... is the Government of India not filled with such moronized bureaucrats, cops, judicial officers?*

RM: This is very important. People don't want to hear this. People want to hear good news *ki ham* cricket *ka* match *jeet gaye* (we won a cricket match). Or that five thousand years ago we were (a) great civilization, etc. They want to feel good. They don't want to be realistic and do something about it because they don't want to face responsibility.

My book is telling them that this addiction to social media, dependence on what will retweet more, how or what will please Twitter more or any social media, makes us more dependent on it. The reliance on such measures of social media for your prestige, making it the barometer of prestige, of matrimonial value, job value, political value, your value as an icon, as a celebrity, all determined. All in foreign hands. It's like during the East India Company days, let's say, the raja was more interested in being in the good books of the East India Company because that would affect everything. And if they wanted they could dump him, bring this raja down and bring that raja up and play one against the other if they wanted to. Because they control. These digital giants armed with AI are controlling the destinies of 1.3 billion Indians because we don't have our own platforms like the Chinese do. India sold out to these people. And I have a lot to say. I am very upset at the way India has sold out to these people.

MK: *One of the very intriguing terms you use in this book is 'crash of civilizations'. We are familiar with the term clash of civilizations, but you have introduced a new term, 'crash of civilizations' with an 'r'. Could you please describe this in your own inimitable way to the viewers of this channel?*

RM: You know, I'm glad you picked this up. When I work on a book, it goes through several drafts and many working titles. At one point in time early on, the title was going to be, *Crash of Civilizations.* Publisher after publisher said, *nahin, nahin, nahin, ye to...* (No, No, No) people won't accept No, no, no, what all this b******t. So, I put it inside the book rather than on the cover. Now, we know, clash of civilizations with the 'l' refers to the West versus Islam, and civilization A versus B having a clash. Crash with the 'r', is the civilization crashing. So, what do I mean by civilization crashing? Right now, civilization is held in a delicate equilibrium with many forces. The haves and have-nots reaching an equilibrium; the former are employers; the latter are employees. Or maybe some countries are haves and they have a donor-recipient relationship. There is some kind of balance. Or let's say, in a family, somebody has got power, some dominant person in the family, while others are subservient. But they find a balance. What happens is that balances disrupt and fall apart when there is a new force that gives them unequal benefit.

Artificial Intelligence is going to have unequal impact. Even if A and B are held in balance today through some means. Or maybe A is above, B is below, but they are held in a balance. With Artificial Intelligence, somebody gets to be much more powerful than they were and the other person does not get the same benefit. Some take advantage of weapons more than others. With the advent of cannons, not every army got them right away. Some armies like (Mughal emperor) Babur's brought cannons to India. Similarly, every weapon has had that effect. Every breakthrough in technology has unequal impact. Therefore, equilibrium falls apart. The delicately held equilibrium falls apart. A crash of civilization refers to a kind of a disequilibrium that society will go through and this disequilibrium has never happened before. Because in this disequilibrium, the basic challenge will be that we do not need so much labor. We have machines that can do this work, cheaper, better. They don't fall ill. There are lot of human problems that don't exist with machines. You will have an argument that maybe the world needs to be depopulated. I am convinced that this argument will happen. Not that we need to kill people and holocaust them, but maybe we need to have policies against too many babies.

The point is, right now the world is eight billion. It's going to be ten-twelve billion later in this century. But with AI you could run the whole world with only one billion people. You do not need that many people. India from 1.3 billion is going to go to 1.5 or 1.6, but 200 million, 300 million people, properly educated, good infrastructure, can run this country perfectly well. India used to have no more than three hundred million people during the British era. We have become four times the population. The bottom half is not very productive. The bottom half has to be looked after…

PM: *Moving on from this discourse of data privacy, protection, security, to a very fascinating chapter of your book I really enjoyed reading. And it is around human psyche and thinking. One of the chapters of your book opens with a scary insight and I'll just paraphrase that. As machines get smarter, a growing number of humans are going to become dumber. So, do you think AI will manage to hack into human thinking and psychology, human psychology? And is AI the mastermind behind fake news and the ever-prevalent confirmation bias?*

RM: My book makes a very strong statement. I know it will worry some people, but I want to shake them up so I can discuss it. As machines are getting smarter, people are getting dumber. Let me explain what that means. There is more and more dependence and reliance on Google search, which posts are prevalent on Facebook, the videos that are boosted on YouTube, what does Wikipedia say. People have started shifting their *adhikaar* (rights) to these *devatas*. I call them Google *devata*, Facebook *devata*, Twitter *devata*. These devatas are now the *adhikaris* (ones with rights) and the average person is bowing down (to them) like you bow to the devatas. Now you are bowing down and saying, oh, Twitter, don't ban me, don't shadow ban me. I'm a good guy. I'll comply with your protocol. Like you comply with some very scary devata in the past, some deity who wants you to perform this sacrifice and the other.

Primitive societies perform blood sacrifice and animal sacrifice and give up all kinds of things to please this devata, what they call gods and goddesses in their culture. Now it seems like we're scared. We are scared of Twitter devata. My god, if Twitter devata doesn't like me, I am in trouble. They could ruin my reputation. Whereas if Twitter devata likes me, I'll be a hero. My matrimonial value will go up, my job value will go up, my prestige, my political value will go up. My movies will do better. My entire success depends on what this devata thinks of me. So, I better be in their good books. This is ridiculous. I call this the moronization of the masses.

The masses are becoming morons. Moron, *buddhu*, dumbed down. Because we are accepting the authority of this kind of an alien, new force in our lives. And this is discussed in tremendous detail in this book. What this whole thing is about, how they are addicting us, how they are understanding our information, our private data, hacking into our lives because the Natural Language Processing (NLP) allows them to understand the meaning of what we are writing. Private messages, whatever I am writing, posts I am putting up, they can understand if I am Left-wing, Right-wing, am I old, young, am I into this movie, that movie, what my hobbies are, who my friends are, what all I like, what makes me angry, what makes me happy. They are understanding everything and building a very complicated profile. Facial recognition can allow people to look at social media, and photographs people put up. Who you are with, are you hugging them, is it a distant relationship, is it a friendly relationship, who are your friends and who are your friend's friends, what is your social network.

This hacking of emails, looking at the scandals you are involved in, some kind of hanky-panky you are doing which could be used for blackmailing you. This business of understanding a whole population better than social scientists of that country. The AI-based machine learning systems know different communities in India and what their hot buttons are and how they can be mobilized to fight each other. They understand all that psychology better than India's social scientists. This is a shame. Certain individuals... let's say, Prachi, systems understand more about you than your own parents and your good friends. The AI systems know you better than your best friends. I would say, in some way, they know you better than you know yourself. Because AI never forgets. It has more memory. All kinds of things you have said, and may be things that you want to deny, things that you wish you hadn't said and things that you said long ago (and) have forgotten, AI doesn't forget. It's able to dig into your psyche and figure you out and that's what the genius of neural network, deep learning is all about. And once people understand that they are being hacked, they are voluntarily giving up all this data, they (will realize) are making a fool of themselves.

This is the scariest new revelation or the scariest part of my thesis that I have exposed in this book, that machines are getting smarter, people are getting dumber. They are getting dumber because they don't understand that under the garb of giving you free services, free email, free everything, they are the ones actually making trillions of dollars. Imagine the richest people in the world today and the largest and richest companies in the world today, are giving things free. WOW! Imagine that! What an irony. Imagine that by giving things free they are making the maximum amount of money. Why aren't smart people thinking about it? Why aren't smart people able to say, how is this happening? What is the secret? This is brilliant. This is so brilliant what is happening, but it is making a fool of the masses and that is what I am calling moronization of the masses, meaning make morons out of the masses. Everybody is very proud and saying, oh, I'm this tough guy, they can't do anything to me. But the point is, they're able to influence what you buy. If they were not able to do that, advertising would fail and they will lose money. They will go out of business.

The reason these big companies are making money, more money than anybody else ever did, is because of their ability to convince you what to buy. If they can convince you what to buy, which holiday to go for, what person you should date or get married to, what kind of a political ideology you should support, they are able to hack your brain. They are able to put in fake news to make you do things. They are able to post certain news, may be valid and boost it, and some other news which may be valid, not boost it and even suppress it. They are able to decide what you should be fed, given your profile. Given Prachi's profile of what kind of person she is, what she likes, what else she will click, what she will not click, where she is vulnerable. There are algorithms figuring out all this, how do we hack into Prachi's mind, how do we hack on behalf of a client. There is an advertiser, there is a political party, there may be a church, there may be all kinds of people who want social media to hack into Prachi's mind and make her think a certain way. The AI systems are incredibly smart in doing that.

This is a human rights issue. This is something that affects social policy, and not just political policy and I don't think leaders of India are sufficiently educated and sufficiently awake to this reality.

PM: *Which leads me to a very simplistic question. Why is Artificial Intelligence so underplayed? If it's under our skin already, why don't we see it, why can't we feel it? It's everywhere.*

RM: There is a section in my book titled, *Aestheticization of Power.* Which means that this is actually a Marxist theory. It was used to interpret how Hitler came into power and to interpret many kinds of power which people accept without fully understanding. You should read that. This is quite complex, quite a detailed theory which I have explained. In a nutshell, there is a certain way to sneak into your life without you knowing it. It's called ambient AI, which means it's all over the place. It's always there. Siri is always listening. This camera is always watching and they are able to do facial recognition and figure you out and you are not conscious (about it). It's not like there is an AI guy knocking at the door saying, hey, I am AI. I am here to look at you. It's not like that. It's permeated all your shopping, all the Netflix movies you watch, all the messaging that you are doing. All the traffic lights where they are capturing pictures, they are looking for troublemakers and known criminals through facial recognition.

The use of AI is so ambient. People do not realize when they use their thumbprint to open their phone, that's AI because in the old days you needed fingerprint experts and some human being would do measurements and it would take a few days. Then they would match and tell you something about the fingerprint. Nobody needs to do that now because AI can figure it out like that (in a jiffy). Artificial Intelligence can not only do facial recognition, but voice recognition, speech recognition, image recognition better than human beings, faster than human beings, cheaper than human beings.

This human intelligence of recognizing objects and voices and different kinds of things has been superseded by AI and gives the AI system a huge sensory ability like senses, harbor senses. Artificial Intelligence has got what they call sensors. There are billions of sensors today connected to AI systems. Billions! The camera on your phone is one of them. What you click, where you click, what you do, is transmitted somewhere. Wherever you are going, there is a traffic light. The CCTV camera working. The number of sensors is so huge and now the bandwidth to bring all of this Big Data and process it and figure things out is amazing. This says why it's important for these people to give you free things that they look like the nice guys. We'll give you everything free. And, you know, content is free, what else can you want. This is great. You can't afford to be outside this connectivity because then you will be (no audio) a nobody and nobody will know about you. So, you have to join. Because once you hit critical mass, who are members of this kind of a thing then everybody else has to join. Because if you are not joining, you are an outsider. You will suffer. It's very difficult to defeat this system because it's gone too far.

The ambient, ubiquitous, ever-present AI is there, not only in surveillance capturing the data about you, but also in using your profile, using the model about you back to influence you. You are supplying the data to the AI system without knowledge, without being conscious and you are taking instructions into your subconscious; you are taking instructions on what to do, what not to do. The AI systems are training you. So, Prachi is being trained by the system on what you do, what you don't do, what you like. And when you like certain things, you will get rewarded. Your rewards are governed by how you behave according to their idea of behavior. This is a very huge problem.

I am surprised that people are talking about global warming and climate control, which (of course) are serious problems. And they are talking about Genetically Modified (GM) foods and about water shortage. Those are all very important problems. But AI is a problem that requires as much discourse in society as any of those. But I don't see that.

UC: *Let's turn to the third battleground. You had mentioned that this is addressing AI controlling our hot psychological desires and agency. And I think you have gone as far as to say that the psychological, emotional, and mental hijacking that is underway by AI and AI-driven technology, is resulting in the moronization of human beings. That is big. That is huge. So, what do you think should be the role of consumer protection groups as well as spiritual leaders and other keepers of society's moral compass in balancing the use of AI?*

RM: Societies across the world face this problem and India is my case study, but the problem is not just limited to India. The good thing for Americans is that there are (a) lot of them that are understanding this problem. I don't know how many people have seen the docudrama *The Social Dilemma*. Some X leaders from tech companies like Google and Facebook and others, have quit and started a movement to expose what was going on when they were working in those companies. There are insiders within Google, insiders within Facebook and also within Amazon, who have come out and started talking about these things; they are whistleblowers. Then there are people on the outside.

I'll show you this book by Harvard professor and social psychologist, Shoshana Zuboff. It is a six-hundred-page book, *(In the Age of the Smart Machine: The Future of Work and Power)* exactly exposing what is going on in this field of psychological hijacking. I mean, she is calling them thieves. She is calling them all sorts of things because they are stealing your insights without fully warning you. And I am quoting a lot of these people quite heavily in my book. There are the Susskind brothers (Richard and Daniel); one of them is into the AI impact on politics, the future of politics, how it is being influenced, and the other is into the future of jobs. They're both into the kind of thing I am talking about. People in the West are doing this. People in India are not doing it. People in India are going gaga, you know, Google come and invest in us. We are so pleased. Google devata, oh wow, we are doing so well. You know!

I am surprised at the lack of understanding of the Indian consumer groups. You would think that the Left would complain. And the Right would say it is hijacking our culture and civilization. But both of them are going gaga. We are running… we are successful on the Twitter platform. I've got so many lakh users (followers). I'm successful on such and such YouTube platform. I have more views. What we don't realize is that we are doing a dance on a platform, the strings of which are being controlled by someone else and they are making us dance. We think we are dancing freely, but we are not. Somebody is controlling which tweet of mine becomes popular, which will be shadow banned, somebody is controlling all of that.

The book is meant to shake up all our thought leaders including the people who are running manthans and literary festivals and who are the icons of social media and the big shots who are very popular… defining our success in terms set by another person in another country where we have no control over what their rules are, but we are placating to those rules. Those are the new devatas. We are bowing to them. We are practicing all the rituals that will make them happy. We want the devata to be happy with me. Twitter should like me. Because God forbid if they ban me, my competitor will get ahead. It's like the rajas, who at one point in time, were competing for British attention. Which raja gets to sit on an elephant and gets a twenty-one gun salute. He feels very proud while the British are the ones organizing all this. So, they lost their selfhood. And India is running the risk of losing its selfhood. As are many other countries… most countries.

India is far too large to just become a colony again. That's the risk I am concerned about and that's what I am shaking people up for. I want awareness. I want all these Twitteratti and all these people who are setting up these great channels on foreign platforms to know that what they are doing is feeding Big Data to those people and giving them more power over us. They will decide who gets the reward, what their views are, what their ideology is. They are controlling the discourse. We are getting free services. We are so happy those guys are giving me free email. Those guys give me free search. But why are the richest people in the world today, the people who are worth hundred billion or more, why do they happen to be the same people who are giving me everything free? I mean, this is amazing. You know, the people who are giving us all the free things are the ones that have amassed the biggest wealth in the last decade. This is strange. So, you would expect intelligent people to wonder. Intelligent people to ask these questions. And since they haven't, I am writing this book.

Battleground Self: Algorithm vs Being

PM: *You have mentioned one major battleground, which is very fascinating. It's about the real clash between algorithms and being. Could you please elaborate on that?*

RM: A huge part of my book comprises discussions around algorithm versus being. I started with a philosophical question… I am a philosopher by habit. As a physics person long ago, as a physicist and then as a computer scientist, one of the earliest metaphysical questions I have asked myself is, is the cosmos an algorithm? The whole cosmos is the algorithm. *Bhagwan ne* algorithm *bana diya.* (God made the algorithm.) It is Bhagwan's algorithm. If you look at what physics says, this is how an electron will move in a certain way according to the conditions.

The laws of physics for an electron are like an algorithm which the electron is following. It's sort of like nature has algorithms. It seems like that. Laws of physics are nature's algorithms in a sense, they are not manmade algorithms, they can think of it like that. Then the question is, where is freedom? Because a large part of nature is algorithmic. Planets move a certain way, there is high tide, low tide, you have all kinds of things. Physics is able to predict outcomes very precisely and that's because nature is behaving in an algorithmic way. It's not random. It's not chaos. It's algorithmic. These algorithms can be discovered and then using these algorithms, you can invent your own machines. That is what science and technology is all about. It's a discovery of nature's algorithms and we make technologies using those algorithms.

Then the question is, what about being, the consciousness, where is the consciousness in all this? What is the relationship between consciousness and algorithm(s)? That's one of the major issues. One of the battlegrounds, is unfortunate for me. In my next book, the one after this, I discuss ways to counter that. I am not giving (away) all the secrets in this book. I am raising issues, but I have a lot more to say. I am writing other books too. One of the things I am addressing has to do with this issue of algorithms becoming very powerful presently.

Our tradition says that your bliss, your *anand*, your joy should come from within. You should do yog, you should meditate, you should achieve a certain state of consciousness and that will give you your anand. That is what one should aspire for. That is what your tradition says, my tradition says. I have spent my whole life pursuing that. But now, we are approaching a situation where you will be wearing Augmented Reality (AR) goggles and it will take you on a virtual holiday, it will give you this excitement and that excitement. You will be sitting next to your favorite movie star and having a meal (with him/her), you will think. And with wearables you will have more and more experiences. Elon Musk (CEO, Tesla, SpaceX) has got these implants, the US military has got these implants going. China is developing these implants. With all of this technology, you will be getting a lot of your excitement, your gratifications, your desires through external simulation, through AI-based, machine learning-based mechanisms that have figured you out, have figured out what you need, when you need it, how to make you happy, how to make you dance, how to make you cry and so on. This will have great applications. Some mental health problems will be solved. Depression, bipolar disorder, Post Traumatic Stress Disorder (PTSD) in the military, all kinds of issues will be solved with AI hacking into your brain to give you happy experiences.

Artificial Intelligence will also have huge application for tourism. There will be virtual vacations. You will download the vacation and you will imagine that you're flying in the sky or you have gone to (the) moon or something like that. This business of fantasy will happen. But as you become more dependent on AI to give you the experiences that you aspire for, you will keep aspiring for more of these experiences. It will be habit forming. What does it do to your practice of yog? What does it do to your meditation? Do you still need all that? Or maybe you don't even need all that.

Some of these AI people are claiming that what the yogis took decades to do and what the rishis took hundreds of years to achieve, we'll plant a chip and give you that experience. This is (a) kind of an artificial rishi in a sense. Imagine Artificial Consciousness. This is fairly scary. Because, what happens to the spiritual movement? How do you counter if a guru says, you come here, study this and do this practice and this and that and you will get joy? This AI system being marketed says, listen, you buy these goggles, you wear these gloves, you do this implant, and actually your life will be very happy. All your friends who are doing it are saying, we are enjoying life, this is great. A lot of people will go in that direction. That is the new economy. That is why Apple is selling at such a high multiple. Not because it's 5G, it's because they are a platform for AI. That is why all these tech companies that are into AI are so rich. Because the knowledgeable people know that this is the future of entertainment. This is the future of defense. This is the future of medical treatment.

As you solve human problems at a certain level using AI, spirituality is almost out the window. You don't need it. Because the biological model of human beings, the mechanistic model of human beings has won. Artificial Intelligence does not need anything; it does not depend on knowledge of *Advait Vedanta* or *Vedas*. It does not. This is a battle between algorithm and being. This is the ultimate clash of civilizations. The ultimate clash of civilization we are having right now is an AI-triggered battleground of algorithm versus being. I have a whole lot written in this book on this subject and I have a subsequent book coming which takes this further and offers solutions.

The solution is not to stop AI, you are not able to be do that, but I have some innovative ideas on how the spiritual movement can get ahead with AI also present. This is my thought for which you will have to wait for another book.

PM: *Are we gradually transferring our* prarabdha (past karmas), *our* purusharth (human pursuit) *to machines? Is that the case?*

RM: There was a period in history when people would say, everything God's is doing. God is making the rules and I am just following what God says. They had a blind obedience to God. Then in Europe came (the) renaissance, scientific renaissance, scientific revolution, Liberalism, Humanism. The idea was that humans are in control of discovery. Humans discover and we have our own values and we come up with the meaning of the world. What is the world all about? We are going to discover it ourselves. It's not some God, (or that) some priest told us about; we are going to discover it for ourselves. This helped. For the last five hundred years it brought lot of discoveries, lot of science and moved forward.

With AI, it is a kind of a new God. There is new external authority that's going to tell me what my values should be. It's almost like the grand narrative is now becoming an algorithmic grand narrative. This algorithm is going to constantly update and fine tune the grand narrative, and there will be a certain version for you and a certain version for other people. People are becoming almost like slaves. There is a social merit system like karma, which is saying, you do good things and the AI system remembers and you get a gift. You'll be sent on (a) holiday and if you run a traffic light or you are doing bad things and a camera showed you are pushing people, then your application for something will be denied. Some of it you don't even know; you are not aware of.

Just as we say that because of bad karma I fell down and because of good karma, I won a lottery. But I don't really know which karma caused what. I don't know that. China has pioneered this social system based on AI, kind of like the Chinese government being the managers... the admin for karma. There is a karma system in China that the government is managing your karma, telling you the right karma, wrong karma, giving you points, telling you what your prarabdha is, what *phal* (fruit) you will get. If you do this karma, what's the fruit of that. So on and so forth.

You can't take this trivially because China is exporting this to Pakistan. Pakistani military is controlling the karma of citizens to keep themselves in power. China has sent this surveillance system to Zimbabwe as an example and placed thousands of cameras and with facial recognition and NLP are helping the dictators stay in power, suppress the people. What you are seeing is China is spreading its footprints for this kind of technology, which will allow it to decide who is going to rule. Who is going to rule in Pakistan? Who is going to be defeated because China has the weapons to secure their authority? And if China doesn't like this particular ruler, they can get him out because they have scandals on him. They know all the scandals on him and they know how to compromise him; how to blackmail him. So, he will stay honest. This is why in this book I say like the rajas were made to fight each other by the British because the British knew how to make one win and how to make one lose. The British knew all the secrets; they knew your vulnerabilities, your weaknesses. And the British used it to win over all of them.

Now I see people in US, some of these big AI companies and I see people in China playing this game with the whole world. And so, the future is challenging. I want people who are smart like you to wake up and figure this out and help. I am trying to figure this out. Because we cannot give up. We have to outsmart this whole thing on behalf of our civilization and keep our civilization moving properly.

Student: *In Chapter 5, the Battle for Self, you have explained how AI and life sciences is combining. How will it affect our spiritual life?*

RM: Chapter 5 is like a whole book (in itself). It's a topic, huge topic. The gurus are afraid to deal with it. I talked to some gurus offline, they don't want to come face to face. Only one or two young fellows, young swamis are very interested and they are learning about this and we are having a good time. But the senior gurus, the old gurus that are very established, worldwide famous and all, they don't know much about this. They will either give some simple answer or a trivial answer, but this battle for self is a battle for who I am, am I the *adhyatma*, which yog teaches *ki andar jao* (go within yourself), meditation karo (do meditation), *andar se andar khojo* (find yourself within) and you will find *sachitanand*, you will find bliss inside. That is what yog gives you. And believe me, it works. Meditation works. It puts you in touch with your real self.

As far as the body is concerned *neti, neti* (not this, not this) you just don't worry about it. Your body will run on its own. You do your duty that you are meant to do. But that is not who you are. You are not really this body. Opposing this is biological gratification, sensory gratification, pleasures, bodily pleasures. Now AI gives you more of that. With AR goggles you will be fantasizing, going here, going there, having sex, virtual sex, going to some fancy restaurant, going to the moon, going to Mars, going in space. All that you will be able to imagine, fantasize about. It will be able to give your mind experiences which are not real but fantasy, which you want to call entertainment. This is the future of entertainment. Future of entertainment is AI-based, Augmented Reality, wearables, eye glasses, implants that will all give you these amazing experiences. But these experiences are not connected with the self.

The Vedic tradition based yog, meditation, *sadhana* goes in one direction, which is more and more inward, while AI-based mechanized pleasures biologically manipulating you, psychologically manipulating you to give you gratification and pleasure, going in the opposite direction. This is the fight between who I am in terms of self, versus who I am in terms of this machine that wants pleasures. The idea that Rajiv is a biological machine—I have these hormones, I have endorphins, I have all kinds of things that a machine can trigger in my brain. I have these fantasy memories or traumas, bad memories. That kind of identity of who I am is what AI is going to manage, and make it good for me or at least looks good for me.

This is a very serious battle for self. If we lose this battle from the Vedic point of view, we'll become machines, like zombies. Elon Musk is developing these implants. He has a company called Neuralink, which is developing Brain Machine Interface where they're making lot of advancements using AI to put some implant that will measure the thought in your brain, what is the mood, what emotion, good, bad and they can intervene. They can change it. They can take nightmares, a bad memory, bad attack, mental health attack, sadness, violence, something like that, and replace it with something happy, joy, make you good, okay. This business of AI-based manipulation of your thoughts and your moods and your habits is basically the battle for the self.

Our gurus are sleeping. They don't know this. Our whole generation is moving in this direction. So, you become slaves. You become slaves, but happy slaves. They'll keep you happy. Not slaves with *danda-shanda*, beating, giving you pain, no, no, no. This new slavery will be very happy. People who are happy, who will be digital slave. They will say, *arey bhaiya*, Rajiv, *aap kya keh rahe hain. Main to vaise hi khush hun. Mere ko to pahunch hi pahunch hai. Mereko kuchh karna warna nahin hai. Main baitha hun. Date kar raha hun. Mereko sab maje aa rahe hain.* (I'm happy; I have a lot of reach; I'm having a lot of fun.) I am enjoying everything. *Sara din main yahi karta rehta hun.* (I do this all day long.) This is what's going to happen. So, *aise log to khush to rahenge lekin* (these kinds of people will be happy but) they will not be qualified to have productive jobs because the robots will do it. So, why will they want to work themselves?

Let me now give you a very provocative answer, which many people will be afraid of, but the smart ones among you will like it. I am saying, you don't need a large population because you don't need them as laborers because you have robots. If they are out of work, they are not going to be consumers because they have no money. How will they buy? They can't be… they are not producers of anything and if they are not producers because robots are producers, then they don't have money to be consumers. Now these people are not producers and not consumers. So, who are they? They are useless people, third grade people. *Inko… inka pet bharne ke liye* subsidize *karne ke liye* (to food and clothe them), why should we be wasting all our wealth. This is what the rich will say. So, how do you keep them happy? You keep them happy with the virtual self. You give them this artificial self that is enjoying life and *wo nashey mein hai* (they are intoxicated).

Like Netflix, this will be some kind of artificial pleasure service. So many rupees per month and there will be a silver plan, gold plan, platinum plan, depending on how much you pay. You actually become managed as a zombie or as a sort of a person who has no will, no free will, no agency, you think you have all that. They are making you feel you're in control, but you're not. This is the crash of civilization. This is the crash of civilization when selfhood crashes. And this will be a state India will go through from 2030 onwards to 2050. Between now and 2030 you will see some basic things happening like Breaking India 2.0 and all that. From 2030 onwards to 2050, you people, you'll still be young, you know. In thirty years, you'll still be, you know, (a) fraction of my age. In your midlife, you will see all this happening. You will see that there will be this algorithmic devata running your life. And you will be happy with it. Many of you will be just happy with it. But ultimately, the idea is to control you, manage you, depopulate you, reduce your population because you'll be seen as a nuisance.

This is the future I am predicting and I am also telling you how to avoid it. I am writing more books to tell you how we can avoid this. It is not that it has to happen. It will happen if you don't change. It will happen under the current policies. But we can change. And that is what I want, why I am writing this to wake up people so we can make that change.

Student: *Will it be possible to build artificial emotional intelligence?*

RM: Of course! There is already artificial emotional intelligence. You know, when the system knows ... Mahima's likes and dislikes... Mahima likes to click on this, this is her weakness. So, they can put more of that to make you feel happy. When they don't want you to be happy, they put less of that. They block it. What they show on your screen is different than what they show on my screen. Because my profile with them is different from your profile. If you search for something and I search for something and Nancy searches for something and Devansh searches for something, ten other people, different things will pop up. Some of them will be same but a lot of things will pop up differently.

Go on YouTube and search something, you get so many things on the side, on the right-hand side and they are different for different people. Because your profile is different, your weakness is different. What they want to do with you is different. This is the power of AI, which you can't do with ordinary technology. This is artificial emotion management because they know you emotionally and have an emotional profile of you, they are able to manipulate that profile accordingly. Gradually as they learn more and more, the artificial emotion management will become even more so. This is happening already, but it will happen even more so.

UC: *As you mentioned earlier when you were giving us a summary of the battlegrounds, that this battleground covers the metaphysics of the self and its ethics. In other words, it's the battle between algorithms and the self, between consciousness and AI's challenge to spirituality and so on. So, in light of these AI-augmented mental functions, what do you think is the future of the mind sciences?*

RM: Brilliant! This is a field very close to me. I have called this algorithm versus being in the book. The algorithm side says that I am basically a bundle of biology. That's all I am. Each biological part of me is nothing but algorithm. And then the parts of me like the lungs and the liver being algorithms can be broken into smaller parts with algorithms. So, the being…there is no being in me. There is no soul, self, any of that in anyone…. None of that really exists. I am a material entity. I can be broken into parts and sub parts and sub-sub parts and all those are algorithms.

Machine learning can figure out how all these algorithms work and we can replicate these algorithms. Certainly, we can inject joy, sorrow, pain, you know, we can give you happiness, unhappiness because we are figuring out the neuron patterns which corresponds to different experiences and we know how to stimulate them artificially. It's like drugs without any physical material… substances. These are sort of internally triggered, electronically triggered. This is going to give a large generation of people, a whole generation of people through AR goggles, which are coming with more and more intrusive variables. This is going to create a generation with artificial desires, artificial joy.

The interesting thing is that when they break down a human being into parts, there are different vendors. One is going to give you fantasy vacations, one is going to give you sex, one is going to give you your chocolate without having to eat the chocolate and having the calories, but you will feel like you have enjoyed it. So, different parts of the being, different parts of the person are being decomposed and very highly specialized vendors providing these benefits.

This is the future of consumerism. It is going to another level, kind of turning the individual into an artificial creature and catering to the joy of the different parts of the creature means that it is totally the opposite of yog, which means unity. Yog is not to break up and give each part separate stimulation. It is to unify. In the unity there is joy. Anand is inside, within. Anand is not something that somebody supplies. Anand is our nature. This is our *tattva*. Sachitananda is who we are. We don't have to add it. It is who we are. We have to undo things that are covering up. This is a contest between the sachitananda model of consciousness and the Artificial Intelligence model of biology. This is the ultimate battle that's going to happen.

(And) I feel that gurus are unequipped. I have talked to them. They don't know. They are just into their own kind of advice, but this is the future and we need spiritualists… we need gurus who understand this and who can counter it. I am going to write a sequel to this book. In this book I am exposing problems. It takes five hundred pages just to explain all these problems. This book gives hints about solutions, but I am writing a sequel to this book already, where I will offer my solutions.

TWO

The Winner of the Fourth Industrial Revolution Takes It All: India's Role in the Battle for World Dominion

Velina Tchakarova

Post the collapse of the Soviet Union in December 1991, the global system became almost completely capitalist for the first time in human history. Once again, the cycle of globalization was determined by the geoeconomic and geopolitical expansion model of a single nation-state (United States of America), which had managed to establish global dominance based on unique technological breakthroughs, similar to what happened with Great Britain in the nineteenth century. Needless to say, both states achieved a dominant position in global affairs by riding the wave of previous Industrial Revolutions. (Tchakarova, 2021)

The country that will emerge victorious from the ongoing Fourth Industrial Revolution is yet to be seen, but the winner will certainly assert its dominance over both, competitors and allies, in the future by setting the new norms and rules in global affairs. Logically, there can be only one winner in such a decisive competition. Attempting to achieve dominance during the Fourth Industrial Revolution will require a quest for increased self-sufficiency in Artificial Intelligence (AI), critical technologies, and global supply chains. Inarguably, the battle for world domination will be between the US and China, but India's role will be critical to the final outcome.

Artificial Intelligence fascinates many, but few are concerned with its potential geopolitical implications for the future of global order. In his latest book, *Artificial Intelligence and the Future of Power: 5 Battlegrounds,* author Rajiv Malhotra argues that 'the new AI-based power centres are located firmly in the U.S. and China'. (2020: 107) He further outlines the struggle for world domination based on AI-driven technological breakthroughs:

> A new era of colonization — namely, digital colonization — is already underway. The associate economic, social and political effects will devastate other countries, which will be relegated to the status of colonies or satellites. (2020: 107-108)

If there is one country that has not only successfully dealt with colonization but also applied a unique approach in the struggle for world domination during the Cold War (1947-91), it is India. How will India meet the challenges of global competition for digital dominance, and what role might New Delhi, the seat of the country's political power, play in the systemic rivalry between Washington and Beijing to ride the wave of the Fourth Industrial Revolution? This essay outlines some ideas about the geopolitics of technology and focuses on sketching scenarios for the future.

Who is Riding the Wave of the Fourth Industrial Revolution?

Technology, along with international norms, political economy, and geopolitical alliances, is one of the main domains of global power competition. In this context, the US is pursuing a decoupling, or a disengaging, of the 'Chimerica', but China is also seeking to break its dependence on US monetary, financial, economic, trade, diplomatic, and technological networks. (Tchakarova 2021a) The process of systemic decoupling can take years, even decades, and in the long term not only considers markets or technologies, 'rather, it requires confronting China's thoroughgoing revisionism that seeks to reorder both the global distribution of power and the normative structures in place since 1945'. (Andrew A. Michta, 2021)

In this current, highly complex and uncertain environment, the Fourth Industrial Revolution entails a contest over supercomputers, data collection and mass use, AI, connectivity, and supply chains. Moreover, a global power competition is already taking place over excellence in various areas such as trade, supply chains, space or defence, and is expected to witness new technological breakthroughs.

The term 'Artificial Intelligence' was coined by John McCarthy, (American computer and cognitive scientist) in 1956, after which it was defined as 'the search for computer programs that reproduce intelligent but not necessarily human behavior'. (Hoos & Kersting, 2020) Artificial Intelligence is the engine driving the global power struggle based on the myriad technological breakthroughs that will shake the foundations of states and societies. Malhotra applies a broader term of AI, encompassing 'the entire ecosystem of technologies that AI propels forward as their force multiplier. This cluster includes Quantum computing, semiconductors, nanotechnology, medical technology, brain-machine interfaces, robotics, aerospace, 5G, and much more'. (2020: xv)

Technological supremacy is the sine qua non of world domination, as the nineteenth and twentieth centuries have taught us. The Second Industrial Revolution enabled Britain to surpass its European rivals and become the world's greatest empire, a position it held for nearly two hundred years. (Malhotra 2021: 106) A century later, the US and the Soviet Union were the main rivals amid the Third Industrial Revolution in the 1970s. One can see parallels between the rise of Britain and the US as a world power, and Chinese ambitions to emerge as a winner from the Fourth Industrial Revolution. In this context, 'Artificial Intelligence is to China's twenty-first-century rise to power what the Industrial Revolution was to Britain's ascendance in the late 1700s'. (Malhotra, 2021: 107) However, the author argues that China's 'rise is not its first experience of historical greatness', but, in fact, 'a redevelopment'. (2021: 107)

Digital Revolution with Chinese Characteristics

China officially announced its goal of becoming the world's leading nation in AI over the next decade. Beijing must be seen as 'a full-spectrum peer competitor of the United States in commercial and national security applications of AI'. (Allison & Schmidt, 2020) This technological revolution is expected to be dominated by the domain of AI, as it will have a similar transformative impact on global trade, economic, and security networks as semiconductors, computers, and the Internet have had over the past quarter century. (Allison & Schmidt, 2020) In addition to being the most significant driver of digital transformation, AI will help the Chinese Communist Party (CCP) develop immensely efficient tools to strengthen the authoritarian model of government, reaching new, more sophisticated heights in data monitoring, collection, and analysis applied to its own, and foreign, populations and governments.

Austrian social scientist Bernhard Seyringer outlines the three stages in China's AI based on the 'New Generation Artificial Development Plan'. In the first stage, completed in 2020, China achieved parity with the most 'advanced nations' in the domain of AI. Next, by 2025, the country aims to improve its competitiveness in various AI fields and set new technological standards based on major breakthroughs in foundational research. In this way, China could become the world leader in AI-driven applications. Finally, by 2030, 'China is expected to have matured into the global innovation center for AI'. (Seyringer 2021) Beijing relies on easy access to vast collections of data to develop machine learning algorithms much faster than is the case in open democratic societies, where data storage, collection, and security are still major concerns. In addition, China has strengthened national, scientific, and military expertise in Artificial Intelligence by establishing centers of excellence, investing in academic and security programs, and launching state-funded programs for national, local, and university teams (Seyringer, 2021). Beijing is catching up not only in AI, but also with applications in facial recognition, fintech, armed drones, and 5G networks. Meanwhile, the country has also surpassed the US in becoming the world's leading AI nation in specific areas such as fintech, speech tech or facial recognition because of ethical, moral, constitutional, or normative barriers and constrains in the case of the US or other open, democratic political systems. (Allison & Schmidt, 2020)

Dr Kai-Fu Lee's (chairman and CEO, Sinovation Ventures) book on AI superpowers (*AI Superpowers: China, Silicon Valley, and the New World Order*) and Rajiv Malhotra's book *AI and the Future of Power*, provide a realistic overview of China's progress and goals in AI. The speed, scale, and determination of China's efforts to achieve AI supremacy warrant serious scrutiny. The volume of investment, the growing number of scientists and patents in AI technologies, and the boom in private sector funding are indeed telling. From fintech and facial recognition to commercial platforms and the Internet of Things, China is leading the way in multiple ways. In addition, AI-enhanced drones and 5G networks are giving China further global advantages due to growing demand from the Middle East and Africa. In the current global context, China is on its way to becoming a second center of gravity for power, and in the process has also begun to challenge existing international structures and networks.

Digital technologies such as Artificial Intelligence and data science will undoubtedly lead to technological breakthroughs in various domains of the global commons such as public health or climate issues. Concurrently, 'the actual use of these tools raises a number of ethical, legal, and societal questions' (Coeckelbergh, 2020), which are tackled differently by the US and China. The transformation of digital technologies could lead to the creation of permanent surveillance societies in which all data collection and storage is under state control. In this respect, China can play a role model function for future authoritarian regimes in the Middle East, Africa, and Asia. Andrew Michta (2021) argues:

> ...we must recognize that we are facing not 'China' as a civilization, but rather a communist power whose ideology has always been at its core totalitarian. What is unfolding before our eyes—and has been underway for three decades since the end of the Cold War—is the second, and possibly decisive and final stage of conflict between liberal democracy and communism.

Can the US Become an Artificial Intelligence-driven Superpower?

The United States of America remains the only international actor with global power projection capabilities. While America seeks to preserve its institutional legacy, technological influence, and geoeconomic clout in cooperation with transatlantic allies and regional partners, China will clearly aim to establish, and promote, alternative structures and systems to counterbalance and challenge US dominance. These competing strategies cannot lead to a win-win situation. Ultimately, systemic competition between the US and China will fragment the interdependent and globalized world by unleashing the centrifugal forces of bipolarity, profoundly affecting the entire global system.

The bilateral race in all relevant socio-economic systems will be determined by the supremacy over AI-driven superpower status. 'The United States will compete with China in applying AI across all domains, including the economy, military, and society. But in governance, because of systemic differences between the two countries, 'the Party is running a leg of the AI race in which the United States has rightly chosen not to compete'. (Allison & Schmidt, 2020) Undeniably, Artificial Intelligence will be a major multiplier of future warfare technologies, leading to comparative advantages for those who can deploy it extensively. From killer robots, AI-dominated drones, space and satellites to disruptive hardware and software in military technologies, the digital revolution is here to stay. It will impact the future of warfare in unpredictable ways followed by unimaginable cascading effects. Axiomatically, the race for AI-driven military applications and technologies will significantly shape the systemic rivalry between Washington and Beijing.

Clearly, China is aiming for 'AI supremacy' by 2030, but US leadership in big tech and semiconductors gives it an edge for now. (Borrett, 2021) Given that 'China will have the largest domestic market for AI applications' (Allison & Schmidt, 2020), it is up to Washington to initiate an extensive network with like-minded countries to boost the alternative market for AI applications and build a significant counterweight to the China-dominated technological race. In this regard, the US will rely on the transatlantic community to broaden and deepen AI expertise. In addition, America will focus on building a resilient network in the Indo-Pacific region in response to China's technological advances in this area. Only through valuable and sustained cooperation with trustworthy and loyal partners can the United States maintain its technological leverage against China over the long term. A pessimistic scenario implies a more radical and consistent mutual technological decoupling, while an optimistic view reveals a more peaceful systemic coexistence in which Beijing focuses on China-friendly partnerships and commitments to strengthen its domestic development until it builds a counterweight to the overwhelming US influence. The US has been the greatest source of China's rise (Schell, 2020), however, Washington could also become the greatest source of Beijing's demise through technological disengagement.

India's Role

Following the outbreak of COVID-19, the year 2020 marked the apparent manifestation of an Indo-Pacific decade in which the US, China, and India are the major players in an emerging competition. The unfolding of regional power centers gives the deceptive impression of multipolarity, when in reality, the bifurcation of the Global System is a consequence of the systemic rivalry between the US and China. (Tchakarova, 2022b) With the emergence of two systemic power centers — the US and China — the global order could transform from a unipolar, to a bipolar, world. In this context, the US is increasingly turning its attention to the Indo-Pacific region, and specifically to India, with the goal of expanding its network of partnerships and allies in this region. Gurpreet S. Khurana (2007), director, National Maritime Foundation describes this geopolitical space as one that stretches from the Indian and Western Pacific Oceans to the coastal regions of West Africa and East Asia—geographical areas where the power projection of all state actors involved will be most concentrated.

In key areas such as space exploration, Artificial Intelligence, defense technologies, and the cyber domain, there will be a variety of strategic investments within the new regional power centers enabled by different constellations of actors. This is important because any significant breakthrough in these areas will bring major competitive advantages and geoeconomic benefits. Moreover, competition between the US and China will be shaped as much by technological, geoeconomic, and institutional decoupling as by the oscillating alliances of the middle powers. Any major regional player, such as India, could shift the balance in favor of either of the two main rivals. Thus, in the coming decade, the Indo-Pacific region will become a major battleground for any progress toward the Fourth Industrial Revolution with India playing a key role in the bifurcation of the Global System by offering a valuable alternative.

The Quadrilateral Format (QUAD) between the US, Japan, Australia, and India - a geopolitical constellation aimed at building counterweight to China's presence in the Indo-Pacific region - began to yield successes in the field of AI as well. India and Japan, for instance, signed an agreement to cooperate on AI-driven initiatives. (Raibagi, 2020) The US-based National Security Commission on Artificial Intelligence advocated for the formation of a US-India strategic tech alliance (*The Financial Express, 2020*). Other formal AI cooperation agreements could be negotiated with Australia, Japan, New Zealand, South Korea, and Vietnam, which would open up a huge space of new business opportunities for India. New Delhi could become the missing strategic puzzle in the new equation with digital powers like the US and the European Union (EU), initiating a formal tech alliance that draws on the world's largest democracies and economies to adequately address the challenges posed by China's advances in AI.

India will play a key role in the geopolitics of technologies due to several factors. The country represents the largest open data market in the world with the highest per capita consumption of data (Chaudhuri, 2020). Artificial Intelligence is expected to have a significant impact on the Indian economy in the coming years. It is estimated that AI could add $967 billion to the Indian economy by 2035 and $450-500 billion to India's Gross Domestic Product (GDP) by 2025, which would represent approximately 10% of India's target GDP of $5 trillion. (*The Economic Times, 2022b*) The adoption and integration of AI technologies is expected to bring numerous benefits to various sectors of the economy, such as improving efficiency, productivity, and decision-making, as well as enabling the development of new products and services.

India is working on a Personal Data Protection Bill (PDP Bill 2019) and has been invited by the G20 (includes nineteen countries and the EU) to sign the Data Free Flow with Trust (DFFT). The Asian giant will also seek to improve its AI infrastructure and is counting on strategic US investments to expand its technological reach to address challenges to its territorial and cyberspace integrity from China. New Delhi is seen as an indispensable member of recent multilateral efforts centered around AI (*The Financial Express, 2020*). One of the most significant developments is the establishment of the Global Partnership on Artificial Intelligence (GPAI) with nineteen international partners. The goal is to join forces to advance technological developments and the use of AI among like-minded countries and organizations (GPAI, 2021). This coalition includes India but excludes China, as it 'aims to ensure that artificial intelligence is used responsibly and respects human rights and democratic values' (OECD, 2020). In 2022, India will be taking over the chair of the GPAI soon after assuming the presidency of the G20, a group of the world's largest economies.

India's current Artificial Intelligence initiatives span thirteen areas. (AI Policy Initiatives for India, 2021) A WhatsApp chatbot was launched to disseminate trusted information about COVID-19. India's Department of Telecommunications initiated a committee to standardize AI technology. The Ministry of Commerce and Industry established an Artificial Intelligence Task Force to advance the use of AI for India's economic transformation. It also launched the Indian Biological Data Centre via the Department of Biotechnology to define guidelines for sharing data generated by scientists in India using advanced biotechnology tools and methods. The Centre of Excellence included start-ups, innovators, companies, and the government involved in AI. In addition, the National Artificial Intelligence Resource Portal is a web-based system for searching and browsing AI resources. Furthermore, national ethical guidelines have been initiated to address the emerging ethical issues related to AI in India. Gene therapy products are being systematically evaluated for safety and efficacy considering potential ethical and scientific concerns. The National e-Governance Division, the Ministry of Electronics and Information Technology, and Intel India launched a national program on responsible AI for government schools. Finally, two programs were conducted on the potential of AI to transform the Indian economy and the need to regulate the use and application of deoxyribonucleic acid (DNA) technology in India. (*AI Policy Initiatives for India*, 2021) According to the Global AI Index (2021), India currently ranks eighteenth and is in the 'waking up' group of nations when it comes to the use of AI. When it comes to national talent, the country is second after the US; however, its biggest weaknesses are related to the lack of infrastructure (ranked fifty-eight), the operating environment (ranked thirty-three), and government strategy (ranked thirty-six).

At the same time, the reconfiguration of global supply chains away from China is becoming a reality amid the COVID-19 pandemic. (Tchakarova, 2021) The disruption of global supply chains has implications for all regions and state actors worldwide, in addition to a compromised rules-based global order and eroding international structures. However, the reconfiguration is mainly initiated by the US to bring production and supply chains back home or to trusted partner countries. Shifting manufacturing from traditional to new hubs will take time and effort but will certainly create new geoeconomic and technological advantages for India, which is forecast to become the world's third largest economy in the next decade (*The Economic Times*, 2020). In this context, India must ensure that it becomes a regional center of trade and digitization in the Indo-Pacific region, where New Delhi can draw on its strong relationships with the US, Japan, Australia, European powers, amongst others.

The Geopolitics of Technology

The current global situation is marked by a high level of uncertainty and volatility. Russia's war against Ukraine has exacerbated the global energy and food crisis and caused China to show comprehensive support for Russia while the West provides aid to Ukraine. (Tchakarova, 2022a) Additionally, technological changes are occurring at a rapid pace that policy makers are struggling to keep pace with. All of this is happening against the backdrop of the ongoing COVID-19 pandemic, which the world is still trying to recover from while also preparing for future health threats. (Mergenthaler & Chugh 2022)

The Global AI Index (2021) places America and China first and second, respectively, in a list of sixty-two countries, based on an examination of the forces accelerating AI development through three pillars of analysis: investment, innovation, and implementation. Once again, two powers are engaged in a fierce technological arms race, with Artificial Intelligence being not just another technology but, in the words of Prof. Pedro Domingos, (professor emeritus of computer science and engineering, University of Washington) the next stage of technology itself. (Armbruster, 2020) The power that dominates in Artificial Intelligence is likely to dominate global affairs both economically and militarily. Therefore, the political economy, defense alliances and partnerships, and the impact on global norms and rules will likely be a function of the speed, scale, and number of breakthroughs in this technological realm. Here, India must catch up with China, which still lags behind America. In the long run, two parallel supply chain networks are likely to emerge—one centered around the US, the other facilitated by China. (Tchakarova, 2020)

Artificial Intelligence plays a pivotal role in the battle for power in the new global order as Rajiv Malhotra outlines in his book on AI. He argues that 'China is using AI as its strategic weapon to leapfrog ahead of the United States and achieve global domination'. Thus, there is this 'special battleground, where the geopolitical competition between China and the US is playing out. Both superpowers recognize the AI as the most prized summit to conquer in their race for leadership in economic, political, and military affairs'. Artificial Intelligence is:

> ...the force multiplier that brings them together and catapults them to new levels. Both countries are heavily invested in AI, and between them they control the vast majority of AI-related intellectual property, investments, market share and key resources. (2020: xviii).

Moreover, disruptive technologies could not only strengthen state control through mass surveillance, but also weaken open democratic systems by destabilizing fragile political equilibria.

In the technological domain, India must play a balancing act between the US and China without getting entangled in the systemic rivalry between them. The adversarial relationship between China and India will further complicate the existent security triangles in the Indo-Pacific region.

A rapprochement between China and Pakistan, and in a broader context between China and Russia (the Dragonbear), are key examples of the fluid regional formations due to ongoing systemic changes. (Tchakarova, 2021a) It is expected that a major geopolitical shift in the region will take place in this decade, caused by Washington's efforts to establish a comprehensive strategic relationship with New Delhi, due to China's rise in the Indo-Pacific region and beyond. Logically, the US regards India as a reliable partner to create a counterweight to China's overwhelming presence in South and Southeast Asia. The political elites in New Delhi are increasingly in favor of closer relations with Washington, but also continue to rely on friendly relations with Moscow amid the intensifying tensions with Beijing.

What kind of digital alliances might emerge from these fluid geopolitical constellations? In the event of a further escalation of conflict, the US will take every opportunity to support New Delhi against Beijing, while Russia will rather seek to remain officially neutral in future tensions between China and India but mediate between both sides via diplomatic channels. From a geopolitical perspective, the new power competition will take place primarily in the South China Sea and the Indian Ocean due to the increasing tensions between the two Asian giants and the race between China and the United States. The outcome of the geostrategic competition between China and India, however, is not yet clear. The geopolitical approach of both countries reflects a constructive pragmatism when necessary, and all-out competition whenever possible, including the domain of Artificial Intelligence. Their relationship will be increasingly characterized by economic and technological competition, geostrategic rivalry, and a certain willingness to confront each other in their quest to shape their shared geoeconomic space. Looking ahead, AI will play a key role in this balance of power.

Rajiv Malhotra's notion of digital colonization will become increasingly relevant as we witness a struggle between the authoritarian model of governance with a closed data market and the liberal model of governance with an open data market. 'The political, ideological, and economic tensions between, and within, these categories of actors shape what might be called the geopolitics of technology'. (Chaudhuri, 2020) India can be seen as the world's largest digital democracy. New Delhi stood up to the big tech companies by defying their questionable behavior while no other leading democracy did so. (Roy, 2021) The very same big tech companies are often restricted, or even banned, in digital authoritarian systems such as China. Given that AI is the sine qua non in the global battle for technological supremacy, the choices India makes to fight digital colonization and ally with like-minded partners will tip the balance in the battle over digital dominion in favor of the model of governance New Delhi stands behind.

It has been predicted that data will be the new oil of the twenty-first century. (Arthur, 2013) In this regard, AI will become a significant enabler in the geopolitics of technology. (Raibagi, 2020) To prevent digital colonization, the most plausible scenario would be for the US and India to join forces and coordinate actions and measures against China's growing influence. United States president, Joe Biden has maintained former president, Donald Trump's efforts to isolate China from global trade and technology networks, despite concerns about potentially causing a 'new Cold War' in light of ongoing tensions between Russia and Ukraine and China's military actions in the Strait of Taiwan. In 2022, the US signed the CHIPS Act into law in an effort to increase production of domestically-made semiconductors, boost economic and national security and target China. (Calabrese, 2022) The Act prohibits funding recipients from expanding semiconductor manufacturing in China for a period of ten years from the receipt of the award. Later that year, the US Commerce Department's Bureau of Industry and Security (BIS) implemented a set of export restrictions targeting China's domestic development of critical technologies, with a focus on semiconductors. (ibid) Under these rules, US companies must obtain a license before supplying Chinese chipmakers with semiconductor manufacturing equipment (SME) and SME components that can produce relatively advanced chips. These regulatory measures reflect the Biden Administration's concern that advanced chips and equipment could help China develop new weapons and improve its digital surveillance network. (ibid)

India may currently be behind both China and the United States in terms of technological advancement, but it is aligning itself with the US in order to counteract China and also leveraging its own domestic potential. This is particularly relevant when it comes to technology. However, India will need to carefully navigate between the two powers while strategically aligning with Washington on AI and other relevant military-technological issues. On 15 June 2020, a violent conflict between Indian and Chinese soldiers took place in the Galwan Valley, resulting in fatalities on both sides for the first time in nearly forty-five years. This marked a significant escalation in the tensions between China and India. More recently, in 2022, their troops faced-off again in the Yangtse region near Tawang in the eastern portion of their disputed border. (Ramachandran, 2020) Against this backdrop, India's geopolitical choices are to either join the US-led bloc of predominantly

Anglosphere allies and close partners like Japan and Australia against China or, once again, build partnerships of non-aligned middle powers that can navigate the complex relationship between Washington and Beijing without taking sides. Nevertheless, this will require technological excellence in AI and enormous military advantages to defy the growing Chinese dominance in the Indo-Pacific region and beyond. This goes beyond banning Chinese apps or considering how India can absorb the slow move to diversify global supply chains. This is about ensuring India's evolving domestic data architecture supports its international interests, with the clear view to benefit from the same. The aim must be to negotiate its weight in data and find the right balance for India's future between localisation and internationalisation. (Chaudhuri, 2020)

In 2022, Prime Minister Narendra Modi stated that India may have missed out on being a part of earlier industrial revolutions, but with the right combination of factors such as demographics, demand, and effective governance, it has the potential to lead the Fourth Industrial Revolution. (*The Economic Times*, 2022). The International Semiconductor Consortium, a joint venture between the United Arab Emirates and Israel, invested in the establishment of India's first semiconductor manufacturing plant in Mysuru, Karnataka. (Calabrese, 2022) The United States will further seek to deprive Chinese tech companies of advanced chips and equipment while also promoting cooperation with India and other like-minded allies and partners to develop and maintain access to reliable and trusted semiconductors and other top-notch technologies. (ibid)

According to Peak's DI maturity scale, the United States was an early leader in the development and adoption of AI technologies. (INDIAai, 2022) However, in recent years, India has also made significant progress in preparing its businesses to adopt AI and become a more mature market in this regard. (ibid) India has a large and growing pool of technical talent, a robust start-up ecosystem, and a supportive policy environment, which are all factors that have contributed to the country's progress in the field of AI. Additionally, the Indian government has made AI a priority area for development and has initiated several initiatives and programs to promote the adoption and development of AI in the country. These factors have helped to position India as a major player in the global AI landscape.

When it comes to India's future role, its place is clearly at the forefront of strategic alliances with other digital democracies to prevent AI from becoming an accelerator of global power competition and an enabler of direct confrontation between the United States and China.

Bibliography

Allison G., Schmidt E. (2020) Is China Beating the U.S. to AI Supremacy?; *Belfer Center for Science and International Affairs.* https://www.belfercenter.org/publication/china-beating-us-ai-supremacy

Armbruster A. (2020, 7 September) Wer in der KI führt, dominiert wirtschaftlich und militärisch; *Frankfurter Allgemeine.* https://www.faz.net/aktuell/wirtschaft/digitec/usa-gegen-china-ki-fachmann-zur-kuenstlichen-intelligenz-16942865.html?GEPC=s9

Arthur C. (2013, 23 August) Tech Giants may be Huge, But Nothing Matches Big Data; *The Guardian.* https://www.theguardian.com/technology/2013/aug/23/tech-giants-data

Borrett A. (2021, 10 May) The US is Losing Ground to China in the Global Race for AI Leadership; *Tech Monitor.* https://techmonitor.ai/ai/us-losing-ground-to-china-global-race-for-ai-leadership

Braml J., Schlie U., Gärtner H., Tchakarova V., Hartweger S., Steiner A., Leitner M. (2020) Geopolitics; *The Defence Horizon Journal.* https://book.designrr.co/?id=61960&token=702129411&type=FP

Buckley C. (2021, 3 March) The East Is Rising: Xi Maps Out China's Post-Covid Ascent; *The New York Times.* https://www.nytimes.com/2021/03/03/world/asia/xi-china-congress.html?smid=tw-share

Chaudhuri R. (2020, 4 December) India and the geopolitics of technology; *The Hindustan Times.* https://www.hindustantimes.com/analysis/india-and-the-geopolitics-of-technology/story-dd2DGyVvuhH7XmOfVSpLwL.html

Calabrese J. (2022) CHIPS on the table: Escalating US-China tech war impacts the Mideast; *The Middle East Institute.* https://www.mei.edu/publications/chips-table-escalating-us-china-tech-war-impacts-mideast

Coeckelbergh C. (2020, 19 May) Corona-App: Ethische, rechtliche und gesellschaftliche Fragen; *Der Standard.* https://www.derstandard.at/story/2000117457544/corona-app-ethische-rechtliche-und-gesellschaftliche-fragen

Fleming S. (2020, 13 February) World Order is Going to be Rocked by AI – this is how; *World Economic Forum*. https://www.weforum.org/agenda/2020/02/ai-looks-set-to-disrupt-the-established-world-order-here-s-how/

Goldberg M.L. (2020, 23 April) How COVID-19 is Accelerating Geopolitical Shifts; *UN Dispatch*. https://www.undispatch.com/the-geopolitics-of-covid 19/?utm_campaign=shareaholic&utm_medium=twitter&utm_source=socialnetwork

G7 to D-10, India Included: The Significance of New Coalition of Democracies Proposed by British PM; (2021, 21 January) *Times Now News*. https://www.timesnownews.com/international/article/g7-to-d-10-india-included-the-significance-of-new-coalition-of-democracies-proposed-by-british-pm/709940

Hoos H., Kersting K. (2020, 14 December) Die dritte Welle der Künstlichen; *Frankfurter Allgemeine*. https://www.faz.net/aktuell/wirtschaft/digitec/die-dritte-welle-der-kuenstlichen-intelligenz17100377. html?premium=0x4dacdc693efcd75e57d25c85bcce852e&GEPC=s9

India to Become 5th Largest Economy in 2025, 3rd Largest by 2030; (2020, 26 December) *The Economic Times*. https://economictimes.indiatimes.com/news/economy/indicators/india-to-become-5th-largest-economy-in-2025-3rd-largest-by-2030/articleshow/79964750.cms

India to Overtake Japan to Become 3rd Largest Economy in 2025; (2019, 12 July) *The Economic Times*. https://economictimes.indiatimes.com/news/economy/indicators/india-to-overtake-japan-to-become-3rd-largest-economy-in-2025/articleshow/70193869.cms?from=mdr

INDIAai (2022, 1 November) India overtakes US to become world leader for AI ready market. https://indiaai.gov.in/news/india-overtakes-us-to-become-world-leader-for-ai-ready-market

Iwamoto K. (2020, 15 November) Asia Forms World's Largest Trading Bloc RCEP After Years of Talks; *Nikkei Asia*. https://asia.nikkei.com/Economy/Trade/Asia-forms-world-s-largest-trading-bloc-RCEP-after-years-of-talks

Jaipragas B. (2021, 7 February) Advantage China, as Democracy Slides From View in Southeast Asia; *This Week in Asia*. https://t.co/SNOtm8pGgB?amp=1

Khurana G.S. (2007) Security of Sea Lines: Prospects for India–Japan Cooperation; *Strategic Analysis*, 31:1, 139-153, DOI: 10.1080/09700160701355485.

Lee K. (2018) *AI Superpowers: China, Silicon Valley, and the New World Order;* Houghton Mifflin Harcourt Publishing.

Luttwak E. (2021, 27 February) How to Stop China's Long March; *The Post.* https://unherd.com/2021/02/we-dont-need-a-long-telegram-on-china/

Malhotra R. (2021) *Artificial Intelligence and The Future Of Power: 5 Battlegrounds;* Rupa.

Mergenthaler S., Chugh A. (2022) Strategic Intelligence Outlook 2022: navigating complexity and interconnected systems. *The World Economic Forum.* https://www.weforum.org/agenda/2022/12/building-strategic-intelligence-how-foresight-and-future-readiness-prepares-you-for-an-uncertain-world/

Michta A.A. (2020, 7 May) The Building Blocks of a China Strategy. *The American Interest.* https://www.the-american-interest.com/2020/05/07/the-building-blocks-of-a-china-strategy/

Michta A.A. (2020, 13 September) Can China Turn Europe Against America?; *Wall Street Journal.*
https://www.wsj.com/articles/can-china-turn-europe-against-america-11600013768?page=1

OECD to Host Secretariat of New Global Partnership on Artificial Intelligence; (2020, 15 June) *OECD.*
https://www.oecd.org/going-digital/ai/oecd-to-host-secretariat-of-new-global-partnership-on-artificial-intelligence.htm

Prasanto K.R. (2021, 29 June) Dharmendra Chatur: Twitter Executive Resigns Amid Tussle with Government; *BBC News.*
https://www.bbc.com/news/world-asia-india-57577268

AI Policy Initiatives for India; *OECD Policy Observatory.*
https://oecd.ai/en/dashboards/countries/India

Raibagi K. (2020, 10 November) The Role of AI Collaboration in India's Geopolitics; *Analytics India Magazine.*
https://analyticsindiamag.com/the-role-of-ai-collaboration-in-indias-geopolitics/

Ramachandran S. (2022) India and China Face off Again, This Time at Tawang; *The Diplomat.* https://thediplomat.com/2022/12/india-and-china-face-off-again-this-time-at-tawang/

Schell O. (2020, 3 April) The Ugly End of Chimerica; *Foreign Policy.*
https://foreignpolicy.com/2020/04/03/chimerica-ugly-end-coronavirus-china-us-trade-relations/

Seyringer B. (2021, 10 June) Artificial Intelligence: A Chinese Assassin's Mace; *The Defence Horizon.*
https://www.thedefencehorizon.org/post/artificial-intelligence-a-chinese-assassin-s-mace

Taylor C. (2021, 27 May) Coronavirus is Accelerating a 'Capital War' Between China and the US, Investor Warns; *CNBC News.*
https://www.cnbc.com/2020/05/27/coronavirus-is-accelerating-a-us-china-capital-war-investor-says.html

Tchakarova V. (2020, 8 July) Covid-19 and the Indo-Pacific Decade; *Observer Research Foundation.*
https://www.orfonline.org/expert-speak/covid19-and-the-indo-pacific-decade-69356/

Tchakarova V. (2021) Is a Cold War 2.0 Inevitable?; *Observer Research Foundation.*
https://www.orfonline.org/expert-speak/is-cold-war-2-inevitable/

Tchakarova V. (2021) The Dragonbear: An Axis of Convenience or a New Mode of Shaping the Global System?; *Irmo Brief.*
https://www.aies.at/publikationen/2020/the-dragon-bear.php

Tchakarova V. (2022a) Enter the 'DragonBear': The Russia-China Partnership and What it Means for Geopolitics, Observer Research Foundation.
https://www.orfonline.org/research/enter-the-dragonbear/

Tchakarova V. (2022b) Bifurcation of the Global System, Envisioning Peace in a Time of War: The New School of Multilateralism Ten Essays.
https://www.amazon.de/dp/370892309X/ref=cm_sw_r_tw_dp_NZ23ZAPP1Y8B6DXW9H5Z

The Economic Times (2022a, 8 October) India can lead the fourth industrial revolution, says Prime Minister Modi.
https://economictimes.indiatimes.com/news/india/india-can-lead-the-fourth-industrial-revolution-says-prime-minister-modi/articleshow/94705225.cms?utm_source=contentofinterest&utm_medium=text&utm_campaign=cppst

The Economic Times (2022b, 20 November) India to take over Chair of Global Partnership on AI for 2022-23
https://economictimes.indiatimes.com//tech/technology/india-to-take-over-chair-of-global-partnership-on-ai-for-2022-23/articleshow/95641022.cms?utm_source=contentofinterest&utm_medium=text&utm_campaign=cppst

The Global AI Index; *Tortois.*
https://www.tortoisemedia.com/intelligence/global-ai/

The New US-China Superpower Rivalry; (2020, 4 April) *East Asia Forum*. https://www.eastasiaforum.org/2020/04/04/the-new-us-china-superpower-rivalry/

US Body on AI Calls for Creating India-US Strategic Tech Alliance; (2020, 14 October) *The Financial Express*. https://www.financialexpress.com/industry/technology/us-body-on-ai-calls-for-creating-india-us-strategic-tech-alliance/2105383/

US, Indo-Pacific Allies Pledge to Boost Covid-19 Vaccine Supply at Quad Summit; (2021, 13 March) *France24*. https://www.france24.com/en/americas/20210313-us-indo-pacific-allies-pledge-to-boost-covid-19-vaccine-supply-at-quad-summit

here that the US is not a normal nation-state in the traditional sense of the word, like Poland, Ethiopia, or Thailand. Not only is it a superpower with near-global hegemony, the American political system is akin to a commercial entity which has, over time, cunningly acquired an army and navy, thanks to its system of legalized corruption, euphemistically termed 'lobbying'. In a process of state capture, private corporations fund policymakers in exchange for state institutions and public resources being deployed to deliver an environment favorable to corporate interests, both domestically and abroad. In relations with such a hegemonic power, the US' so-called 'allies' and 'strategic partners' are expected to become captive markets for American goods and services, in exchange for the illusion of security under the pre-eminent superpower's nuclear umbrella.

With time, the interests of these states and companies will align, and they will collude to numb the masses to the heinous inequality, poverty, and suffering around them, prescribing and administering a comforting opiate to the people, so that they do not question the status quo. This is exactly what soft power is. Soft power, contrary to popular imagination, is not the aspirational value of a country's cultural products in overseas markets, such as Coca-Cola, blue jeans, or yoga. Instead, soft power is merely an extension of hard power. True soft power exists when a state can make the institutions and society of other countries act as extensions of its national interests, enthusiastically on their own accord, without any coercion, thinking it is their own idea.

Presently, in certain countries, there is a fetish within the media and public discourse around celebrating their supposed soft power, based on the popularity of their cultural products abroad, but often without the hard power to back it up in a manner relevant to actual foreign policy. For instance, anime, Bollywood, and K-pop serve this 'soft power' fantasy for Western-oriented commentators in Japan, India, and South Korea respectively, or among their diasporas across the Anglosphere. Unfortunately, this is often simply a coping mechanism for countries too weak to pursue their own interests. Soft power is not about trying to win hearts and minds abroad or brownie points from other countries. It is rather about making other countries act in your interests without them even realizing it. When a vassal acts in the interests of its hegemon, out of grudging obligation or fear of coercion, that is hard power. When a notionally sovereign country or its elite act in the interests of others, enthusiastically and in the absence of coercion, thinking it is their own 'free will' and based on their own ideas, that is soft power.

The concept of 'free will' itself has always been an illusion, as all human behavior is, in reality, a response to the incentives around us. What we call culture, society, institutions, law, or the economy, are all invisible incentive structures related to our physical, mental, and material well-being. People then act in ways designed to maximize their welfare or interests within these structures, without questioning or even realizing the existence of any such structure. Even when people believe they are exercising their own choice, it is often still a reflection of years of conditioning, to constantly calculate the likelihood of reward or punishment, and of targeted messaging by society, the state, media, and advertisers.

The only way individuals and societies will be able to take control of their destinies is by becoming aware of, and then dismantling, the false prisons we are all trapped in. It is only by being able to comprehend how our minds are being massaged to think and act a certain way and our consent being manufactured for outcomes that may not always been in our interests, that we can we begin to challenge these structures and think outside the box. It is only then that an individual or a society can develop the courage to invent the future.

The Impending Collapse of the Façade of Sovereignty and Democracy

It is an unfortunate reality that like free will at the individual level, national sovereignty at the societal level has never existed for most countries in the first place. The social and political fractures in the Artificial Intelligence (AI) era will lead to the eyes of more and more people being opened to the sham their national sovereignty really is. Sovereignty only has meaning if a state can enforce it. Prized and ostensibly 'universal' concepts such as democratic values, fundamental rights, elections, or the rule of law are, at the end of the day, socially-constructed. They only came into being because enough people chose to, and continue to, believe in them, and would cease to exist if not enforced by the state.

Contrary to modern Western political philosophy, or what is left of it today, these values and rights do not exist or exert power merely by being written down on a sacred piece of paper. They only exist if and when the state has the sovereignty, ability, and willingness to deliver, enforce, and defend them. Such an understanding dates back to ancient times, as the

Indian political philosopher Kautilya wrote in the *Arthashastra* (fourth century BCE-third century BCE):

> The king, the minister, the country, the fort, the treasury, the army and the friend are the elements of sovereignty. The acquisition and security [of rights] are dependent upon peace and industry. Efforts to achieve the results of works undertaken is industry. Absence of disturbance to the enjoyment of the results achieved from [these] works is peace.
>
> Strength is power, and happiness is the end. Strength is of three kinds: power of deliberation is intellectual strength; the possession of a prosperous treasury and a strong army is the strength of sovereignty; and martial power is physical strength. The end [goal] is also of three kinds: that which is attainable by deliberation is the end of deliberation; that which is attainable by the strength of sovereignty is the end of sovereignty; and that which is to be secured by perseverance is the end of martial power. The possession of power and happiness in a greater degree makes a king superior to another; in a less degree, inferior; and in an equal degree, equal. Hence a king shall always endeavor to augment his own power and elevate his happiness. A king who is equal to his enemy in the matter of his sovereign elements shall, in virtue of his own righteous conduct or with the help of those who are hostile or conspiring against his enemy, endeavour to throw his enemy's power into the shade. (Kautilya & Shamasastry, 1915)

This understanding lives across Asia in modern political philosophies and state institutions, reflecting both classical Indian and Chinese thinkers on sovereignty and statecraft. In their modern avatar, these principles form a core belief in what Singapore's first prime minister, Lee Kwan Yew, called 'Asian values', and was popularized and institutionalized with the 1993 Bangkok Declaration on Human Rights, signed by over thirty countries spanning the continent and beyond, from Cyprus in the West to Samoa in the East. A short overview of 'Asian values' is as follows,

> The 'Asian values' theory, in brief, makes four claims:
>
> First, human rights are not universal and neither can they be globalised. They emerge differently according to the context of particular social, economic, cultural and political conditions.

> Second, Asian societies are not centred on the individual but on the family. The nation is like a big family. It supposedly comes naturally for Asians to let the combined interests of the family and the nation go before the interests of each individual.
>
> Third, Asian societies rank social and economic rights over individual political rights.
>
> Finally, the right of a nation to self-determination includes a government's domestic jurisdiction over human rights. This implies that other nations should not interfere with the internal affairs of a state, including its human rights policy. (Hoon, 2004)

This has also been acknowledged for decades by the realist school of international relations, with its leading theoretician, Hans Joachim Morgenthau, writing in 1948:

> The individual state has the right to give itself any constitution it pleases, to enact whatever laws it wishes, regardless of their effect upon its own citizens, and to choose any system of administration. (Morgenthau, 1948)

Based on this understanding, in today's world, it is only superpowers that enjoy true sovereignty, while minor powers have the choice between either giving up some amount of sovereignty in order to become client states, or adopting a defensive sovereignty backed up by armed neutrality.

In addition to sovereignty, the comforting bourgeois aesthetics that we mistakenly call 'democracy' today are no more than a sham, designed as a pressure valve to channel the aspirations of the people into policies acceptable to the elite. True popular democracy, on the lines of Switzerland's bottom-up, participative model, is non-existent in most countries, as there are a series of technocratic, judicial, and extra-constitutional institutions, actors, and incentives that seek to dilute and distort the people's aspirations into policies that are in line with the interests of the established elite.

Despite the revolutions and reforms that birthed their modern political systems, people in these democracies do not enjoy *lokniti* (people's policy) or *lokshakti* (people's power). They suffer under *rajniti* (state policy) and *rajshakti* (state power), to use the terms developed by the Indian freedom fighter and political reformist Jayaprakash Narayan.

> The central issue in all revolutions is that of power, and though they are all made in the name of people's power, power comes invariably to be usurped by a handful of the most ruthless among the erstwhile revolutionaries. Nor can it be otherwise when power comes out of the barrel of a gun and the gun is not in the hands of the common people … And that is also why after a revolution, a new privileged class of rulers and exploiters grows up in the course of time to which the people at large are once again subjected. (Narayan, 2005)

The sooner we all realize that modern democracy and its institutions are a façade, the sooner can people demand to build a model of governance that is in their own image. While deluding oneself from the true nature of reality can be comforting in the short-term, in the long-term, it numbs one from reaching the realization needed in order to take control of it and shape it. As Oscar Wilde wrote in *The Soul of Man Under Socialism:*

> [T]he worst slave-owners were those who were kind to their slaves, and so prevented the horror of the system being realised by those who suffered from it, and understood by those who contemplated it. (Wilde, 1891)

A New, Artificial Intelligence-enabled Cold War

The age of Artificial Intelligence being built around us, in addition to creating new socio-economic realities at the individual level, will have a profound geopolitical impact on how states interact with each other over the twenty-first century. We are entering what appears to be a second Cold War: an era of great power rivalry between the United States of America and People's Republic of China (PRC), with the two having created parallel systems in the digital sector, with their own internet, surveillance systems, and online ventures, as well as a network of client states and international trade infrastructure.

To understand the advantage that China holds in the coming decades, we need to understand the fundamentals of the Chinese economy, society, and polity. In the 1980s, the PRC under Deng Xiaoping abandoned its foundational ideology of purist Maoism, which was based on rural-led 'People's Revolution' and the fostering of a proletarian consciousness within the populace. Instead, the Communist Party of China (CPC) acknowledged that a feudal society and economy could not leapfrog to socialism without the state accelerating capitalism first. In his speech entitled *Building a Socialism with a Specifically Chinese Character,* Deng said,

> As they develop, the people's material and cultural life will constantly improve. One of our shortcomings after the founding of the People's Republic was that we did not pay enough attention to developing the productive forces. Socialism means eliminating poverty. Pauperism is not socialism, still less communism.
>
> Our political line is to focus on the modernisation programme and on continued development of the productive forces. Nothing short of a world war could tear us away from this line. And even if a world war broke out, we would engage in reconstruction after the war. The minimum target of our modernization programme is to achieve a comparatively comfortable standard of living by the end of the century. (Deng, 1984)

Breaking the taboo around bourgeois capital accumulation that characterized the class warfare of the Maoist era, Deng said that it was necessary to 'let some people get rich first' (Wong & Zheng, 2001), in order to build an economy and state that could deliver desirable outcomes to its citizens. The country thus sought to harness the power of markets towards long-term civilizational goals, related to overcoming the legacy of colonialism and imperialism, which is remembered in China as the 'Century of Humiliation'. This traumatic period of Chinese history encompasses the forced opening of the country, the Opium Wars, the Boxer rebellion, the Eight-Nation Alliance of colonial powers against China, the end of the monarchy, a descent into an era of anarchy and warlords, a short-lived republican era, and Japanese invasion. This period is regarded as a historical aberration, where China — which has historically seen itself as the 'Middle Kingdom' and thus the primary centre of civilization — was degraded and defiled by 'barbarian' foreign powers, who set aside their differences and rivalries to drag China into a state of poverty, anarchy, and dependency.

Deng's 'socialism with Chinese characteristics', or socialist market economy, channeled the state's energies towards economic and social consolidation, while cementing the stability and monopoly of the CPC in the political sphere. This hard-nosed approach came to be seen when in 1989-90, even as almost every communist country in Central and Eastern

Europe reformed and adopted the neo-liberal consensus both politically and economically, the People's Republic of China stuck to its own long-term vision, crushing the Tiananmen Square (4 June 1989) demonstrators who questioned the party line, whether on economic or political doctrines.

Meanwhile, Western policymakers and experts naïvely surmise that China embracing certain aspects of capitalist thought would naturally lead to demands for political liberalization and democracy, as people turned their aspirations from material basics to political representation. However, this undercounted the strength of the Dengist social contract, wherein citizens trust the party to deliver collective economic prosperity in exchange for accepting a limited set of individual rights, which are anyway seen as a Western and bourgeois social construct, incompatible with collectivist Asian values and a proletarian republic, while also not having existed in a meaningful manner at any point in modern Chinese history. After all, one cannot miss what one has never enjoyed in the first place.

In the light of this social contract, the Chinese policymaking elite uses India as an example to its own citizens, of the risks of what it calls 'bourgeois democracy', proclaiming that India is not capable of the kind of economic, social, or geopolitical power consolidation that China has delivered to its citizens because such a Western-style democracy is simply a continuation of colonialism, designed to hinder the upliftment of the masses and the pursuit of their civilizational interests. This is why, it is a cornerstone of Chinese foreign policy to exploit the fractures in Indian domestic politics for its own ends. The party has thus, invested heavily into the failure of the Indian political and economic systems. With this objective in mind, the CPC has successfully cultivated considerable influence among political parties and major media outlets within India over a decades-long process, starting from the Sino-Soviet split during the Cold War. As a result, India's Beijing-affiliated political parties and intellectuals are rendered either unable or unwilling to learn from Chinese best practices as an export-driven industrial country or revisionist geopolitical player, but rather see their role to be that of ensuring India does not compete with China economically, politically, or intellectually. It is as though nothing has changed since the 1970s, when Soviet and American diplomats and intelligence agents stationed in India remarked that 'it seemed like the whole country was for sale', based on how easy it was to buy influence among the English-speaking political, academic, and media elite. (Andrew, 2010)

By the late-2000s, when the US and its network of client states woke up to the possibility that China's economic and geopolitical consolidation had poised it to challenge the post-Cold War unipolar order, it was too late to act. They had offshored most of their manufacturing capacity to China, and could not pull out without economic disruption, so instead began deploying a digital propaganda war, on the lines of what they did during the Cold War using Central Intelligence Agency (CIA) front platforms such as Radio Free Europe/Radio Liberty. (Mickelson, 1983) The key difference today is that the digital age allows for the targeted use of the internet for such psychological warfare, disguised as neutral analysis in the so-called 'free media' of the West. As explained by Noam Chomsky and Edward S. Herman in their seminal 1988 work, *Manufacturing Consent: The Political Economy of the Mass Media:*

> In effect, the large bureaucracies of the powerful subsidise the mass media, and gain special access by their contribution to reducing the media's costs of acquiring the raw materials of, and producing, news. The large entities that provide this subsidy become 'routine' news sources and have privileged access to the gates. Non-routine sources must struggle for access, and may be ignored by the arbitrary decision of the gatekeepers. It should also be noted that in the case of the largesse of the Pentagon and the State Department's Office of Public Diplomacy, the subsidy is at the taxpayers' expense, so that, in effect, the citizenry pays to be propagandised in the interest of powerful groups such as military contractors and other sponsors of state terrorism.

However, these endeavors at psychological operations and information warfare have proven futile against the People's Republic of China, as the country has insulated itself from foreign influence in the digital sphere, to the extent that Western propaganda efforts do not even create a ripple at the ground level within the country. In fact, this misguided propaganda strategy arises out of Western hubris, assuming that they won the Cold War against the Soviet Union through their ostensibly 'superior' Western values, and that this victory marked the 'end of history' (Fukuyama, 1992), to use the American political scientist, Francis Fukuyama's infamous term. However, this was a misreading of how the Cold War ended. The West did not win the Cold War through soft power, but through hard power: an expensive arms race, funding and arming the Afghan *mujahideen* against Soviet troops, and control of international financial institutions such as the International Monetary Fund (IMF) and World Bank. Having been economically and militarily exhausted by attempts to keep up parity with the West, the Soviet Union no longer found it viable to compete with the Western bloc's industrial capacity, and gave up on its geopolitical ambitions, to focus on domestic consolidation through Mikhail Gorbachev's (general secretary of the Communist Party of the Soviet Union, 1985-1991) *glasnost* (openness) and *perestroika* (restructuring). This international withdrawal and domestic restructuring under Gorbachev are what caused the USSR to make overtures of peace towards the West, as partners rather than rivals. Hence, it is fair to say that the Western bloc did not actually win the Cold War at all, but rather that the Eastern bloc chose to no longer compete.

Today, the People's Republic of China is in a much more advantageous position vis-à-vis the United States, compared to the Soviet Union in the 1980s. It is armed with the lessons of how the Soviets were treated upon giving up their adversarial relationship with the US, being turned into a neo-colony in the 1990s under Boris Yeltsin's (president of the Russian Federation 1991-9) American advisors and handlers, causing a catastrophic collapse of life expectancy and living standards that set back Russian and Central Asian economic and human development indicators by a generation.

In a 2012 speech, President Xi Jinping asked CPC officials why the Soviet Union disintegrated, saying 'An important reason was that their ideals and convictions wavered. In the end, nobody was a real man, nobody came out to resist.' (Armitage, 2021) The Indian strategic affairs analyst Kunal Sharma, has summarized the policies pursued by Beijing to avoid overextension and internal fault lines, saying,

> Since its short war with Vietnam in 1979, China has not been involved in any proxy warfare that requires a substantial investment of resources. Taking a cue from the USSR's mistakes, China has gradually developed tools and mechanisms to undertake unconventional or hybrid warfare in the form of cyber attacks and information warfare, which are often difficult to prove in terms of their origin. The strategy of building artificial islands has been particularly proved helpful in advancing the expansive Chinese claims over the South China sea.
>
> In a nutshell, learning from the mistakes of USSR during the Cold War, China has very tactically camouflaged its fault lines, whether they be in Xinjiang, Tibet, Hong Kong, or Taiwan, in pursuit of its broader strategic goals. (Sharma, 2021)

Old Powers during a New Cold War: Russia, Germany, France

In this new age of an AI-powered Cold War, states will start to assert a new form of sovereignty — digital sovereignty. The days of a single, worldwide web will end, and we will see a fortification of multiple internets, divided on national or ideological lines. This means an American internet, a Chinese internet, a Russian internet, and possibly even an Indian, Iranian, and French internet existing in parallel to each other. The new Cold War will see the division of the world into ideological blocs, client states, and spheres of influence. China will focus on asserting its long-term goals through hard power, while accelerating the revision of the Western-designed 'rules-based international order' to carve institutional power for itself in global governance institutions. During the Trump administration's (2017-21) withdrawal of the US from its multilateral commitments, China was more than pleased to fill the vacuums of both funding and high-profile positions at various international organizations. Should this not be enough in the long-term or other countries do not accommodate its new status, China could instead create its own World Bank, its own IMF, its own military alliances on the North Atlantic Treaty Organization (NATO) model, and create an incentive structure that some countries could consider more attractive than the old Washington-controlled institutions.

The solution to digital imperialism is threefold: digital sovereignty, digital protectionism, and digital information warfare. Of the old European powers, the Russian Federation has the capacity to engage in all of these, and may well follow the path of China in setting up barriers to foreign digital encroachment, while continuing its efforts at promoting its own platforms, both domestically and abroad. With one of the strongest IT talent pools in the world, a rich ecosystem of locally-owned digital platforms and media, and a strong *souverainiste* tendency across all mainstream political factions, Russia today is both capable and willing to resist the country being once again turned into a Western neo-colony or puppet state, as experienced during the 1990s under Boris Yeltsin and the 'shock therapy' reforms of his American advisors. Despite its resource-dependent economy and declining demographic trends, the Russian Federation has a strong geopolitical, military, and nuclear legacy inherited from the Union of Soviet Socialist Republics (USSR), which means it can hold its own as a sovereign state, and extract concessions from either of the two new superpowers, in exchange for its support or cooperation with their interests.

Meanwhile, Germany is an incredibly weak state in terms of both the capacity and willpower needed to resist digital colonization. Despite performing a huge public drama around the crimes of the *Stasi* (the East German Ministry for State Security), which spied on millions of citizens of the former German Democratic Republic (GDR) from 1949 to 1989, the only lesson learnt has been with regards to the privacy of individual citizens, and not the security of the state or society as a whole. Also, with the absorption of the GDR into the German Federal Republic (colloquially known as West Germany during the Cold War) in 1990, it has become easy to explain away such abuses as a foreign phenomenon that took place in another country with another system, and which could never happen in a liberal democracy. In recent years, Germany has barely registered a murmur when it emerged that US intelligence agencies had tapped the phones of former chancellor Angela Merkel and two hundred of her top ministers and bureaucrats. Or that the new headquarters of the German intelligence services (BND) in Berlin are suspected to have been infiltrated and bugged during its construction. In May 2021, new revelations exposed that Germany's own NATO ally Denmark had deployed its intelligence agencies for years in espionage against Germany, including Merkel, on behalf of the US. (Deutsche Welle, 2021) As a result, Germany is already a digital colony of the US, and prefers to not challenge this status, in exchange for being allowed to exert regional economic hegemony over other European Union (EU) member states, using its export-driven industrial model, fuelled by currency manipulation and enforced fiscal austerity throughout the Eurozone, thus turning peripheral EU member states into both cheap labor sources as well as captive markets for the German industrial sector.

Similar to Germany, the simplest option for France would be to remain aligned with the West, and thus protect itself from Chinese digital colonization, but reconcile itself to being incapable of effective digital power projection abroad, instead simply sticking to traditional diplomacy and economic links, in Francophone Africa. However, this would demonstrate a lack of ambition and a betrayal of what the iconic founder of modern France, Charles de Gaulle, called *la politique de grandeur* (the policy of greatness), which sees France as a great power, one that must never rely on other superpowers for its defence or prosperity. It is important to remember that France was a leader in digitization until the late-1980s, and their policy of strategic autonomy during the Cold War, such as withdrawing from the US-led NATO command structure or maintaining an independent nuclear arsenal (with protocols to be used solely to defend French sovereignty and not that of NATO allies), could well be revived and adapted to the new geopolitical reality ahead. President Emmanuel Macron has made clear his dissatisfaction with France's ambitions being tied to the political compulsions and domestic turmoil of the Anglosphere (Onishi, 2021), as well as the risk aversion and status quo-ism of Angela Merkel's Germany. (Kauffmann, 2019)

The post-war German reluctance to wield hard power, combined with the withdrawal of the United Kingdom from its role as the American-sponsored internal saboteur at the EU, provides France a long-awaited opportunity to reassert itself as Europe's pre-eminent geopolitical engine. If the US is to focus on a great power rivalry with China in the coming decades, it will mean a redeployment of strategic resources away from the European theatre to the Indo-Pacific theatre. This implies that European powers need to wean themselves off dependence on NATO and assert their own foreign and defence policy, based on their own national interests, rather than being directed by the US-UK consensus. This is complicated by the fact that France, unlike other EU states, has extensive territories and a significant population of citizens within the Indo-Pacific itself, and has found its supposed Anglosphere allies to be unreliable. Australia's surprise decision in September 2021 to cancel a fifty-six billion euros submarine deal with France — to instead buy American submarines as part of an Indo-Pacific security pact with the UK and US — has only heightened the French impression of Anglosphere unreliability. The gravity with which this news was received in Paris was made clear by the reaction of the French foreign minister, Jean-Yves Le Drian, who accused the United States of 'betrayal' and Australia of 'back-stabbing'. (*France 24*, 2021) One can already see how after Brexit, France has been looking East in its foreign policy, working closely together with fellow EU member-state Greece to partner with countries such as Armenia, Egypt, India, Saudi Arabia, and the United Arab Emirates. This unorthodox partnership has been tailor-made to counter Turkey and its close ally Qatar, as President Recep Tayyip Erdoğan intensifies his 'neo-Ottoman' influence in the Eastern Mediterranean and West Asia, as well as his strong leverage over German foreign policymakers, France's traditional continental rival in Europe. The end of the Merkel era in Germany in 2021, and the long-awaited shedding of the dead weight of the American-vassalized United Kingdom from the European Union, provides Macron's France a once-in-a-generation opportunity to reassert itself as a great power with an independent foreign policy, along the lines of Charles de Gaulle's vision.

Socio-economic Unrest in the Global North and Its Export to the Global South

The entire concept, structure, and social contract of supposedly 'benevolent' welfare states in the developed world are built upon maintaining the current economic relations with the developing world. The entire post-war international system is designed to keep certain countries rich, stable, and powerful, by forcibly keeping others poor, chaotic, and dependent. Regardless of which party is in power in any given Western 'democracy', there is complete consensus on what the nature of their country's relations with the rest of the world should be. This undisputed consensus underlying all of their economic and social policies (often clothed under liberal or progressive aesthetics) is their economic need to facilitate extraction, exploitation, and access. That is, extraction of resources from the developing world, exploitation of their cheaper labor pools and lax regulatory environments, and access to their markets for the export of industrial goods, financial services, excess population, and social conflicts.

Any change in these relations leads to a tremor in the very foundations of society in these industrialized countries, as we saw after the World Wars and the first waves of decolonization in Africa, Asia, and the Caribbean. Wealthy states pulled the strings to ensure that newly-independent countries remained economically dependent on them and continued to supply them with the resources needed to maintain their industrial economies while act as markets for their value-added goods and services.

> Economies structured around agriculture and resource extraction—i.e., the production of basic commodities for export to the industrialised West—were the most significant hangover of imperial rule. As a result, these countries were forced to import back manufactured goods, including the basic machinery for their own producer industries, resulting in a disastrous crisis in their terms of trade. What they were exporting was always necessarily less valuable than what they were required to import. Capital could be accessed in the form of aid or loans from international financial institutions or directly from richer countries, but this method posed a risk to national sovereignty: states would be forced to create policy for the benefit of their international creditors, rather than the immediate needs of their own populations. (Maisey, 2021)

After the post-war economic boom in the West and the neo-liberal 'Washington consensus' of the IMF and World Bank from the 1980s onwards, these relations were restored and reinforced, in a slightly more subtle avatar, and form the basis of Western prosperity, much more so than any modern myth around these countries owing their success to superior values, work ethic, or neoliberal policies.

> The IMF ... made access to capital contingent on the deregulation of markets, the end of subsidies on basic goods, and the mass privatisations of public services and state industries.
>
> The 'structural adjustment loans' rolled back years of social progress within the national liberation states, returning them to the kind of gross poverty not seen since the most tyrannical days of the old empires. Many nascent industrial economies quickly snapped back to raw commodity production, or even subsistence farming, as the state's assets were cannibalised in the name of 'restructuring'.
>
> By the 1990s, the ruins of the Third World were acting as a direct subsidy to the economies of the First, in which all pretence of social and economic development was sacrificed in favour of servicing unimaginably huge debt burdens'. (Maisey, 2021)

As a result, today, leveraging cheap labor for manufacturing in the developing world is the basic foundation of international trade. In the coming years, as Artificial Intelligence and automation make it cheaper to produce greater outputs with less labor and at better margins, investors will move productive assets to environments that give them tax breaks or guarantee digital sovereignty, not based on where labor costs are cheapest or industrial norms are the weakest.

The economic inequality that such a system will create will then be exacerbated by the social tensions around what Russian-American evolutionary anthropologist Peter Valentinovich Turchin has termed 'elite overproduction'. In this phenomenon, elites in many countries seek to self-replicate and over-produce through the established educational and economic systems. As more and more individuals are equipped with the aesthetic trappings of the elite, they find themselves lacking the actual core of elite status – access to power. Such notional elites may multiply rapidly through the market forces behind the expansion of access to elite education, but that does not imply that actual elite jobs situated at the levers of power expand at the same rate. In fact, the custodians of power jealously guard their roles, and seek to prevent any dilution through increased access to newcomers. This leads to frustration, as increasing numbers of individuals and communities feel that they are entitled to a place within power structures which steadfastly refuse to accommodate them.

> You have a situation now where there are many more elites fighting for the same position, and some portion of them will convert to counter-elites. The excess elites become counter-elites, who then try to make alliances with the lower classes that usually don't work out. (Mauldin, 2020)

> The final trigger of impending collapse, Turchin says, tends to be state insolvency. At some point rising insecurity becomes expensive. The elites have to pacify unhappy citizens with handouts and freebies—and when these run out, they have to police dissent and oppress people. Eventually the state exhausts all short-term solutions, and what was heretofore a coherent civilization disintegrates. (Wood, 2020)

This impending collapse will lead to a situation where, just as developed countries place protectionist tariffs and taxpayer-funded subsidies for their agricultural sectors (in order to prevent social upheaval and to insulate themselves from international competition), they will also start giving state incentives to promote automated production in their own countries. They will then use the resulting efficiency gains to institute a universal basic income to quell any discontent among the (erstwhile) working class. Meanwhile, the frustrated professional managerial class will be mollified through meaningless, glorified clerical roles both at home and abroad. This is very similar to the condition of the United Kingdom during its industrialization in the nineteenth century, which served as a major factor for their push towards colonialist and imperialist ventures overseas.

In the developing world, this series of new economic relations will lead to further social stratification and inequality, as both the rural and urban working class are robbed of even a limited chance to lift themselves out of poverty through export-driven manufacturing. As we saw in the twentieth century, these countries will remain colonial outposts of extractive industries such as mining, quarrying, lumber, and fuel extraction, or low-regulation paradises for sectors considered undesirable in the developed world, such as ship-breaking and garbage processing. These changes will also exacerbate the divide between the elites and the masses, as a handful of native compradors or middlemen will be picked up by foreign companies at home and abroad, being thus cultivated as agents of imperialism, while the poor struggle for crumbs from both foreign and domestic elites. This will lead to a shift in the Overton window (the range of policies seen as acceptable within mainstream opinion), as the masses, being locked out of economic and social mobility, will express themselves through their numerical advantage, in politics – either through support for new strains of populism and nativist ideologies, or through revolutions and civil wars.

This combination of skewed socio-economic relations is in line with what Kwame Nkrumah, the first prime minister and president of independent Ghana, termed as 'neo-colonialism' in the 1960s,

> [N]eo-colonialism, like colonialism before it, postpones the facing of the social issues which will have to be faced by the fully developed sector of the world before the danger of world war can be eliminated or the problem of world poverty resolved. Neo-colonialism, like colonialism, is an attempt to export the social conflicts of the capitalist countries. (Nkrumah, 1965)

In this light, what does this new economic and geopolitical future mean for non-Western countries? Is this a new age of imperialism and colonization? The answer is that colonialism never ended, even after ostensibly successful independence movements from the 1940s to 1960s. The same colonial mentalities and relations only took a new form. The old colonial powers still exert their economic and geopolitical paramountcy over their former possessions, but have been able to disguise it as 'democracy promotion', 'shared values', 'structural adjustment', and 'free trade'.

These new forms of colonization seek to entrench the interests of the colonial powers in their former colonies, turning them into helpless dependencies, while disguising this process as altruism to audiences both at home and abroad. Nkrumah, upon coining the term, wrote:

> The neo-colonialism of today represents imperialism in its final and perhaps its most dangerous stage … The essence of neo-colonialism is that the State which is subject to it is, in theory, independent and has all the outward trappings of international sovereignty. In reality its economic system and thus its political policy is directed from outside.

> Neo-colonialism is also the worst form of imperialism. For those who practise it, it means power without responsibility and for those who suffer from it, it means exploitation without redress. In the days of old-fashioned colonialism, the imperial power had at least to explain and justify at home the actions it was taking abroad. In the colony those who served the ruling imperial power could at least look to its protection against any violent move by their opponents. With neo-colonialism neither is the case.
>
> Neo-colonialism is based upon the principle of breaking up former large united colonial territories into a number of small non-viable States which are incapable of independent development and must rely upon the former imperial power for defence and even internal security. Their economic and financial systems are linked, as in colonial days, with those of the former colonial ruler. (Nkrumah, 1965)

The core goal of colonialism remains the same: to maintain certain countries as weak, stagnant, and dependent on the powerful hegemon, so that they continue to serve as a source of cheap labor and raw materials, as well as markets for finished goods. There is almost complete consensus within the Western world as to the necessity of such relations, across the full political spectrum. On one hand, Western Right-wing parties invest in maintaining and defending imperialism, to help their companies and donors maximise profits by using Africa, Asia, and Latin America as hubs of extraction and captive markets. On the other, Western Left-wing parties also invest in maintaining and defending imperialism, so they can push the same companies to share the resulting profits with the working class and trade union members, in order to create 'capitalism with a human face' and prevent social unrest and radical political revolution through a social democratic welfare state. This is the same mercantilist model perfected by the East India Company (EIC) in the first wave of modern colonialism, simply in a new garb. This phenomenon was excellently summarized by Thomas Sankara, the revolutionary, anti-colonial president of Burkina Faso (1983-87):

> Imperialism is a system of exploitation that occurs not only in the brutal form of those who come with guns to conquer territory. Imperialism often occurs in more subtle forms, a loan, food aid, blackmail. (Kamau, 2019)

Applying this unchanging goal to the era of AI means it is still very much in the interests of superpowers to turn African, Asian, Caribbean, and Latin American countries into sources of Big Data, while opening up their markets to foreign digital platforms that serve the interests of the colonial metropole.

If Nkrumah and Sankara are correct and neo-colonialism represents the final, most dangerous, stage of imperialism, the question arises, as a newly-minted superpower, will China act as an imperial power and seek to supplant the US? As things stand, it is not possible to supplant the US wholesale. A sensible course of action for China would be to first seek to create a bipolar world order, and demonstrate that it is in the interest of the West to seek *détente* (an easing of tensions) with the Sinosphere (China and its satellite states). A restoration of a bipolar world order is the medium-term goal, after thirty years of a US-led neo-liberal victory heralding the 'end of history'. What China can then count on is that their model of a civilization-state, which is already planning for a restoration of China's pre-eminent place in the world by the year 2100 CE, will prove to be more risk-proof and resilient than Western democracy and neo-liberal capitalism that only plan for four-year election cycles and three-month business quarters, respectively. Superpowers do not seek to go to war with each other; they seek to bleed the other side dry, and China sees itself as having the strategic advantage in such a long-term strategy. So, it is not that China seeks to supplant the US, but rather that Chinese policymakers see the US as inherently so weak domestically, that it is inevitable the US will suffer from imperial over-reach, causing domestic turmoil, and leading to their withdrawal from unipolar and hegemonic status, to focus on domestic consolidation, much like the USSR under Gorbachev.

In Africa, where there has been the most public Chinese diplomatic and economic outreach in recent years, one still cannot say that China has sought to supplant the US, simply because the US was not present apart from military and strategic partnerships. Rather, it would be more accurate to say that China seeks to replace the roles of France, Portugal, and the United Kingdom in their former colonies, by going deeper than before in investing in infrastructure and productive capital, while also selling their goods and exporting their surplus labor.

In Latin America, the US will seek to jealously guard its sphere of influence from Chinese overtures as well as the rise of Brazil as an economic and geopolitical power in the region, whose aspirations may be opposed to the region's neo-colonial status quo of American hegemony, as had been attempted under President Luiz Inácio Lula da Silva between 2003 and 2010.

In Asia, one will see the most friction between the two superpowers, a combination of the 'Scramble for Africa' of the nineteenth century and the 'Domino Theory' of the twentieth century, involving the cultivation of new client states, by engineering regime change, separatism, and civil wars in countries perceived as not servile enough to superpower interests.

India in This New Cold War: The Strong do What They Can, the Weak Suffer What They Must

In the case of India, neo-colonialism has been a free-for-all from independence itself, with unreformed colonial-era state institutions being designed for the convenience of foreign powers, and native comprador elites happily selling access to the corridors of power to the highest bidder. With economic growth, as India becomes both a more lucrative market for foreign capital and a potential threat to the geopolitical status quo, such interference may intensify ahead. This could lead to a 'Scramble for India' in the twenty-first century on the lines of the infamous 'Scramble for Africa' in the late-nineteenth century or the colonial-era 'Great Game' between Britain and Russia for influence in Persia, as foreign powers seek to carve out India into clear spheres of influence and settle upon a formula that satisfies all of their ambitions, without considering the consent, permission, interests, or opinions of the people of the Indian subcontinent as relevant. The first step in this long-term plan was the successful Partition of India in 1947, and the timidity with which independent India accepted this as a permanent settlement (not even reintegrating Bangladesh into the Union of India after the 1971 Liberation War), has signalled to the world that there are no consequences from the Indian state, should foreign powers once again attempt such a Balkanization.

India, in this new Cold War, will thus have a choice to make: submit, resist, or exit.

- **Submit** means that the country is reduced to serving as a digital colony or client state of one of the superpowers, China or the US.
- **Resist** means the country radically changes the foundations of the state and re-engineers its institutions to becoming a *Realpolitik*

power player like Bismarckian Germany or early-twentieth century Japan, seeking its rightful place in the international community, through consolidation at home and intensified power projection abroad.

- **Exit** means the country turns inwards, closing itself off from influence from external powers, to focus on consolidating its own massive internal economy. The goal would then be to become a fully self-sufficient country, and to build a digital garrison state, focused on defending its *Sonderweg* (special path) from the threat of neo-colonialism.

Aligning with either of the new blocs will be difficult, since both are inherently hostile to Indian interests and do not want to share their geopolitical power with an emerging country like India, lest they enable its further rise to itself become a potential rival to them.

However, neutrality or non-alignment only work when a state is both capable and willing to defend it, such as Sweden or Switzerland during the two World Wars and the Cold War. Historically, countries that declared themselves neutral but depended upon the goodwill of others to guarantee their neutrality and sovereignty, such as Belgium, Denmark, or Cyprus, found themselves easy prey for predatory neighbours.

It is also important to remember that superpowers do not have allies in the traditional bilateral sense of mutual assistance. Instead, they have client states, who are sworn to defend the superpower, do its dirty work for them overseas, and offer a captive market for its military-industrial complex, in exchange for a mere promise of protection. Thus, superpowers view the rest of the world as client states, potential client states, and rogue states.

For better or worse, India is perceived as too big, poor, chaotic, and diverse to be considered a reliable client state, as superpowers traditionally only trust those countries capable of acting in the superpower's interests with a minimum of fuss. For example, the closest US allies since the Second World War have been authoritarian polities such as Gulf monarchies, Latin American dictatorships, or ethno-linguistic European nation-states which were beholden to a superpower for their role in historical liberation or defence. A small minority of policymakers and opinion-shapers in the PRC and US view India with sympathy, but even the full extent of their limited vision is merely to convince their policymaking establishment that India has the potential to become a credible client state in the future.

As a result, the foreign policy establishment insiders in both the PRC and US view India as a larger version of Yugoslavia during the first Cold War: a multi-ethnic, multi-religious, federalized, secular, and socialist country that was non-aligned between the two superpowers, but which could be incentivized to act as a buffer state without openly antagonizing the other superpower. The USSR supported Yugoslavia and its communist partisan army in its liberation from Nazi occupation during the Second World War, but soon fell out following disagreements on post-war policies. Following this split, the US happily offered diplomatic and economic relations to communist Yugoslavia under President Josip Broz Tito, in order to cultivate a friendly, Western-oriented socialist state in Eastern Europe. With access to Western loans and aid, combined with a unique form of hybrid socialism known as *radničko samoupravljanje* (worker's self-management), Yugoslavia experienced a strong post-war economic recovery and one of the highest standards of living in the region. However, such a buffer state is only useful when there is tension between the two superpowers. In the case of *détente* between the superpowers, as was seen in the 1980s through the efforts of Mikhail Gorbachev and Ronald Reagan, the two blocs overcame the need for a successful, stable, and prosperous buffer state. The US thus pulled the plug on its support for the country, began harshly enforcing repayment of the loans it had provided to the country, and engaged in 'sub-national diplomacy'. This took the form of encouraging richer, industrialized regions such as Slovenia and Croatia to secede from Yugoslavia, promising Western financial support and diplomatic recognition to separatists, while portraying either the federal capital in Belgrade or poorer rural regions such as Bosnia-Herzegovina, Macedonia, Montenegro, and Serbia, as the cause of the debt crisis, economic stagnation, and currency inflation. This has parallels today in how certain Western-backed Dravidian and Khalistani supremacist and separatist movements in India portray the rest of the country in their political discourse. This forms a phenomenon that historian Emmanuele Dalle Mulle calls the 'nationalism of the rich',

> [A] type of nationalist discourse that aims to put an end to the economic 'exploitation' suffered by a group of people represented as a wealthy nation and supposedly carried out by the populations of poorer regions and/or by inefficient state administrations. The core elements of this rhetoric are: a claim of economic victimisation according to which a backward core area holds back a more advanced periphery. (Dalle Mulle, 2019)

Like Yugoslavia, once India has served its purpose in the new Cold War and has nothing left of value, the superpowers will prefer to Balkanize the country in order to create manageable spheres of influence – small, easily managed, authoritarian client states, beholden to the powers that supported their successful separatist movement. There is already a successful precedent for such a strategy after the Second World War in India, through Partition in 1947, creating a loyal authoritarian Western client state in the form of Pakistan. A civil war or repeat of the Partition in the twenty-first century would be a catastrophe from which recovery will be almost impossible. Hence, India needs to equip itself with the tools and information needed to anticipate and counter this strategy on a war-footing.

This is particularly concerning in the light of key policymaking institutions in the West warning of exactly such a situation, accelerated by the effects of climate change and rising sea levels on the Indian subcontinent:

> As Pentagon reports have warned, even much more limited rises in temperature however will have a disastrous effect on more vulnerable societies in heavily-populated parts of the world, leading to famines, civil wars, and the collapse of states. This applies above all to South Asia and western Africa, where temperatures are already close to the limits of human survivability for parts of the year, and where societies and agricultures are already facing severe and growing water shortages. The World Bank has warned that if climate change continues at present rates, by the middle of this century Indian economic growth will go into reverse, plunging hundreds of millions of people back into deep poverty. (Lieven, 2021)

Werner Menski, emeritus professor at the School of Oriental and African Studies and Muneeb Yousuf, research scholar at Jamia Millia Islamia, echo this prediction with a grim outcome, writing,

> If Bangladeshi citizens now quietly infiltrate certain parts of India's borderlands, silently changing the religious demography of Bengal, this looks like reclaiming ground lost in the unsatisfactory partition of family assets of 1947. This could pose future risks that a Muslim-dominated West Bengal may in due course opt, together with Bangladesh, to form the large, strong Bengali nation some people wanted during the 1940s. (Menski & Yousuf, 2021)

As things stand, a federal, artificially 'secular' republic, with a weak rule of law in the face of multiple domestic separatist groups capable of exerting a 'veto through violence', gives India a very weak hand. If India does not build state capacity through massive constitutional, administrative, police, and judicial reforms, India will find itself as the new Yugoslavia in this new Cold War, as discussed above. Like India today, a neutral country which tries to play along with both the East and West, so as to focus on domestic consolidation, Yugoslavia, despite being on the border with Eastern Bloc states, enjoyed Western investment, trade, and movement. However, as soon as the country stopped being useful as a bulwark against the Eastern Bloc, the Western Bloc were very happy to put economic pressure on the country, causing stagnation and discontent, and then to support ethnic separatists in splintering the country.

A massive warning sign for India's future was in February 2021, with the Center for Strategic and International Studies (CSIS), an American foreign policy think tank, publishing a report titled, *Subnational Diplomacy: A Pivotal Tool for Biden's India Strategy*, which recommends that the Biden administration in Washington DC 'encourage participation of nonstate actors, including industry, academia, investors, research institutes in order to build a nimble, dependable network' in India. (Jain, 2021) What this means is that US state actors will seek to cultivate their own assets within Indian civil society and politics, in parallel to traditional state-to-state diplomacy with the government. These assets, over time, can be used to influence elite opinion and state policies to align with US interests, often to the detriment of public welfare.

If India's current Yugoslav-inspired policy of non-alignment, dating to the bonhomie between Josip Broz Tito and Jawaharlal Nehru, independent India's first prime minister, is ill-suited to the new Cold War, and neither superpower sees a use for India within their bloc, the question arises, what other options does the country have?

Another model of neutrality from the first Cold War is the 'Finlandization' model, from another neutral country that bordered one of the superpowers, the Soviet Union. This term is given to the process by which one powerful country makes a smaller neighboring country orient its economy and society towards the former, while allowing it to keep its nominal independence and its own political system. Or, as the Finnish political cartoonist Kari Suomalainen termed it, 'the art of bowing to the East without mooning the West'. (Macintyre, 2019) A situation where the political elite of the country themselves deploy state institutions to control, censor, and foster positive public attitudes and preferential trade relations to avoid antagonising the superpower neighbor, in the hope that appeasement and approval would result in lenient treatment.

Finally, there is the classical Swiss/Swedish/Austrian model of armed neutrality. Wherein a country ensures its neutrality by zealously defending its sovereignty through the involvement of every citizen against foreign domination. The digital equivalent of armed neutrality in the new Cold War would be to turn India into a self-sufficient digital economy, closed to the world in terms of online platforms and AI technology, and with a large, well-trained, and highly-motivated information warfare conscription system.

India's Path Forward: Reform, Revolution, or Collapse?

It is essential to acknowledge that the alternative to change is not the status quo; it is the catastrophic collapse of the old system. Nothing is permanent, everything collapses in the end. The question is, do we want to control the pace of collapse or just pretend all is okay as it collapses on us?

Unless there is a massive course correction, India will be left behind, competing merely for the crumbs of the new AI world – getting subcontracts, creating backend offices, and offering cheap services to the real hubs of innovation abroad.

While this may be enough to deliver a few years of Gross Domestic Product (GDP) growth, it will be meaningless if the state and private sector have neither any long-term strategic or civilizational ambitions nor any effective tools for achieving them.

It may seem reassuring to look at GDP statistics and say, 'Oh, everything is alright, India is just fifteen or twenty years behind China's level, and is finally on the right path now after liberalization and globalization.' However, such a comforting analysis does not necessarily mean it will take India only fifteen to twenty years to catch up. In fact, it is not possible for India to catch up to China, on any measure, unless the entire system and mentality of governance is dismantled and replaced from the bottom-up.

In the best-case scenario, India can maybe reach the per capita income level of Iran or Mexico in twenty years, and become a middle-income economy and a minor regional power. But even in that best case, this ostensible success will only last a decade or so. At that point, nobody within the international community will want to encourage, or even allow, a rising power to reach any higher. The US will have no qualms in using its financial leverage to ensure India's long-term economic stagnation in order to then engineer a Yugoslav-style break-up. Meanwhile, China will use the threat of a two-front war (in cooperation with Pakistan) to demand a submissive trade and diplomatic policy from India. In addition, Pakistan on their own, as the country succumbs to its internal challenges of economic stagnation, religious extremism, and climate change, may be encouraged to use nuclear weapons against Indian urban centres and civilian targets in a last-ditch effort to level the playing field with their historical rival in what former prime minister, Zulfikar Ali Bhutto, called their '1000-year war'. (Haqqani, 2005). Ever since acquiring nuclear weapons, Pakistan has maintained a first-use policy with the blessings of both the US and China, so that if India creates a large enough socio-economic or military gap relative to Pakistan, they will have the means to cut India back down to their level, betting on India being too pacifist and image-conscious to retaliate in kind. Thus, despite the theoretical threat of Indian nuclear retaliation in such a scenario, going ahead with first strikes may still seem attractive to Pakistani military planners, as the pusillanimous track record of the Indian state may suggest to them that New Delhi could instead pursue the Gandhian pacifist 'moral high ground' and seek foreign validation at the international level by highlighting itself as the victim of aggression instead of embarking on a proportional retaliation.

As a result, current institutions and ideologies of governance in place in India are akin to a boxing match against three simultaneous opponents, but where the country had one arm chopped off in 1947, and the other arm tied behind its back since then as well. In such a case, it is impossible to even land a single punch on one's opponent; the best one can hope for in such a situation is to dodge and evade, buying time while waiting for the timer to run out. However, there is no timer on history; it does not end, as contrary to Fukuyama's famous statement, there is no end of history.

If the Chinese policymaking elite today claims that India is under a semi-colonial state and semi-feudal economy, one which is incapable of delivering popular welfare and civilizational goals, it is simply because they are correct, and understand India at a fundamental level better than the West or even most Indian policymakers and intellectuals themselves. Today, India is trapped in unimaginative incrementalism, not allowing itself to dream beyond what others have destined it to be. Instead of re-imagining the outdated and ossified Constitution, Penal Code, courts, police, bureaucracy, education system, armed forces, or trade strategy, the country's decision-makers and opinion-shapers spend their time and energy on how to make these a little bit more comfortable or a little more efficient. But what is the point in improving efficiency of a system, when the very purpose and outcomes it is designed for are in fact poisonous to its own society?

When the state institutions are akin to an axe, designed to be wielded with brute force, and useful only to cut down trees, it does not matter how pure-hearted or tree-loving the one holding the axe is. Even trying to improve the system, merely sharpens this axe to make it more efficient at cutting down a whole forest. As the ancient Confucian philosopher Mencius wrote,

> When a minister lives among calumniators, flatterers, and sycophants, though he may wish the State to be well governed, is it possible for it to be so? (Mencius & Legge, 2011)

Instead of limiting oneself to dreaming merely of putting the axe in the hands of someone who resembles or thinks like the natives, what post-colonial societies should aspire to is reforge that axe into a shovel or a plough, that will allow them to replant and restore their sacred groves, both literally and figuratively.

As a result of these structural weaknesses, India today is an exact example of what its neighbors do not want to be: a post-Partition rump state, traumatized and ashamed after losing (or more accurately surrendering) its civil war in 1947 by accepting Partition without a whimper, and still ruled by colonial-era bureaucracy, police, and judiciary, with no shared civilizational identity, common goals, or social contract between citizen and state.

If there are any thinkers or leaders of twentieth century India whose thoughts and legacies will have an impact on the country in the twenty-first century, it is Mohammed Ali Jinnah and Huseyn Shaheed Suhrawardy, the founders of Pakistan, for proving that India's unreformed, colonial-era state institutions are both incapable and unwilling to prevent partition, civil war, or extortion by a violent domestic interest group or external power. If the country does not address the weaknesses they exposed, there will not be an India by 2100.

It is also important to recognize the deep roots of colonial-era laws and institutions in 'independent' India, because the state is much more than just Parliament and the Cabinet of Ministers at any given point of time. Those are simply the managers at the head of a system designed to suppress and subdue native assertion, after the attempted Indian War of Independence in 1857 proved that Indians were capable of self-organization and armed resistance against the East India Company. India's Penal Code, policing standards, judiciary, and educational system all date back to the takeover of the Company's colonial possessions by the British Crown in 1858. Clothed in alleged concern for the native subjects, these institutions were designed to prevent a native rebellion on the lines of 1857 from ever repeating. Together, they destroyed an indigenous tradition of civic engagement and political resistance that had developed at the grassroots over millennia. This is explained by Jayaprakash Narayan in his Foreword to the iconic Indian scholar Dharampal's book, *Civil Disobedience in Indian Tradition:*

> Whether it was to assert the 'dignity of the State' or for the 'maintenance of the public tranquility' or for 'upholding those sentiments of respect which it appeared so essential that the community should entertain for the public authority' the traditional right of the people of peaceful resistance had to be given no quarter. The reason Shri Dharampal gives, with which I am in agreement, is the feeling the British rulers had of extreme insecurity. They could not feel safe until they had beaten the people into a state of unquestioning obedience. The ultimate sanction they relied upon to achieve this end was military force. Thus was brought about the spiritual death of the people of this country.... (Narayan, 1971)

In addition, even the democratic institutions of 'independent' India were not created from the ground-up with the Constitution of India in 1950, but were simply a rebranded and expanded version of the British-supervised 'managed democracy' set up by the Government of India Acts of 1919 and 1935.

As a result, the Indian state today remains primarily the unelected and undemocratic colonial-era bureaucracy, police, and judiciary, all designed to degrade and demoralize its 'native subjects' rather than deliver rights to empowered citizens, while the elected Parliament and the Cabinet, for all their good or bad intentions, generally lack the capacity to act upon the people's aspirations at a structural level.

As the Croatian political philosopher Srećko Horvath says, 'The current system, with its never-ending war against the majority of people, other species and nature, is already more violent than any revolution.' (Anthony, 2019) The developing world might be pursuing some well-intentioned policies within the constraints of the system, but the truly righteous policy would be to accelerate the end of the current system. To place itself in the driving seat of a new system that seeks to give people the sovereignty and dignity imperative to create a society where poverty and powerlessness is not the default state, but an impossibility.

The Chinese understand this; it is a part of their philosophy, and incorporated into their understanding of the world today. As Mencius said, 'If you know that the thing is unrighteous, then use all despatch in putting an end to it – why wait until next year?' (Mencius & Legge, 2011)

The same sentiment is also a part of Indian philosophy, but under the hybrid Mughal-Macaulayan neo-colonial republic since 1950, the state has continued almost every British-era effort to strip Indians of these tools. Even after the long-awaited national liberation had been achieved and the British bureaucracy had been taken over by native managers, the mentalities of this new ruling class remained almost unchanged. Jayaprakash Narayan, building momentum for his attempted 'Total Revolution' *(Purna Swaraj)* in the early-1970s, drew a straight line between the attitudes of British colonial administrators and the new post-colonial Indian elite,

> During the British period, the needs of imperialist rule dictated that Indians be pictured as an inferior people in respect to material, moral and intellectual accomplishments. This deliberate denigration of the Indian nation was furthered by the incapacity of the foreigner to understand properly a civilisation so different from his own. So, in course of time, as our political subjugation became complete, we happened to accept as real the distorted image of ourselves that we saw reflected in the mirror the British held to us … After the first few years of euphoria since Independence, a period of self-denigration set in during which educated Indians, particularly those educated in the West, took the lead. Whether in the name of modernisation, science or ideology, they ran down most, if not all, things Indian. We are not yet out of this period. (Narayan, 1971)

Similarly, Samora Machel, the leader of the Mozambique Liberation Front and first president of independent Mozambique, summarized the state institutions he inherited from the Portuguese colonial administration in his country, which resonates clearly with India's seven decades of nominal independence:

> Some people, with a certain nostalgia, the worshippers and admirers of the colonial system, cherish and nurse its structures instead of smashing

> them. This is typical of a mentality in bondage to decadent values, negative values ... The structures in the state apparatus are infiltrated and disorganized. We do not punish indiscipline, we tolerate it. We do not punish saboteurs, we coexist with them and still pay them salaries.
>
> We do not remove or combat those who hanker for colonial structures, hierarchies and methods. Quite the reverse, we use them as if they were good cadres.
>
> Our structures are infiltrated by elements who are irresponsible, negligent, incompetent, thieving, malicious, dishonest, and the faithful servants of colonialism. Our structures shelter opportunists and the power-seekers who, under the banner of racism, tribalism and regionalism, stir up confusion, division and chaos, to satisfy their own personal, selfish and petty secondary interests. They are the mud on our boots that we must take off and clean.
>
> The antagonists within the society facilitated colonial occupation. Representatives of the exploiting strata betrayed the national cause and made an alliance with the foreigner to continue the domination and exploitation of their own people. (Machel, 1980)

The Courage to Invent the Future: Breaking the Shackles of the First Republic

The African freedom fighter and anti-colonial revolutionary Thomas Sankara famously said,

> You cannot carry out fundamental change without a certain amount of madness. In this case, it comes from nonconformity, the courage to turn your back on the old formulas, the courage to invent the future. It took the madmen of yesterday for us to be able to act with extreme clarity today. I want to be one of those madmen. We must dare to invent the future. (Jacobs, 2008)

In order to invent the future, one must first understand the past and present. Truth be told, India never achieved true decolonization, national liberation, or sovereignty; only a power transfer from the British elite to a British-trained native elite. As a result, the country has barely enjoyed the fruits of sovereignty over the past seventy-five years, only nominal independence. This is a direct result of the circumstances of the so-called 'non-violent' independence movement and post-colonial power transfer.

It has become an article of faith in both academia and politics that Mohandas Gandhi won Indian independence through non-violence. However, it was only non-violent for the colonizers, who then wrote this self-serving account of history from their perspective. For the millions of Indians jailed, tortured, killed in the freedom struggle, famines, and Partition, it was very violent indeed. 'Non-violence' only has meaning when one has the capacity to deploy violence, but one chooses not to use it. Otherwise, it is simply meekness and cowardice, clothed in a specious and vacuous morality.

The 'non-violence' myth was the colonizer's parting gift, emasculating the ancient Indian civilization instead of letting the blood of the fallen martyrs fertilize the soil for its long-awaited civilizational rebirth and regeneration. Instead of being able to say that the sacrifices of millions of ordinary Indians were not in vain, their suffering, trauma, and memories were thrown to the side in order to please the elite, denying a once-proud people the chance to reclaim their dignity and self-respect. Instead of being able to say that Indians won their freedom themselves, they were reduced to beggars who were 'granted' independence by a benevolent overlord, only after proving themselves worthy. Just like the inscription above the entrance of the Central Secretariat buildings of Edwin Lutyens and Herbert Baker's colonial capital of New Delhi reads:

> Liberty will not descend to a people, a people must raise themselves to liberty, it is a blessing that must be earned before it can be enjoyed.

However, during the Ghanaian independence movement, Kwame Nkrumah reminded his followers of the true nature of power dynamics around freedom, criticizing the 'semi-responsible government' that the British offered his people instead of true self-rule and sovereignty, 'Freedom is not something that one people can bestow on another as a gift. They claim it as their own and none can keep it from them'. (Nkrumah, 1953)

The question then arises, whom did this narrative of non-violence serve? Not the poor, not the oppressed, not those who sacrificed all they had in their struggle for dignity and freedom. Only the Anglophile, comprador bourgeoisie of the Indian National Congress (INC) who sought to inherit the privileges and tools that their colonial masters enjoyed, in exchange for arranging a 'non-violent' independence movement. As the West Indian political philosopher and pan-Africanist Frantz Fanon wrote on national liberation,

> [I]t is clear that in the colonial countries the peasants alone are revolutionary, for they have nothing to lose and everything to gain. The starving peasant, outside the class system is the first among the exploited to discover that only violence pays. For him there is no compromise, no possible coming to terms; colonization and decolonization is simply a question of relative strength. (Fanon, 1963)

The Congress leadership cravenly surrendered millions to their deaths at the hands of the feudal landowners, colonial collaborators, and compradors behind Jinnah's Muslim League, who cooperated with the British to use colonial state institutions to 'free' them from having to share power with *kafirs* (non-Muslims) considered inferior. Did Jinnah and his eclectic alliance of feudal landlords, Anglicized Bombay lawyers, and street goons achieve their prized goal of an ethno-religious theocracy by begging? No, they built up a 'veto through violence' by radicalizing and mobilizing their grassroots supporters and deploying them against their perceived enemies in the pursuit of maximalist political demands, which the cowardly colonial administration and 'non-violent' Congress leadership were unable (or unwilling) to counter.

Through this decision to avoid a full-fledged civil war by instead accepting Partition, Independent India did not guarantee peace; it only emboldened non-state actors and extremist leaders that they can extort state institutions by exerting violence. As a result, India has been trapped in a one-sided, low-intensity religious civil war since the pre-independence era, exemplified by the Moplah Rebellion, Direct Action Day, and Noakhali massacres, during which organized Islamist mobs conducted large-scale, inhuman atrocities upon unarmed Hindu civilians, while the state institutions were unable or unwilling to intervene. This very same phenomenon was repeated well after Partition and 'independence', during the ethnic cleansing of the Kashmiri Pandit community from the northern state of Jammu & Kashmir at the hands of terrorist groups and local collaborators in 1990, which rendered hundreds of thousands of Hindus homeless and refugees in their own country. Yet, throughout the past century, the state has been in denial, instead of addressing the root causes behind the ability and impunity of extremist elements to deploy violence as a political tool, the Republic of India is reduced to trying to prevent the helpless victims from 'provoking' any further escalation through their demands for truth, reconciliation, or justice. Owing to lack of state capacity and fear of a backlash that could easily undermine the limited power of top-heavy colonial-era state institutions, policymakers assume their only option is to buy (or more accurately, rent) harmony, instead of imposing costs on violence. As a result, they spend all their energy on ensuring order instead of delivering justice. Such a rented form of 'harmony' is merely what the American civil rights activist Martin Luther King Jr. called a 'negative peace', saying,

> [The] great stumbling block in [our] stride toward freedom is … the moderate, who is more devoted to "order" than to justice; who prefers a negative peace which is the absence of tension to a positive peace which is the presence of justice. (King, Jr., 1963)

The contemporary fetishization of Gandhi or Nelson Mandela as 'non-violent heroes' is bourgeois liberal propaganda, designed and encouraged by the elite to degrade and demoralize the masses. After all, from the perspective of the elite, non-violent protests are the easiest for the establishment to ignore, undermine, or appropriate, and act as a pressure valve to prevent radicalization and violent rebellion. George Orwell, the Indian-born British journalist and author, wrote about this phenomenon with regard to Gandhi soon after Indian independence, saying,

> [S]ince in every crisis he would exert himself to prevent violence — which, from the British point of view, meant preventing any effective action whatever — he could be regarded as 'our man'. In private this was sometimes cynically admitted. The attitude of the Indian millionaires was similar. Gandhi called upon them to repent, and naturally they preferred him to the Socialists and Communists who, given the chance, would actually have taken their money away. (Orwell, 1949)

Kenneth Kaunda, the African freedom fighter and first president of Zambia, renowned for his peaceful and non-violent path both to and out of power, wrote:

> Some people draw a comforting distinction between force and violence. I refuse to cloud the issue by such word-play. The power which establishes

> a state is violence; the power which maintains it is violence; the power which eventually overthrows it is violence. Call an elephant a rabbit only if it gives you comfort to feel that you are about to be trampled to death by a rabbit. (Kaunda, 1980)

This cult of non-violence also leads to a unique situation wherein countries that achieved independence through non-violence, such as India or South Africa, face what can be called the 'bigotry of high expectations', being treated to a different standard than those which used violence as a tool of decolonization and national liberation, such as Algeria or Vietnam. The former is constantly reminded that being inheritors of a non-violent legacy, they have a greater burden than others to uphold Western expectations of acceptable behaviours, ideologies, and policies.

> From the land of snake charmers, India became the land of Gandhi, nonviolent, non-aligned, and a non-entity, almost. For the global powers, nonviolence became a stick to beat India with. If India went to war, someone would say, "How can the Land of Gandhi indulge in wanton violence?" Testing a nuclear device? Gandhi and nonviolence. Shoring up border defenses? Gandhi and nonviolence. Correcting architectural colonialism? Gandhi and nonviolence. Celebrating Navrātri? Gandhi and nonviolence. Hitting a six in cricket? Gandhi and nonviolence. Worshipping Mā Kāli? Gandhi and nonviolence. (Kansara, 2020)

> India's pernicious founding myth gave rise to a pacifist country that believed it could get peace merely by seeking peace, instead of building the capability to defend peace. (Chellaney, 2019)

Meanwhile, anti-colonial and anti-imperialist thought leaders and nation-builders elsewhere had a very different take on the morality and reality of how power and violence works:

> Africans are constantly being reminded that they are a peace-loving, tolerant and communalist-minded people. The African is projected as an individual who has always been loath to shed blood. The corollary of this argument is that it would be immoral and against our nature to engage in revolutionary warfare. The moral argument is easily destroyed. Centuries of liberation wars, wars of conquest, revolution and counterrevolution in the west were not considered to be moral or immoral. They were simply

> part of western historical development. Our armed struggle for freedom is neither moral nor immoral, it is a scientific historically-determined necessity. (Nkrumah, 1968)

> At the level of individuals, violence is a cleansing force. It frees the native from his inferiority complex and from his despair and inaction; it makes him fearless and restores his self-respect. Even if the armed struggle has been symbolic and the nation is demobilized through a rapid movement of decolonization, the people have the time to see that the liberation has been the business of each and all and that the leader has no special merit. From thence comes that type of aggressive reticence with regard to the machinery of protocol which young governments quickly show. When the people have taken violent part in the national liberation they will allow no one to set themselves up as "liberators". They show themselves to be jealous of the results of their action and take good care not to place their future, their destiny, or the fate of their country in the hands of a living god. (Fanon, 1963)

When a country is 'granted' independence from above by the colonial master or external forces, instead of taking it by force, the new elite remain beholden to their 'benevolent' masters, a form of mental colonization that continues to protect the interests of the colonizers even after their physical departure.

> Imperialism leaves behind germs of rot which we must clinically detect and remove from our land but from our minds as well. (Fanon, 1963)

Turkish academic Ayşe Zarakol, in her seminal work, *After Defeat: How the East Learned to Live with the West,* discusses how once a nation is stigmatized in international perceptions, or at least the perceptions of the cultural hegemon, it can lead to an internalization of such stigma and a sense of shame. Wherein the people of that nation begin to believe in foreign portrayals of their culture as inferior, and constantly reinforce this impression through their behavior, in a phenomenon which can be called 'auto-Orientalism' or 'self-Orientalism'. This leads to their intellectual and policymaking elites being rendered extra-sensitive to foreign criticism or approval, who then shape state policy based on these sensitivities around status.

> [S]tigma has the same effect on states that it has on individuals: it colors and therefore motivates every subsequent interaction. Not being of the "West," being behind the "West," not being "modern" enough, not being developed or industrialized or secular or civilized or Christian or democratic enough – these are examples of designations (and, later, self-evaluations) that have essentially functioned as stigmas for states … Once the peoples of the old empires started accepting this worldview, it was inevitable that they too would embrace its judgment: they found themselves as coming up short, not just materially but socially and culturally. (Zarakol, 2011)

The Nehruvian dynastic state, despite the aesthetics of being a 'Sovereign Socialist Secular Democratic Republic', was never truly any of these labels, just as the 'Holy Roman Empire' was neither holy, nor Roman, nor an empire (Voltaire, 1756). Rather, Nehruvian India merely offered a cruel and cynical two-tiered 'feudalism with a human face', hoarding all the economic and social capital at the top and throwing just enough crumbs at the poor to keep them alive and dependent on the feudal *mai-baap* (patronage-based) state and its political elite. A post-colonial policy akin to applying a band-aid onto a gangrenous wound, and then praising one's own generosity and magnanimity for this supposed act of charity and altruism. Offering a Nordic-style welfare state and 'honorary white' status for the rich, while delivering brutal, soul-crushing feudalism to the poor. The Nobel Prize-winning American novelist John Steinbeck famously said the American poor 'see themselves not as an exploited proletariat, but as temporarily embarrassed millionaires'. (Wright, 2004) Meanwhile, the Indian elite see themselves not as native *compradors* or cheap imitations of their white masters, but as future US or UK citizens, temporarily inconvenienced by Indian passports. Yet, like in the past, they are only useful to Western powers as compradors, middlemen, and fixers that help colonial administrators navigate native politics, history, and culture. Despite all their proximity and utility to Western power structures, these compradors know that they are not seen as equals, and that if they stop toeing the imperialist line, they will be shown their place almost instantly. For in geopolitics, just like in their own homes in urban India's posh gated communities, servants do not get to eat at the table.

As Fyodor Dostoevsky wrote of Russian elite society and its craving for Western approval in the mid-1800s:

> You see, our whole life, from earliest childhood, has been geared to the European mentality. Is it possible that any of us could have prevailed against this influence, this appeal, this pressure? How is it that we have not been regenerated once and for all into Europeans? That we have not been so regenerated I think all will agree, some with joy, others, of course, with anger that we have not grown up enough for regeneration. (Dostoevsky, 1863)

Sri Aurobindo, the Indian revolutionary and philosopher, identified this fatal flaw in the self-appointed Indian intelligentsia and bourgeois leadership as early as 1907, who found themselves so embedded within the intellectual and socio-economic incentive structure of Western imperialism and colonialism, that far from dismantling it, they could only dream of a greater role for themselves within it:

> In this country, however, there is a class of wise men who regard the rule of the British bureaucracy as a dispensation of Providence, not only to create unity but to preserve it. They preach therefore a gospel of faith in the foreigner, distrust of our countrymen and acquiescence in alien rule as a godsend from on high and an indispensable condition for peace and prosperity. Even those whose hearts rebel against a doctrine so servile, are intellectually so much dominated by it that they cannot embrace Nationalism with their whole heart and try to arrive at a compromise between subjection and independence – a half-way house between life and death. (Aurobindo, 1907)

The Irish intellectual, poet, and playwright, Oscar Wilde, writing about the morality of British liberalism in the age of industrialization and colonialism in 1891, also accurately predicted the situation of India today, whose elite are still trapped in the cage of the very same Victorian-era political debates and false morality.

> They find themselves surrounded by hideous poverty, by hideous ugliness, by hideous starvation. It is inevitable that they should be strongly moved by all this. The emotions of man are stirred more quickly than man's intelligence; and, as I pointed out some time ago in an article on the function of criticism, it is much more easy to have sympathy with suffering than it is to have sympathy with thought. Accordingly, with admirable, though misdirected intentions, they very seriously and very

> sentimentally set themselves to the task of remedying the evils that they see. But their remedies do not cure the disease: they merely prolong it. Indeed, their remedies are part of the disease.
>
> They try to solve the problem of poverty, for instance, by keeping the poor alive; or, in the case of a very advanced school, by amusing the poor.
>
> But this is not a solution: it is an aggravation of the difficulty. The proper aim is to try and reconstruct society on such a basis that poverty will be impossible. (Wilde, 1891)

What makes this upcoming era of digital colonization so crucial is that it can open India's eyes to these uncomfortable realities. The multiple crises India has already faced at the start of the 2020s—be it the COVID-19 pandemic, anti-Hindu riots in New Delhi, horrific political violence in West Bengal, or the revival of Khalistani separatism in Punjab—and the toothless state response to them, have exposed that the country is finally reaching the limits of its current political and administrative system. A system which can easily be held to ransom by foreign intervention, extortionist extremists, and internal saboteurs.

As the limits of the current system's utility are reached, it is important to remember that nothing is permanent. Everything eventually ends, even the unquestionable foundations of the Ambedkarite-Nehruvian Republic through which the country is trapped into incapacity and inaction. India has to radically change – to match the world around it and the goals its people have for their civilization, in order to not just survive but thrive for centuries ahead. If a polity does not radically reform itself in its own interest, the alternative is not the status quo continuing to last indefinitely, the alternative is catastrophic collapse, and changes on the terms of others instead of its own. Without massive constitutional, administrative, judicial, police, and educational reforms, India will remain a semi-feudal society and semi-colonial polity. Naively sleepwalking into another partition, civil war, and Balkanization that others have planned, regardless of who wins elections to merely manage the broken system.

With this in mind, the new India that needs to be built could take many forms: it could be a *Mahājanapada* based on ancient Indian political conceptions of a republic, a Sanskrit revivalist dharmic homeland akin to Israel, a Sri Lankan-style unitary state with a dharmic constitution and executive presidency, a post-socialist restored monarchy like Cambodia under a *Cakravartin Samrāt*, a Malaysian-style *bhūmiputra* state (with special rights and protections for recognized native communities and faiths), a welfarist state based on an indigenous 'socialism with Indian characteristics' such as *sarvodaya* or *antyodaya*, a second republic based on the ideologies put forth by pre-independence leaders such as Subhas Chandra Bose, Manabendra Nath Roy, Vinayak Damodar Savarkar, or Bal Gangadhar Tilak, or a hybrid democratic model on the lines of recent constitutional reforms in Chile, Poland, Russia, or Turkey.

There are several models that would appeal to many people within the country. The exact form it takes is to be driven by the people themselves, on the foundation of a unifying ideology of national liberation and a decolonization of hearts, minds, and institutions. It is essential to note that the political system of a country is merely a superstructure built upon the foundation of state sovereignty and individual dignity. A country can only build its political system upon this basis, be it democracy, communism, or even a monarchy. Without this foundation, political debates are reduced merely to aesthetic choices for the elites. As long as the new India can protect sovereignty from neo-colonialism and deliver on the people's socio-economic and cultural aspirations such as their pursuit of *dharma* (moral righteousness), *artha* (material prosperity), *kāma* (human desires), and *mokṣa* (spiritual liberation), such a change should be welcomed and embraced, no matter the model that the people choose for themselves.

Citizens should feel empowered to lead their country towards a constitution that creates an enabling environment for the fulfilment of their aspirations. Combined with state institutions that deliver rights, protection, and a social contract, instead of a callous and cruel bureacracy sinisterly hovering above them, offering either patronage or punishment in its 'civilizing mission'.

A roadmap to creating such a state could be constitutional reform that removes the dead weight of colonial-era standards, mentalities, and institutions. The Constitution, Penal Code, Civil Code, and other laws all need to be democratized, by redrafting them all from scratch in simple language, free of jargon, translated into every state language, and made widely available as original sources online and offline, so people can access them and understand laws themselves instead of being dependent on self-appointed custodians such as lawyers, journalists, and politicians.

A common complaint and refrain heard for decades among many jaded middle-class Indians is that the country is dysfunctional because of 'too much democracy'. However, nothing can be farther from the truth. The issue is not that India has too much democracy; it has too little, and what it has is wasted in the wrong places. The current unelected and unaccountable bureaucratic and judicial institutions suffer from a 'democratic deficit' and are all designed to thwart any aspirations of the people that can challenge the status quo. Moreover, the current Constitution, drafted and enacted under British colonial supervision has been turned by Supreme Court judgments into a 'holy book' of sorts, beyond the comprehension, reproach, or questioning of the masses. This ossification is the exact opposite of what Sri Aurobindo saw to be the very basis of Indian polity,

> The one principle permanent at the base of construction throughout all the building and extension and rebuilding of the Indian polity was the principle of an organically self-determining communal life — self-determining not only in the mass and by means of the machinery of the vote and a representative body erected on the surface, representative only of the political mind of a part of the nation, which is all that the modern system has been able to manage, but in every pulse of its life and in each separate member of its existence.
>
> The test of the Indian genius for socio-political construction lay in the successful application of its principle of a communal self-determined freedom and order to suit this growing development and new order of circumstances. (Aurobindo, 1942)

Hence, the coming years can also be an opportunity to democratize the Constitution with this in mind. The first step in such a new Constitution should be a clearer separation of powers, with direct elections for an executive president, who appoints a Cabinet of Ministers and sets government policy. While in a new, unicameral parliament, the role of the Speaker can be reimagined as the elected leader of the legislature, while Members of Parliament (MPs) are made responsible for drafting, passing, amending, and repealing laws and serving on oversight committees, rather than acting as the elected feudal lords of their constituencies, seeing themselves as above the law, and holding court to offer favours to supplicants among their electorates.

On this note, India needs more local democracy and fewer regional satraps. This can be done by reforming the federal structure, which is currently serving only to amplify artificial ethno-linguistic fissures and facilitating foreign powers' attempts at promoting sub-national separatism and Balkanization. By discarding the current Constitution's State List and Concurrent List, and thus ensuring 'One Nation, One Law', the current state governments and legislatures can be dissolved, and in their place, the country's 740 districts can be upgraded into elected *janapadas* (prefectures), a term used for classical Indian republican polities, responsible for the delivery of rights and implementation of policy objectives on the ground, on the lines of prefectures in France or Japan. Each *janapada* can be administered by a directly-elected *nāyaka* (prefect) and a seven-member executive council, akin to Switzerland's cantonal system. Such a set of bottom-up, accessible institutions can replace the current system of chief ministers, Members of Legislative Assemblies (MLAs), and district magistrates acting like local feudal lords, enjoying the trappings of power with no accountability to the public.

In each *janapada*, crime prevention should be assigned to a local *janarakshak seva* (people's protection service) based on the community policing model, accountable to local citizens, having them provide a sense of security and build a working relationship with the public they serve, rather than fortifying themselves in their colonial-era *thana* (station or barracks), waiting for the public to come to them to report crime after the deed. Meanwhile, law and order, crime investigation, counter-terrorism should be assigned to a new central police force, independent of the executive, so that the Ministry of Home Affairs or local elected representatives cannot use it as their personal militia. This can be similar to the independent nature of the armed forces, with democratic safeguards through parliamentary committee oversight, rather than being directly under the control of the Cabinet.

In addition, one could suggest splitting the Supreme Court into a constitutional court and court of final appeal, each with clear and separate functions and duties. Alongside this reform, each *janapada* can be empowered from the bottom-up through a decentralized system of courts and alternative dispute resolution mechanisms, working in local languages and jargon-free, to ensure that justice is accessible at the grassroots.

Finally, the new constitution should allow for national-level referenda for constitutional amendments, organized by the Election Commission at the advice of the president, Cabinet, or Parliament, requiring a two-thirds majority of both voters and *janapadas* to pass, in order to break the deadlock of the current Supreme Court's 'Basic Structure Doctrine' and the obstructionist role of the Rajya Sabha, both of which exist in their current form to the prevent any meaningful constitutional reform.

While many of these suggestions may sound radical or utopian, they exist worldwide, including in the Indian subcontinent—Sri Lanka being an example, which has enacted many reforms despite similar levels of religious, linguistic, and ethnic diversity combined with a British colonial administrative legacy of 'divide-and-rule'. Bhutan, an absolute monarchy with a much poorer economy than India, has also adopted a modern, people-centric Constitution in front of our eyes, based on bottom-up, village-to-village public consultations, and drafted in easy-to-understand language in order to empower its citizens. In addition, the post-socialist countries of Central and Eastern Europe all adopted new constitutions in the early-1990s, often along with lustration laws to purge the institutions of loyalists of the discredited *ancien régime.* Even in the early 2020s, Chile has drafted a new Constitution, based on mass participation, to replace its current outdated document seeped in the legacy of a brutal neo-colonial dictatorship, and put it to a public vote before adoption. As Michael Parenti has put in plain and simple terms,

> There is nothing sacred about the existing system. All economic and political institutions are contrivance that should serve the interests of the people. When they fail to do so, they should be replaced by something more responsive, more just, and more democratic. (Parenti, 2015)

It is truly a shame that India has reduced itself to worshipping the cage left behind for it by its former tormentors, leaving it too helpless to imagine a world outside this cage. As writer and film-maker Radha Bharadwaj has said,

> 'When the slave will whip himself after the master has long gone, the work of colonialism is complete'. (Pandey, 2021)

As long as India allows people with colonial mentalities to act as the self-appointed gatekeepers of the country, the country's decolonization and sovereignty is incomplete. *Svatantrata* (independence) is meaningless without *svarajya* (self-rule); *svarajya* is meaningless without *svabhiman* (self-respect).

Bibliography

Andrew, B.C. (2010, 3 April). Indira's India and the KGB. *The Times.* https://www.thetimes.co.uk/article/indiras-india-and-the-kgb-3c5hp98xttm

Anthony, A. (2019, 24 April). Srećko Horvat: The Current System is More Violent than any Revolution. *The Guardian.* https://www.theguardian.com/books/2019/apr/21/srecko-horvat-poems-from-the-future-interview

Armitage, R. (2021, December 27). China studied the collapse of the Soviet Union and learned three lessons to avoid a similar fate. ABC News. https://www.abc.net.au/news/2021-12-26/ussr-collapsed-30-years-ago-china-tries-to-avoid-same-fate/100705112

Aurobindo, S. (1907, 27 April). *Shall India be Free? The Loyalist Gospel. Bande Mataram.* https://www.aurobindo.ru/workings/sa/37_06_07/0125_e.htm

Aurobindo, S. (1942). *The Spirit and Form of Indian Polity.* Calcutta: Arya Publishing House.

Chellaney, B. (2019, February 3). The non-violence myth: India's founding story bestows upon it a quixotic national philosophy and enduring costs. *Times of India.* https://timesofindia.indiatimes.com/blogs/toi-edit-page/the-non-violence-myth-indias-founding-story-bestows-upon-it-a-quixotic-national-philosophy-and-enduring-costs/

Dalle Mulle, E. (2019). *The Nationalism of the Rich: Discourses and Strategies of Separatist Parties in Catalonia, Flanders, Northern Italy and Scotland (Routledge Studies in Modern European History)* (1st ed.). Routledge.

Deng, X. (1984). *Building a Socialism with a Specifically Chinese Character.* Speech to the Japanese delegation to the second session of the Council of Sino-Japanese Non-Governmental Persons, 30 June 1984

Deutsche Welle. (2021, 30 May). Danish secret service helped US spy on Merkel: report. *Deutsche Welle.* https://www.dw.com/en/danish-secret-service-helped-us-spy-on-germanys-angela-merkel-report/a-57721901

Dostoyevsky, F. (1863). *Winter Notes on Summer Impressions.* New York: C riterion Books.

Fanon, F. (1963). *The Wretched of the Earth.* New York: Grove Press.

France24. (2021, September 21). France's Le Drian asks Europeans to 'think hard' about alliances amid submarine spat. *France 24.* https://www.france24.com/en/diplomacy/20210920-france-s-le-drian-asks-europeans-to-think-hard-about-alliances-amid-submarine-spat

Fukuyama, F. (1992). *The End of History and the Last Man.* New York: Free Press.

Haqqani, H. (2005). *Pakistan: Between Mosque and Military.* Washington DC: Carnegie Endowment for International Peace.

Herman, E.S., & Chomsky, N. (1988). *Manufacturing consent: The Political Economy of the Mass Media.* New York: Pantheon Books.

Hoon, C.Y. (2004). Revisiting the Asian Values Argument used by Asian Political Leaders and its Validity. *Indonesian Quarterly,* 32(2), 154–174.

Jacobs, S. (2008, 15 October). Sankara: Daring to invent Africa's Future. *The Guardian.* https://www.theguardian.com/commentisfree/2008/oct/15/thomassankara-burkinafaso

Jain, N. (2021, 11 February). *Subnational Diplomacy: A Pivotal Tool for Biden's India Strategy.* Center for Strategic and International Studies. https://www.csis.org/blogs/adapt-advance-refreshed-agenda-us-india-relations/subnational-diplomacy-pivotal-tool-bidens

Kamau, J.N. (2019). The Road to Shanghai; A Stranger in Africa's Coffin-Case of Kenya. *Biomedical Journal of Scientific & Technical Research,* 12(4).

Kansara, B. (2020, 4 October). The Non-Silence of Non-Violence. *Kansaratva Chronicles.* https://kansaratva.wordpress.com/2020/10/04/the-non-silence-of-non-violence/

Kauffmann, S. (2019, 7 May). Opinion | Macron Puts Germany on Trial. *The New York Times.* https://www.nytimes.com/2019/05/07/opinion/macron-puts-germany-on-trial.html

Kaunda, K. (1980). Morris, Colin (ed.). *The Riddle of Violence.* San Francisco: Harper & Rowe.

Kautilya & Shamasastry, R. (1915). *Kautilya's Arthasastra.* Bangalore: Government Press

King, Jr., M.L. (1963, 16 April). *Letter from a Birmingham Jail.* University of Pennsylvania. https://www.africa.upenn.edu/Articles_Gen/Letter_Birmingham.html

Lieven, A. (2021, 16 August). *Report reaffirms that climate is the national security threat of our times.* Responsible Statecraft.

https://responsiblestatecraft.org/2021/08/10/report-reaffirms-that-climate-is-the-national-security-threat-of-our-times/

Machel, S. (1980). *Transform the State Apparatus into an Instrument of Victory.* Speech in Maputo, Mozambique, 7 February 1980

Macintyre, B. (2019). *The Spy and the Traitor: The Greatest Espionage Story of the Cold War.* New York: Crown.

Maisey, R. (2021, 13 February). The Real Third World. *Tribune.* https://tribunemag.co.uk/2021/02/the-real-third-world

Malhotra, R. (2021). *Artificial Intelligence and the Future of Power: 5 Battlegrounds.* New Delhi: Rupa Publications India Pvt Ltd.

Mauldin, J. (2020, 30 November). *We are about to mint even more excess elites.* Forbes. https://www.forbes.com/sites/johnmauldin/2020/11/30/we-are-about-to-mint-even-more-excess-elites/

Menski, W., & Yousuf, M. (2021). *Kashmir after 2019: Completing the Partition* (1st ed.). SAGE Publications Pvt. Ltd.

Mickelson, S. (1983). *America's Other Voice: The Story of Radio Free Europe and Radio Liberty.* Westport: Praeger.

Morgenthau, H.J. (1948). The Problem of Sovereignty Reconsidered. *Columbia Law Review,* 48(3), 341.

Narayan, J.P. (1971). *Foreword.* In Dharampal, *Civil Disobedience in Indian Tradition.* Varanasi: Sarva Seva Sangh Prakashan.

Narayan, J.P. (2005). *My Concept of Total Revolution.* In Das, S. (Ed.), *Jayaprakash Narayan: A Centenary Volume.* Delhi: Mittal Publication.

Nkrumah, K. (1953). *Motion of Destiny.* Speech to the National Assembly, Accra, 10 July 1953.

Nkrumah, K. (1965). *Neo-colonialism: The Last Stage of Imperialism.* London: Nelson.

Nkrumah, K. (1968), *HANDBOOK of REVOLUTIONARY WARFARE: A Guide to the Armed Phase of the African Revolution,* New York: International Publishers.

Onishi, N. (2021, 11 October). "Woke" American Ideas are a Threat, French Leaders Say. *The New York Times.* https://www.nytimes.com/2021/02/09/world/europe/france-threat-american-universities.html

Orwell, G. (1949, January). Reflections on Gandhi. *Partisan Review,* 16(1), 85–92.

Pandey, P. (2021, 3 February). *Colonialism in Media: Why is Joseph Biden not a "Christian Nationalist"? HinduPost.* https://www.hindupost.in/media/the-colonial-bias-in-media/

Parenti, M. (2015). *Profit Pathology and Other Indecencies.* Taylor & Francis.

Sharma, K. (2021, December 6). What China Learned From the Collapse of the USSR. *The Diplomat.* https://thediplomat.com/2021/12/what-china-learned-from-the-collapse-of-the-ussr/

Voltaire. (1756). *Essai Sur Les Moeurs Et L'esprit Des Nations.* Voltaire Foundation.

Wilde, O. (1891). The Soul of Man Under Socialism. *The Fortnightly Review,* 49(290), 292–319.

Wong, J., & Zheng, Y. (2001). *The Nanxun Legacy and China's Development in the Post-Deng Era.* Singapore: Singapore University Press.

Wood, G. (2020, 12 November). Can History Predict the Future? *The Atlantic.* https://www.theatlantic.com/magazine/archive/2020/12/can-history-predict-future/616993/

Wright, R. (2004). *A Short History of Progress.* House of Anansi Press.

Zarakol, A. (2011). *After Defeat: How the East Learned to Live With the West* (Cambridge Studies in International Relations, Series Number 118). Cambridge: Cambridge University Press.

FOUR

Artificial Intelligence for National Security

Lt. Gen. P.J.S. Pannu

Introduction

The possibility of machines taking over the lives of humans is easily gauged from the proliferation of smartphones and numerous electronic devices that control our everyday existence. In fact, trends reveal that the first item on a youngster's shopping list is a smartphone. It is also the fastest replaced, and upgraded, item. The millennium generation has been superseded by the neo-millennium, (those born after the early 2000s), that has made the computer, a multifunctional machine, their most proximate companion. This kind of unnatural dependency gives rise to serious questions. The first is obvious: Has a machine taken charge of human life? The answer is an unequivocal, Yes. The second: Is the mind of the neo-millennial being impacted, influenced, and controlled by a smartphone? The answer again is, Yes. This phenomenon is clearly dangerous and alarming, as an individual is oblivious to the fact that a considerable part of decision-making is influenced by a machine.

A similar collective analogy applies to the nation, raising grave concerns about national security. These machines not only influence our minds, they constantly map them and pry on us as individuals, as communities, and as a nation. We are certainly at risk because we have not clearly grasped as to who operates these machines and receives maximum advantage. The main beneficiaries are clearly those that manufacture and program the machine, while the rest remain users and get used in the process.

The term *national security* covers all areas of governance that ensures physical, economic, material, and territorial protection of a nation. It preserves the national culture and value system for the common good of its citizens, which allows them to make choices for overall prosperity. National security provides wholesome support for the protection of a nation's citizens and those that influence them. Machines, on the other hand, provide opportunities and also pose a threat to the individual and collective security of the country. The government of the day is responsible for ensuring that technology must be harnessed, absorbed, and controlled in a manner by which a nation always remains the master and and stays strong, both internally and externally.

Future threats can appear in traditional, and non-traditional, ways; the latter is more likely as machines take over. Future wars will be based on technology. The enemy will control our capabilities either by destroying, or denying, the use of our machines, while simultaneously being able to use theirs with impunity. Wars will be described as trade-, economic- and territorial wars including grabbing materials from existing land and other planets. The use of physical force would include applying both kinetic and non-kinetic means, or non-contact, and contact, battle methods.

Security forces, especially the military, would increasingly use autonomous war and remotely controlled systems. Digital platforms will be operated through wire or wireless networks making huge demands on power consumption to run a plethora of autonomous machines simultaneously. Large digital networks will consume huge bandwidths, achieving high speeds of computing and communication with inbuilt redundancies. Sensors and computers would run neural networks with high cognitive power and require special materials that are tough, light, and responsive. Electronics would revolutionize miniaturization in combination with super-sensitive materials and smart circuits.

Robotics will empower leaders, scientists, administrators, managers, soldiers, commanders alike and equally whereby switching roles would be a possibility. Warfighting would need a very high order of situational awareness, quick decision-making, and intimate control for precise execution. It would be possible to fight battles through digital platforms via remote control. Machines would become smarter; the ones that control would be challenged to stay ahead and be faster. Mistakes, miscalculations or accidents caused by faulty machines will likely run into complications of law and ethics. Given the advantages and challenges of machines, Artificial Intelligence (AI) that will run machines as autonomous systems are here to stay.

The Power of Virtual Domain

Robotics will be seen as the major game changer in the medium- to long-term period. Artificial Intelligence would power machines and humans in an unprecedented way. This will accelerate all processes of growth and economy but result in a sharp divide between humanity. The group of humans powered by AI and robotics, even though smaller in number, could be seen as the 'haves'. In effect, dominating those that do not have access to this 'virtual power' and thus remaining 'have-nots'. This may lead to a contest, more likely a clash, between the two sides, making the 'have-nots' literal slaves of the neo-colonists, i.e., the 'haves'. In this scenario, robotics would replace human beings in several aspects of life. To begin with, the risky, menial and subhuman jobs would be outsourced to machines. Artificial Intelligence will be seen as the *largest outsourcing ever witnessed in global history.* The first shift is likely to happen in the security business, starting from personal, home, community or even national security. Those not employing such machines would remain defenceless and capitulate or surrender. In some ways, this process has already begun. China realized this phenomenon well in time and has deep designs, well prepared plans, and a strategy in place.

The AI-driven military machines would essentially be used for grabbing or protecting resources such as water, rare and precious minerals on earth and other planets, and/or taking over the industrial potential of adversaries. Economy and technology are now seen as the main ingredients of comprehensive national power and nations rich in both have begun to enslave others. Autonomous systems powered by machines will be seen replacing fighting machines, as a result making aircraft, tanks, guns and military machinery autonomous. This would ensure there is minimum risk to human lives in warfighting and even the frontline fighting soldier would be a robot in the privileged forces.

A clear shift in power toward nations employing such means is likely, causing larger instability in global security, and upsetting the balance of power. The desire to covet massive natural resources will make violence a preferred option, more so, with the world population likely to grow to almost nine billion by the year 2050. This contest is currently very visible between dominant powers. The first target for resource grabbing will be defenceless nations that are technologically starved and denied. By 2050, India is projected to be the most populated country in the world with a population of 1.6 billion, leaving China behind at 1.4 billion. One can only imagine the disruption caused by the technological and economic balance of power in the region. Disputes based on territory will become a ready excuse for large land grabs.

What Needs to be Secured?

The power of Artificial Intelligence cannot be realized unless nations invest rightly, and wisely, in digital technology. The security of AI platforms would be of prime concern not only for military application but for all critical infrastructure of a nation such as power grids, airlines, banking systems, strategic industry, and so on. Financial institutions and currency provide financial autonomy and strength to a nation. The digital growth of business and banking services runs the risk of exposure to external control or lack of internal control. The rise of deep and dark web transactions and introduction to tradable crypto currencies need a quick fix. Investments must be prioritized into preparing national budgets where the digital industry gets an urgent and larger piece of the pie. Governments must realize the urgency and necessity in such financial allocations as the survival of the nation would largely depend on how swiftly technology is implemented. Transformation is required in turning analogous systems into autonomous systems, both for critical infrastructure as well as for the military. This cannot be treated as a 'switch solution', as numerous national bodies have to unite to make this transformation a deliberate, and a well-planned, process; one that is diligently implemented. Artificial Intelligence engines are double-edged, super-productive and also super-destructive, when left unregulated or uncontrolled.

China outlined sixteen megaprojects in its medium- and long-term Science and Technology Development Plan (2006-20). This included advanced numeric-controlled machinery, high-end generic chips, integrated circuit manufacturing and techniques, Chinese High-definition Earth Observation (CHEO), advanced nuclear reactors, manned aerospace and moon exploration, and large aircraft. In 2017, the Chinese Ministry of Industry and Information Technology issued a document on goals for building an AI-enabled economy from 2018 to 2020 in line with the vision of the top leadership. This was aimed at China's ability to mass-produce neural-network processing chips by 2020. In 2018, Chinese president, Xi Jinping urged China to speed up its semiconductor strategy in the face of foreign pressure and growing demands on technology. China aims at reducing reliance on foreign technology by the year 2025. It has created a roadmap for milestone contributions to the global scientific community by 2030 and ultimately become a science and technology powerhouse by 2050.

Indian industry needs an urgent re-orientation. To absorb AI into all of our systems, including national security apparatus, industry cannot rely on imported chips/semiconductors. A large-scale communication network is essential which is scalable and has 5G/6G capacities. Digitization and indigenization must go hand in hand, from designing to fabrication, and all, or most of it, must be done on Indian soil. Indian industry has sufficient capacities to scale up Information and Communication Technologies (ICT), provided the budgets and policies are supportive. In fact, ICT will be the main foundation to achieve digitization, providing a baseline to create AI platforms. Data reservoirs will require early fruition to get the machines to crank in the process of 'machine and deep learning'. Data management institutions will take time to get established but must be built in parallel, which might initially consume large manpower. India has a sizeable Information Technology (IT) and business base that can shape up the cyber domain in ensuring it builds exclusive, yet interactive, domains.

Cyberspace has been widely accepted as the fifth domain of war that nations need to protect and exploit for offensive operations. The militarization of cyberspace and development of cyber weapons are raising the spectre of a cyber war.[1] In fact, cyber-attacks are emerging as the concealed war of all wars. The digitization of warfare with applications that connect the human mind to war machines places the cyber ecosystem at the core of all functions. Cyber warfare would mean hitting the electronic or digital nerve of the enemy while securing one's own. It covers a very large canvas ranging from information systems to data that moves the digital platforms which are networked. The cyber domain can be compared to the human body that connects and combines all the vital organs and in particular, a combination of 'brain and heart'. The brain is the nerve centre and the heart is the prime mover of data as power. Any of these get hit, the system gets paralyzed. As cyber networks comprise the number

1. Lt. Gen. Davinder Kumar, *The New Arthashastra, Cyber Security and Imperatives*; p. 273.

of computers interlinked and fused together through the network, if any computer in the network gets compromised, it acts as the weakest link undermining the entire network. The networks and data containing information would remain constant targets. *There are no defined cyber borders: it is all pervasive.* All critical infrastructure such as power supply, railways, aircraft, and military platforms can be attacked. There can be a situation of immense alarm if a major pipeline were to be shut down by a cyber-attack, as another way of enforcing oil embargos.

Electric power grids are regulated and controlled through a network of computers. A knock on the power cyber grid can bring the country to a grinding halt. Worse, as the government is making a rapid shift towards e-governance, ending the need of maintaining physical files, an attack would not only make these files and data inaccessible but also susceptible to theft. Similar attacks can paralyze airlines, banking, defence, health services, logistics-supply chain, e-market, e-governance and so on, triggering a man-made disaster. Even though firewalls, encryptions and protocols are regularly upgraded, what is most concerning is that often, it is the people manning the database developers, administrators and others that end up creating an unsecured environment facilitating a cyber-attack.[2] In recent years, attacks targeting critical infrastructure and businesses have surged. These include the 2017 *WannaCry* and *NotPetya* ransomware attacks, the 2015 attack on the Ukrainian power grid and the 2010 Stuxnet attack on Iranian nuclear reactors.[3] The Solarwinds (a major cyber-security breach, allegedly carried out by Russia) and the Colonial Pipeline (the American oil pipeline system that suffered a ransomware cyber-attack) attacks deeply impacted the economy and financial health of several companies.

A compromise on security of critical infrastructure is akin to handing over command and control to the enemy. For military platforms, it would be essential to build military grade secrecy and protection from interference. The basic 'attack identity' is the Internet Protocol or IP address. It is essential that military equipment and critical infrastructure must create 'non-IP' systems, i.e., systems without addresses unknown and unrecognized by other agencies. The US has been working on IP address-less connections. The Distributed Denial-of-Service (DDoS) is becoming more severe; its speed has increased to over three hundred

2. Data Vulnerability and Security Threats. *Data Sovereignty: The Pursuit of Supremacy*; p. 87.

3. Sameer Patil, Cyber Attacks on Critical Infrastructure: Is India Prepared; *The Hindustan Times* 20 May 2021.

gigabytes per second. The amount of data coming at this speed can easily overwhelm most servers and cause networks to crash.[4] Cyber espionage, cyber terrorism, and social media amalgam adds to the vulnerability of individuals that may not receive any institutional support either due to the lack of, or very nascent, legal provisions.

Data is believed to be the new oil. It is being constantly collected, stolen, spied on, analyzed, or even manipulated. It is being sold at huge prices from various agencies operating under the garb of innocent service providers. Software companies offer multiple freebies that a customer is tempted to purchase, including apps, games, and instant global connection. Increasingly, these companies are collaborating or acquiring other companies to enlarge the database for analytics and deep learning. Machines can process huge amounts of data within a matter of seconds establishing a 'cause and effect' relationship while making a quick comparative analysis. The machines shorten the Observe Orient Decide Act (OODA) loop to an instant process. The speed and accuracy of machine decision-making can beat a conventional competitor effortlessly. Those that employ smarter and faster machines will prevail in 'first draw' engagements.

Conversely, if an adversary employs machines with inferior technology or has inadequate data, they will fall behind in the OODA cycle. The worst-case scenario would be an inferior nation that does not use machines, or has machines with no or low/inferior data or, in spite of having both, allows its data to be manipulated. Such disruption would cause instant loss in all forms of engagement i.e., trade, commerce, targeting of critical infrastructure, and even war. Data security needs careful understanding, planning, and implementation. The consequences of losing machine data are grave, more than in the analog or cosmic world. Over a period of two centuries, we have transited from the cosmic to the cyber world. The cyber age, i.e., the current period, also known as the information age, is typically caused by the Fourth Industrial Revolution. In the cyber domain, the flow of data can be compared to haemoglobin in the bloodstream. The speed and volume of flow of data increases, making a demand for large bandwidths. Any leak in the networks would be catastrophic as the data that powers the AI engines would make all autonomous systems fail or malfunction, just as in a human body, if an unwanted chemical is added or an important one made deficient. The loss of data not only means that information is compromised; it can also imply information being lost

---

4. Arvind Gupta; *How India Manages its National Security; Cyber Security Challenges;* p. 313.

in a manner that it may not be available or accessible to us. Imagine a scenario whereby someone gets control of your bank account without your knowledge, making your account inaccessible, or using your email account with you having access to it. Data protection is achieved by protecting all networks that connect computers, machines and subsystems. Firewalls have been the traditional protection system; however, the software that offers protection is increasingly being used to inject viruses where systems can get compromised after uploading new programmes. Spywares can be induced at the assembly stage of machines. Commercial internet is the easiest mode to attack any machine. Once a machine is compromised, it becomes a slave of the enemy, most often without our knowledge.

The power of cyber networks is magical as it seamlessly connects the entire security, economic, and governance apparatus. Increasingly, e-governance, e-market and the like are making remote processes possible. Machines will require a neural-network with multiple sensors to enable them to get smarter. Heavy duty servers and cloud makes storage of mega data possible when employed with high-speed computers, enabling machines to work with greater speed and efficiency than a human being. A robot is simply a machine that mimics a human in logic and makes any process faster. Human behavior is replicated by a machine with the aid of large volumes of behavioral data collected by the computer. Similarly, details for the military like terrain, weather, enemy's locations, habits, doctrines, personality of commanders, strengths, weaknesses are an endless list that would make a machine present options for decision making, or when permitted, take decisions based on pre-fed parameters and execute actions. This would result in an automated OODA cycle with autonomous functionality as an option.

Even though it is possible to have large nationwide networks, these would be extremely complicated and prone to becoming dysfunctional if any part of the network breaks down. Domain separation would therefore be the ideal way ahead. For instance, the military, paramilitary, border security forces, police forces, and civil defence units should have the ability to unite on a common network like Wide Area Network (WAN), with each entity having its own domain network. This arrangement is referred to as the 'System of Systems'. It is possible to create very small and tight domains, yet configure them to access, and be accessible, by larger domains, making them network-centric.

Imperatives for Network-centric Operations

Technology-based warfare is dictated by new possibilities that the new industrial age (Industry 4.0—the Fourth Industrial Revolution) offers. This effectively means that whoever achieves information dominance will take the lead and conquer the battlefield.

New generation technologies are moving at a fast speed. Revolution in military affairs has been unable to keep pace with the revolution in technology. As innovation and technology grows, the military needs to adapt to newer fields and also guide and customize technology. Problems, however, arise when a country is dependent on foreign technology as a result of which home grown technology remains inferior or absent. The options and outcomes then have systems of varying vintage including imported systems from different origins, thereby impacting system compatibility adversely. Equipment compatibility is essential for Digital and Network Centric Operations. Due to adequate residual shelf life of the legacy systems that are based on analogous/antiquated systems, upgradation becomes cost-prohibitive and replacements very complicated. Though the industry may be competent and specialized, the military often does not guide the trade to the exact specification of the military's battle needs. As a result, while attempts are being made to keep pace with technology, a need to achieve compatibility with legacy systems, we enforce changes with half measures that have created confusion and paralysis in modernization. Military decision makers and budget administrators need to play their roles well and not become the weakest link in this chain.

Digitization and Networking

With digitization and networking, we are entering a period of smart systems where man, machine (digitized platforms and systems) and the weapons system (shooter) are synergized. To fight a battle in the war zone or the Tactical Battle Area (TBA), the war must be brought into the war room to serve as a 'strategic or operational vantage point'. In earlier times, senior commanders would physically climb hill tops to observe the battle unfolding and make strategic decisions. Today it is possible, if the requisite systems are introduced, to bring the war into the war room. The OODA loop can then literally be automated. However, this does not imply shortening the OODA loop, which is a step lower. Automation of OODA means the algorithms have to be thought through by military professionals. Industry can only manufacture systems provided military professionals guide the industry about the outcome required in the battlefield. Hence, military commanders must get deeply involved with technology that can run battle systems ubiquitously. Success on the battlefield can be achieved at all levels of each domain—operations, intelligence, logistics and the like if networked with ubiquitous systems.

Information and Decision-making

For information to be useful, it must be provided to the right quarters, in the right form and at the right time. It has to be accurate. Decisions arrived at must be aided by higher authorities, assisted with machines and not interfered with. Technology may replace humans but not override them. Artificial Intelligence makes a case for robots to become the biggest outsourcing case for the highly critical and delicate jobs. Technology must assist in guarding our borders but presently, are we talking about borders as frontiers that are conventional in nature - where you fight physically? Or hybrid wars? Borders have now been redrawn. Literally speaking, they are limited only by our imagination. In fact, the mind is the first target—psychological warfare—where the mind is key. When the mind is manipulated, more so, of those at the nerve center, then just about anything can be manipulated. Bad news can affect anybody's morale whereas positive news can be made to look adverse when simple truths are manipulated or reported inaccurately. *Once the morale of a soldier is sunk, the military becomes a dead machine.*

A soldier must absorb technology but at the same time not be cluttered or be consumed by it. It is imperative that technology is simple for him to adapt to, and to fight with, rather than create problems. The Battlefield Management System (BMS) must ensure that a soldier is not loaded with complicated wire and hardware systems that hamper his movement and muddle his thought process. Another issue is ownership, privacy and security of data, based on which AI engines are to be run. Since we need to own AI engines, we cannot allow them to be operated or controlled by a third party. Assurances are mandatory that the systems are not being exploited or working for the enemy. One could be fed with information that has been tweaked leading to a flawed decision. In a high tempo of operations, speed is paramount; immediate and instant decisions have to be taken, with no latency permitted. A sluggish military system will lose the first draw. Moreso, the nerve center itself can be targeted if the first draw in battle is lost.

The developing world has been investing in AI-based technology but most of their military commanders have been slow to either absorb it or spell out 'Use Cases' for military AI platforms. Field commanders have a tendency to leave technology to technical experts and neither have the appetite nor the patience to focus on understanding or harnessing it. There is a complete lack of alignment between the millennial world of technology and traditional doctrines of the past. It is up to the senior leadership to realize that in the information age, systems at the apex, strategic, operational, and tactical level must be integrated seamlessly.

Information warfare and psychological operations are a leading pack in modern warfare. Effective psychological operations or psywar, is the ability to present and defend an idea, or to offer a better way that is appealing to the recipient and not merely the giver.[5] Intelligence agencies use soft power as an influence tool. Dislocating the mind of an adversary and capturing it would mean targeting the center of gravity without a physical attack. The 'chaos theory' is the most organized way of fighting this war. A chaotic mind is a defeated mind. Reactions can be mapped by different individuals and groups after applying a shock. This 'reaction repository' data can be used to design the next wave of chaos. The reactions to each narrative are mapped and modified. This form of warfare exploits the existing fault lines in military units, formations, and even nations, and creates subsequent events to accentuate these weak points. Fault lines also erupt based on the different value systems in a nation that define its character. In democracies, due to transparency and open media, it becomes extremely difficult to hide vulnerabilities exposed via fault lines. Data collection and the writing of narratives, counter narratives to suit ideologies and serve various agendas becomes relatively easy.

Presently, Artificial Intelligence applications are being increasingly used for aggregating this data and using it to manipulate minds. Once that is done, the targeted adversary would defeat itself when there is a calibrated application of shock. Information warfare is a combination of cyber, space, electronic, propaganda, psychological, media, and social media wars.[6]

---

5. *The Future of Intelligence; The New Arthashastra*; p. 124.

6. Lt. Gen. Philip Campose, *A National Security Strategy for India: The Way Forward*; p. 33.

Information warfare targets the minds of different segments of people; Starting from young, school-going minds to higher age groups. For each group, it would be difficult to differentiate between truth and lies. Each theme exploits the vulnerability of people in different sections and throws thematic shocks to target human psychology. A marked increase in mass shootings in nightclubs, at concerts, educational institutions, religious and other places has taken place by radicalization of vulnerable minds on the internet, which has now become a potent tool of warfare. Recruitment drives for radical terrorist groups like ISIS amongst others and use of the dark web for supply of arms and ammunition has already been taking place.

Common Operational Picture

Military organizations make a constant shift in their thought process by creating new force structures. Certain models are made to integrate different organs of defence services and platforms. This would be a tall order when intra-service digital integration is lacking. We need to draw up technology-based models and platforms for future battles, which must not be built in isolation as it would create silos and hamper interoperability. Technology will also be unable to correlate with frequent changes in organizational models. Today, an individual service makes its own system; all stakeholders must unite and those who need to see the Common Operational Picture (COP), require a common agenda.

Any system built in isolation in the conceptual, drawing board, evolutionary, and development stages would prevent development of a cogent COP. Figure 1 is a representative model of how systems can be networked and integrated to achieve COP. The model also explains how different elements of warfare such as intelligence, operational, including the Tactical Battle Area, and logistics need to synergize on need-based connections. It also indicates how external links can be created as required. It is imperative that leaders at the apex are provided processed information, even though tactical level instant situations are available to them if they chose to examine. The automation of 'sensor-shooter' systems would make decisions quicker or instantaneous, but would need commanders at all levels to be aware of what machines are doing and control them if required.

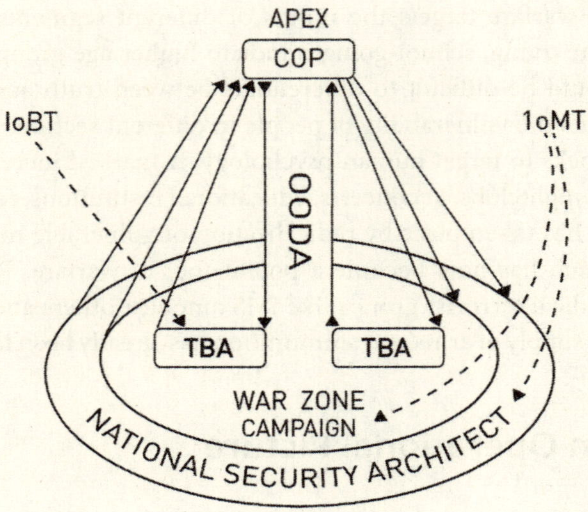

ABBRIVIATIONS

ODDA	OBSERVE, ORIENT, DECIDE AND ACT
IoBT	INTERNET OF BATTLE THINGS
IoMT	INTERNET OF MILITARY THINGS
COP	COMMON OPERATIONAL PICTURE
TBA	TACTICAL BATTLE AREA

Figure 1: AI Based (OODA LOOP)

Bandwidth and Power Requirements

As technology and data connectivity become the prime focus, a clear understanding is mandatory about the data and bandwidth required for each module of a tactical or combat unit. The United States Army has this worked out and how it will grow over a period of time. Similarly, a tactical combat module is needed for giving out data and bandwidth for each current system that may be acquired and operated in the future. Roughly, it will need a flow of terabytes of data per square kilometer to run digital platforms in a Tactical Battle Area. Similarly, data centers and digital platforms would require a huge amount of uninterrupted electricity supply starting from the frontline to the backend communication centers at the apex level.

The Future

Future military systems will be driven by Power, Materials and Electronics. With the size of data and intense connectivity required both in the static and mobile communication segment, every now and then sufficient power (batteries, generators, renewable and revolutionary energy) will be required to ensure all systems have stable power supplies. Security units will need to build secure systems based on quantum technology or blockchain that consume very high power. Nations would need reliable and uninterrupted power in the war zone, equivalent to the amount being consumed today by large modern cities. China is building dams, especially in Tibet, to harness power. Similarly, nations are investing in materials. Currently, most of the military and strategic materials countries like India consume are imported. China has possession of over sixty percent of the world's rare earth materials and is exploring planetary materials from the moon and Mars. It is important to research and source materials; if the design of the product is indigenous, we then need to unearth indigenous material sources.

A thorough understanding of electronics is necessary if we are to talk about reliability, ruggedization and miniaturization. Nations need to secure and own digital systems and hardware. Supply chain infections and cyberattacks have become rampant. Since most nations do not have the capacity to fabricate microchips, they would need to scale up testing facilities for checking the integrity of imported systems. What is also necessary is to look ahead digitally and work on creating and stabilizing organizations, doctrines, and policies. If these changes are made periodically, at no point will technology get fixated to a point of stability.

Additionally, bandwidth needs of tactical fighting and battle support units needs to be identified. Once the technological baselines are clear, it would be relatively easy to get into procurement/Research & Development (R&D)/manufacturing and budgeting. Presently, the annual budget is an enabler for decisions, but allocations need to be congruent to battlefield challenges posed by hi-tech adversaries. An adept eco-system needs to be created between the fighting and supporting entities that would help fight an integrated war, not only in the conventional domain but also in hybrid, non-contact, and non-kinetic battlefields.

Digital Wars

Future digital wars will be configured around C5I2-STAR2. Command, Control, Communication, Computers and Cyber (C-5) will ensure all platforms are connected to the nerve center that would act as communication, data, and a network hub. Information and Intelligence (I-2) will empower decision-making while Surveillance, Target Acquisition, Reconnaissance and Robotics (STAR-2) would ensure that decisions are implemented, modified, and delivered with total impact and transparency. The system of systems approach is required to build security and redundancy. Artificial Intelligence and robotics in warfare will lead to a paradigm shift in the use of technology in warfare. Sensors and seekers would be more efficient and more versatile, giving rise to a billion-dollar industry where applications would be dual-use Internet of Things (IoT) or Internet of Anything (IoA).

Internet of Military Things

Network centricity and Artificial Intelligence make an excellent combination to empower war fighting and national security apparatus. The requirements of the military commence prior to the actual commencement of war. Information, Intelligence and Surveillance (I2S) are the three critical factors for decision making. While information can come from multiple resources, data aggregation and analysis are extremely time consuming and require super specialization. The time lag between information received, and intelligence, needs to be reduced. This would take care of Observe and Orient, the first two letters of OODA. Artificial Intelligence can rapidly process the Observe and Orient and assist in suggesting the decision options, even selecting the best decision. Once machines mature up through deep learning, they can even suggest and/or initiate an action. If allowed to act, machines could be pre-programmed. Most of the 'act' function would lie in the actual battlefield as part of the Internet of Battle Things (IoBT).

In the electronic environment, information would come from multiple seeker sensors deployed in the field. Processing of this information is possible with high-speed processors for aiding decisions. This is the essence of the Information and Decision Support System (IDSS). The Command-and-Control System has data flow that links the Command, Control, Communications, Computers and Cyber systems in a way that the OODA cycle becomes seamless and mature for machine applications.

Information, Intelligence and Surveillance has to integrate with this process as C5I2. Cybersecurity and cyber deterrence should therefore form part of this domain as cyberwarfare.

The military has to manage mega networks, more so, when the nation is at war. It involves integration of war fighting domain services, strategic forces, nuclear command and multiple government and Non-Governmental Agencies (NGOs). In fact, systems will require the military to connect at the national level as war necessitates the 'whole of the nation approach'. The national command centre would need a Common Operational Picture. The war zone will require forces to manoeuvre, as well as control and defend kinetic attacks. Typically, a war zone could have a number of Tactical Battle Areas. Once the digital transformation of the military is achieved, the actual warfighting would be prosecuted by digital and autonomous platforms that lie in the ambit of Internet of Battle Things, as a subset of Internet of Military Things (IoMT). Figure 2 explains how

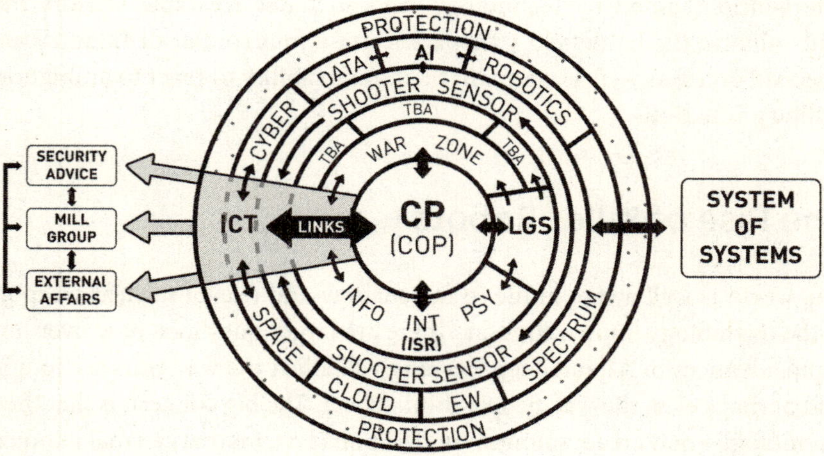

ABBREVATIONS

CP	COMMAND POST
COP	COMMON OPERATING PICTURE
TBA	TACTICAL BATTLE AREA
EW	ELECTRONIC WARFARE
ISR	INT SURVEILLANCE RECCE
PSY	PSYCHOLOGICAL
INT	INTELLIGENCE

Figure 2: AI National Security Networks

both would connect the war zone and the Tactical Battle Areas respectively and yet seamlessly connect with the apex structures forming a COP.

Internet of Battle Things

Remotely piloted vehicles, robots and Artificial Intelligence have announced the beginning of Lethal Autonomous Weapons (LAWs) which will function with minimum human intervention.[7] The targets identified would be kept under surveillance through multiple means. The decision will increasingly be automated, shortening the process of target acquisition. Sensors will increasingly become smarter to connect shooters with such sensors. This would typically form Surveillance, Target Acquisition, Reconnaissance and Robotics. Presently, some of the Reconnaissance, Surveillance and Target Designation is undertaken by the Special Forces. This process is likely to be outsourced to robotics sparing the Special Forces for complicated human interventions aided by technology. This includes wearable sensors that will enhance the battlefield transparency of a foot soldier of Infantry and Special Forces, as well as augment the human ability to react to ambiguous military situations.

The Rise of Killer Robots

The world is well aware of life in the shadow and fear of nuclear weapons —the technology known thus far. There are larger questions now over how rapid advances in AI and deep learning will affect the way wars are fought, and perhaps even the way people think of war. The big concern is that these technologies may create autonomous weapons systems that can make choices about eliminating humans independently of those who created or deployed them. The international 'Campaign to Stop Killer Robots' (a collective of NGOs) is seeking to ban lethal autonomous weapons before they even come into existence. A letter to that effect, warning against an imminent arms race in autonomous weapons, was signed in 2015 by over one thousand AI experts including Stephen Hawking, the English theoretical physicist, Elon Musk, founder SpaceX, and Demis Hassabis, the British AI researcher.[8]

---

7. *Technology and Security, How India Manages its National Security*; Arvind Gupta; p. 146.

8. Special Report: *The Future of War, Great Power Conflict.*

Such a ban seems unlikely to be introduced. However, there is room for debate about how humans should interact with machines capable of varying degrees of autonomy (with a human constantly monitoring the operation and remaining in charge of critical decisions), in the loop. This should be with a human supervising machine that can intervene at any stage of the mission, or out of the loop, and the machine carrying out the mission without any human intervention once launched. Western military establishments insist that to comply with the laws of armed conflict, a human must always be in the loop. However, some countries may be unscrupulous if fully autonomous systems are seen to confer military advantages.

Artificial Intelligence-based technologies are being developed around the globe, most of them in the civil sector, and are bound to proliferate. In 2014, the Pentagon, the US headquarters of the Department of Defense announced its 'Third Offset Strategy' to regain its military edge by harnessing a range of technologies including robotics, autonomous systems and big data, and to do so faster and more effectively than potential adversaries. However, even its most ardent advocates know that the West may never again be able to rely on its superior military technology. Robert O. Work, deputy defense secretary under both the Barack Obama and Donald Trump presidencies, who championed the Third Offset, argues that the West's most enduring military advantage will be the quality of the people produced by open societies. It would be comforting to think that the human factor, which has always been a vital component in past wars, will still count for something in the future. But there is uncertainty even about that.

A modern soldier will be armed with light, wearable surveillance and weapon controlling devices, armed with the option of firing a weapon himself or directing a weapons system to fire which is deployed in an offset/mounted configuration. These weapons would have the capability of firing steerable bullets and projectiles. Robotic systems are likely to be an important part of the blend of future ground-based warfighting capabilities and key contributors to reducing the risks to troops by improving sensing and targeting, and reducing the danger of collateral damage. The boots on the ground would reduce as gradually the robotics- and AI-powered soldiers replace human involvement. There will, however, be a need for 'boots on the ground' if required to interact with the local population. All engagement decisions will have a 'human in the loop' hence employing highly controlled autonomous weapons.

Lasers and energy weapons could well become an important part of the entire defensive system. A soldier in combat would have the luxury of assigning a 'robot buddy' a more dangerous task of delivering a kinetic punch from a greater exposed position. Robot buddies could be assigned to surveillance and vanguard duties.

Unmanned and Autonomous Systems

Unmanned and Autonomous Vehicles (UAVs), aircraft and ships will see an increasingly larger role in the battlefield. The pilot-, driver- or crewless fighting machines would be pervasive. The control stations of these machines could be located underground and far away from the war zone. Such machines would be remotely controlled through secure and stable cable, radio, and satellite communication that are uninterruptible, reliable, and instant. The ranges, or the radius, of action and stamina of these machines would be enhanced through the efficient power of hybrid engines requiring low maintenance or charging. The warheads could be kinetic, high energy or radiological. Nuclear power would run engines in miniature plants empowering these killing machines. These vehicles could be light in weight, smaller in size, and yet have the ability to carry disproportionate loads. The re-arming and refuelling, if and when required, could be executed through an autonomous logistic support system.

Lethal Autonomous Weapons are a type of autonomous military system that can independently search and engage targets based on programmed constraints and descriptions. It is a highly sophisticated autonomous military weapons system with an array of sensor suites and pre-programmed computer algorithms that can independently search, select, designate, track, engage, and eliminate hostile targets. These weapons systems, once activated, can destroy targets without further human intervention. Hence, LAWs on a broad scale can transform the structure of war by bringing in AI into systems governing weapons, where humans would remain out of the loop. The AI-triggered Revolution in Military Affairs is taking place in leading military establishments across the world. Fully-autonomous defensive systems have already been deployed by several advanced countries to intercept air aggression. Defensive weapons systems are deployed to seek all incoming aerial targets, the most common of which is the Missile Defence Systems (MDS).[9] Both the US and Israel have deployed and tested MDS successfully while fire-and-forget systems

9. Commander (Dr) Jayakrishan N. Nair, IDR, Military and Aerospace, 9 April 2020

have been deployed by UK and Israel. South Korea uses SGR-A1, a sentry robot with an automatic mode, in the demilitarized border zone with North Korea. Norway has an offensive autonomous system which will be deployed under the Joint Strike Missile program of the North Atlantic Treaty Organization (NATO). This system can hunt, recognize, and detect a target ship or land-intervention. Both Russia and China are developing similar systems at a faster pace.

Precision Battles

Future battles are poised to be more lethal at the point of punishment, decisive yet highly controllable and economic. A major concern of warfare is that it brings untold misery, avoidable damages, and drains a nation of its resources. Sometimes war is imperative to defend national interests. In doing so, use of military power is always the last resort. Technology would ensure that the militaries of the world do not attack speculatively or make decisions based on hazy inputs. To ensure that the military forces fight economically, without collateral damage, and applies just military power, it is necessary for nations to fight precise battles so that the desired end is achieved earlier without burden on humanity. Target acquisition must be done with calibration.

Remote Controlled Warfare

Keeping the human soldier away from the damages of war, the inherent safety would be provided by fighting from standoff ranges. Remote controlled wars would be an extension of the 'Systems of Systems' Network. The digital arena and industry 4.0 would make it possible to create a network with Command, Control, Communications, Computers and Cyber capabilities and connect machines with the surveillance means of enmeshing ground and aerial platforms including drones and satellites, making ISR a real time possibility. Sky and space would provide a strategic vantage point for a decision maker at operational and strategic levels. There would be enough data and information available for decision-making, cutting short the OODA cycle. It makes it possible for the leadership to not only take decisions but also control operations of strategic importance. With the advent of AI and sensors it would now be possible to robotize the battlefield. This will indeed be a game changer making remote warfare possible. Battles can be fought on pre-programmed 'targeting on appearance'.

Regulating Artificial Intelligence

Artificial Intelligence is clearly the most significant disruptive technology which has already established itself in numerous domains. Presently, a human is still the prime driver of AI. In due course, as machines become empowered with competence to learn, aggregate data, and compile algorithms, human control would be lesser, i.e., in the hands of fewer and fewer owners. Those who lose jobs to the machine initially, might soon become targets of the same machine. Imagine if an autonomous vehicle decides to run amok at a red light when faced with repeated bad traffic management systems, or notices other vehicles breaking rules. Similarly, a 'robot soldier buddy' decides to enslave the human buddy by taking faster decisions and execution of autonomous action that the commander or his buddy cannot influence. Legal impact of an action carried out by a robot or an autonomous system would be beyond human legal jurisdiction. The legal and ethical algorithms will have to be fed into the system. War crimes and social disorders would need quick redressal. A 'machine jury', 'digital conscious keeper' or a 'robot judge' may need to be appointed to assign damages and dispense justice or indemnify losses. The worst-case scenario is if all systems go rogue through virus and cyber-attacks. It would be absolutely essential to ensure that humans remain in the loop and not allow a digital coup.

Dumbing-down of humans in relation to machines is a likely scenario when human beings become dependent on machines. For instance, when calculators were introduced, a shopkeeper could not sell his products as the calculator ran out of battery. Today, the younger generation has forgotten the use of a pen as they grow up using a keyboard. The time is not far when voice control would be a standard way to deal with a machine. Imagine a modern Alexa robot misreading its master's accent and executing something embarrassing, offensive or downright damaging. What would the master do if an 'Alexa robot' is broken or out of control? The master will be unable to understand the machine and its speed.

Teaming

At every stage of execution, human supervision of a robot would be essential. Initially, the ratio between robot to human could be 1:10, which means around ten personnel supervising, controlling, maintaining, and programming one robot. A robot would be defined as any autonomous machine, not necessarily a human robot. Once trust gets established and experience makes refinements to robot-human relationships, this ratio would continue to shift in favour of robots till it gets to a comforting ratio of 1:1. and incrementally reversing the ratio to 10:1. This stage will establish the teaming ratios where the machine becomes the main workhorse and a human is just there to hold the reins. Artificial Intelligence would aim to replace humans in ratios, but will not be able to eliminate it completely. Increase in productivity by machines would need supervision at higher levels, shifting humans from manual to managerial levels and from managerial to strategic level.

Security will be a grave concern as the denial and targeting regime kicks in. This would be quite comparable to the Human Development Index (HDI) and may be seen as Robot or AI Development Indices (RDI/AIDI). A country with lower HDI will most likely have low RDI as the teaming would be with inferior human programming. Technology denial and robot hacking or hijacking will become a possibility where a superior robot would neutralize an inferior robot far more easily. Under such circumstances, a higher human ratio will have to be maintained.

It would be imperative that a country must form a good teaming strategy and build doctrines around it so as to keep the robot growth sustained rather than collapse in an event where robot favoring ratios are attempted in a hurry. Sustained and consolidated progress needs to be crystalized. Control systems would have to be built in layers like 'nuclear command authority' to enable and disable keys for systems and domains. This must come with the overall accountability of the highest political, military or combined authority.

Artificial Intelligence will continue to develop and disrupt society in ways we cannot yet imagine. It is challenging to keep pace with the speed of developments with which AI systems are being deployed. One developer recently described it like a 'sort of peanut butter you can spread' across multiple disciplines and industries. As the peanut butter is spread, organizations must prepare not only for positive but also for the unintended, and likely unfortunate, negative consequences this technology will bring. It is largely unknown how the law will react to this new reality but anticipating what those impacts might be is a timely first step.[10] National security apparatus will face challenges from the adversary as well as machines. Artificial Intelligence, in a way, becomes a 'third party conscript' in the larger milieu of human security. Benefits of AI and its challenges can only be realized by early understanding and adoption of this domain to keep humans from being surprised and exploited.

10. Todd J. Burke and Scarlett Trozo, Gowling WLG, Lexology.

FIVE

The Indian Army Training Command Discuss *Artificial Intelligence and the Future of Power: 5 Battlegrounds*

(Disclaimer: The following discussion has been produced verbatim, except for grammatical changes and those made for ease of reading.)

Participants: Lt. Gen. Raj Shukla, Army Commander, Indian Army Training Command (ARTRAC); Maj. Gen. B.S. Dhanoa (Retd.); Gen. Bansiwal; Gen. Nair; Gen. T.S.A. Narayanan; Brig. Kairo; Lt. Col. Goyal (WARDEC); Capt. Gopanna; Maj. Sumit, and Rajiv Malhotra (author: *Artificial Intelligence and the Future of Power: 5 Battlegrounds*)

Lt. Gen. Raj Shukla: As Army commander of the Indian Army Training Command (ARTRAC) it gives me great pleasure to welcome in our midst, Rajiv Malhotra, internationally acclaimed author and public intellectual whose interests range from physics, computer science, philosophy, history, civilizations, geopolitics, and the futures. That is not only a breathtaking array of interests but also ambidextrous. *Sabyasachi*, as they say. Multifaceted and multitalented. It is an absolute delight that he is with us, along with twenty-six-odd outstations and close to three thousand officers of the Indian Army logged in to discuss his fascinating recent book, *Artificial*

Intelligence and the Future of Power: 5 Battlegrounds. Our compliments for an illuminating book. One, may I say with deep insights, as also for outlining as to how Artificial Intelligence (AI) will revamp our futures, just as personal computing virtually changed humanity. In some ways, the book is much more than AI. It is a grand strategy for India to embrace and emulate. It is a book that should shake us out of our indolence. I do not think we have as yet grappled as to how profoundly Artificial Intelligence will impact our national security and war fighting.

The Indian Army's training command, ARTRAC, looks primarily at training and its multiple dimensions across the Army, and also at doctrinal thought in intelligence, operational philosophies, military futures, technologies, operational logistics, all of which would be impacted by AI. It is a kind of think tank for the Indian Army with some of the finest and oldest legacy institutions, albeit from the old college that frames doctrines. It is working on a roadmap of disruptive technologies and transition to digital era combat to the three technical institutions which look at communications, computer science. And now, AI and Quantum (computing) to Military College of Electronics and Mechanical engineering (MCEME) which looks at electronic and mechanical engineering and is also pioneering forays into autonomous drones to the College of Military Engineering in Pune which is at the forefront of our innovation in combat engineering, the Capability Maturity Model (CMM) which assess our logistic futures. All that is happening in the spheres of intelligence, surveillance, sensors, and shooters. So, a multitude of domains and each, as I said, begging for the infusion of AI. They are all embedded within ARTRAC. The Training Command, in all humility, has some of the finest minds in the Indian Army's rank and file.

May I remind the audience at ARTRAC that we are on the open Cisco web platform. While we debate the subject Artificial Intelligence and associated aspects with passion and insight and depth, no operational specifics may be discussed. We, meaning thereby the Ministry of Defence, the Indian Armed Forces and specifically, the Indian Army have, for a while, been looking very seriously at disruptive technologies, particularly AI. Here I refer to it, as does the author, as an umbrella term, the brains that bring together a wide array of emerging technologies from Quantum computing, blockchain, nano technology, 5G, the military Internet of Things, robotics, aerospace and so on. We have analyzed global trends and key drivers in the domain of Artificial Intelligence. We have, in particular, taken an intimate look at all that China has done, is doing, and is planning to do. Both the Chief of Defence Staff (CDS) and the Chief of Army Staff (COAS) have labored at length on the game changing impact of Artificial Intelligence. We are, in consequence, embarked on a roadmap of our own. We always knew that the gap was considerable but even the first read of *Artificial Intelligence and the Future of Power* drives home the fact that the challenge is indeed humongous. We will undoubtedly redouble our efforts and galvanize ourselves into more focused traction and thought planning, ambition, innovativeness, pace, and scale. We look forward to the sequel (of the book) wherein you intend to spell out concrete ideas not only to catch up on AI innovation but also to leapfrog ahead.

Most of us have read your current book and watched the launch videos. I turn to the first issue I would like to raise, which is about the geostrategic trajectories of India and China in the context of relative AI competencies. One view spelt out by thinkers like the Singapore-based academic and civil servant, Kishore Mahbubani claims from year 1 to year 1820 or so of recorded history. India and China were the world's two foremost economies and consequential powers till colonialism and imperialism exemplified by inferior steel, opium water imposed in China stepped in. The last two hundred-odd years, therefore, in his (Mahbubani) view, were merely an aberration in the longer march of history. The natural inference is that we are now missing the inevitable return of history. If India and China, the world's number one and three economies in terms of Purchasing Power Parity (PPP) managed their geopolitical and geostrategic relationship with wisdom, they both shall prosper and bloom. You seem to suggest otherwise. You say that AI will be the defining metric of the future and China is using AI as a strategic weapon to leapfrog to pole position in the geopolitical competition, as it is heavily invested into AI while India lags (behind) considerably.

To quote some statistics from your book: the AI boost to Gross Domestic Product (GDP) by the year 2030 you estimate for China will be in the order of seven trillion dollars. In India's case it will barely be 1.2 trillion dollars. India, therefore, does not stand a fair competitive chance. How would you reconcile the two standpoints? Will the impact of AI on the prospective Sino-Indian trajectories be significant and game changing? Will AI indeed be the most prized summit to conquer in the race for leadership in economic, political and military affairs between India and China? Over to the author.

Rajiv Malhotra: First of all, I want to thank you for inviting me. I always enjoy interacting with military personnel. I don't have a military background myself, but during my fifty years' stay in the US, I started to appreciate their brains, their audacity, their patriotism, and their scientific prowess. First in the US because I worked with them at top corporate positions in all sorts of hi-tech situations. I then started looking at things in other parts of the world including India and I realized that military personnel are a delight to work with because they are realistic, they are pragmatic. They don't run away from situations. They aren't looking for emotional feel good. They want to know the facts. That's the kind of style I have as a researcher and author. With that I want to say I'm delighted to have this discussion.

The question on India-China, you know, the quotation of the eminent Singapore gentleman (Mahbubani) is absolutely correct as far as history goes. But I think there is a different thinking when you look at a future-oriented understanding rather than a past-oriented understanding. There are disconnects in history. You can extrapolate the past, (be) nostalgic and try to convince the Chinese that this '*Hindi-Chini bhai bhai*' (Indians and Chinese are brothers) should be the way forward. But China, in its thinking, does not take India seriously. China is looking forward, they are looking up, thinking who they have to beat, and that is the United States. They have been doing this for twenty years. India is a side show, kind of 'in the way', if you will. If India didn't exist, it would probably be better for them. The United States is the one that they really need to go after.

To take this deeper, I feel India is in denial of the understanding of the China-Pakistan alliance. How deep it is? They are not two separate borders. If you look at the Pakistan border and the China border as a unified front, India has the world's largest hostile border. There is no border so long in kilometers and I am not even counting Nepal, which is so far, not hostile, but it could be, one day. And I am not counting Bangladesh and Myanmar. They are relatively passive at least for the foreseeable future. I am counting simply the Pakistan and China border. It is just huge and the variety, diversity of terrain involved. When you look at China's investment in Pakistan, China needs Pakistan, firstly, as geography to get through to the Indian Ocean and then to Africa and the Middle East and so on, which is so strategically important as there is no other route. Pakistan is absolutely necessary for China's future and their biggest investment in this one belt and road initiative is in Pakistan. Secondly, beyond just the physical level of needing Pakistan, China also needs Pakistan's military. This is something experts in the US have told me. No matter how successful they are in AI, in building weapons and aircraft carriers, and they are really quite ahead of India for sure and catching up with the US. However, the US feels that one area they score over China is that they have battleground experience. Boots on the ground. Ever since the Second World War, there has never been a period without US fighting wars, very aggressive wars somewhere or the other. Whether it's Korea, Vietnam, the Middle East, Afghanistan, Iraq, the US has been training. They have a highly trained military in terms of training and testing out its latest weapons in real terms, in actual hot warfare. China hasn't had that experience. The US knows that the Chinese army hasn't really gone out to war. They are basically a peace time army. All kinds of things they are developing haven't been tested. Pakistan, on the other hand, has battleground experience. They have hot war experience and they continue to have on their Afghan front and Kashmir and so on. China needs that (experience). China also needs cultural knowledge about the Indian subcontinent, (their) language skills, the climate etc. For them (China), Pakistan is a very good friend, an ally colony. It has pretty much colonized Pakistan.

As far as Pakistan is concerned, they have been up for sale for a long time. They sold out to the Americans, to the Saudis and now to the Chinese. Pakistan…they really don't have too much choice. They have just ended up on China's lap. This is not an alliance that's going to go away. This is not something you can wish away and I feel they're acting in unison, although, it's not very obvious and explicit at this point. When you look at things that way, India has a very serious issue. And China is not going to be an easy one to settle all this. They feel they don't need to. They may not attack India right away, but they may empower Pakistan with weapons and AI and so on. As far as the role of AI (is concerned), I want to preface my comments on the power of AI by showing how technology, in general, has shaped wars and shaped empires and civilizations.

In recent times, a great example is the shoulder missile that the Americans gave to the Afghani *mujahideen* (guerrilla fighters) to shoot down Soviet warplanes. This was the result of semi-conductor miniaturization. What used to take the size of a truck of circuiting, that kind of intelligence, was miniaturized and put onto the shoulder of an uneducated human, a person who could be trained on how to use just this, didn't need brains, didn't need a whole lot of infrastructure. He could just carry it around, and wherever he went if he saw a plane, up to fifteen thousand feet high, he could shoot it down. Now, this is what caused the Soviets to lose because they didn't have any air support. Air support would have given them superiority over the local Afghanis, without which the Soviets were finished. And that defeat ultimately culminated in the collapse of the Soviet Empire. So, you see, technology can have a dramatic implication. Remember Babur, (the founder of the Mughal Empire) brought cannons for the first time to the Indian subcontinent and then the Europeans brought them on ships by the sea route. India wasn't prepared. These cannons existed in other countries for a long time and India could have sent spies. India had the money and other resources to study other people but didn't bother to do so. This business of being introverted and content with oneself, poses a dilemma, because one becomes complacent. You don't do what Indian tradition calls *purvapaksha*, which means study the other. Purvapaksha is a term very highly regarded in Indian *shastras*, which means you must always be studying the other, with respect, don't knock him down, but take him seriously. Don't trivialize your opponents. We, historically, haven't done purvapaksha. And so, we got invaded over and over again. We didn't anticipate who these people were, where they were coming from, their ideologies, their strengths and resources, and could we go after them. We never did the hot pursuit, even though we had the power to do so. I call that an emotional psychological weakness when it comes to hard power. We can glorify it as moral superiority. But wars have not been fought and won and lost based on morality. That has never been the case. History would otherwise have been different. So, we got to be extremely pragmatic.

I see the use of AI today as traumatic, seeing the shoulder missile with the mujahideen or with the cannons that Babur brought. This is going to be a game changer. This is not only at the military level; it is at the civilization level, at the economy level, employment or all kind of stuff we can get into. I am convinced that whoever wins this Artificial Intelligence (race, will lead the world). And we are right in the middle of it; it's not a fifty-year-long thing, it's not science fiction, I am talking about by 2025. By 2025, things would be in place with Artificial Intelligence, highly militarized weapons, new kind of industry and economy, a new wave of hacking human brains and hacking networks. If you've lost it, you've lost it. And the lead we have to catch up is pretty big right now. I welcome more questions.

Lt. Gen. Raj Shukla: Before I get in General Dhanoa, there is one more issue I would like to delve into, that of comparative strategic systems and their impact. And this is once again from your book, where you talk of China's surge in AI and otherwise in technologies, deep technologies and compare it with India. You make the point that China's surge in AI is of course about its intimate connect with technology, but it is also about its ability to think long and deep. Also, the Chinese resolve to retain their deep civilizational connect in thought and action. You talk of their connect with the Han (founded in 202 BC) culture and with Confucian (named after the Chinese philosopher Confucius) thought. You also draw this comparison between the leveraging of Indian and Chinese talent and cheap labor with the West and the manner in which the two countries did it. That was interesting. And you refer to the fact that China leveraged this labor arbitrage much more smartly, and even as it offered cheap labor to the West it remained focused on moving up the value chain and creating a vast ecosystem of domestic Intellectual Property Rights (IPR) in next generation technologies. India gave away its cheap labor to the West, but by way of lazy thought or strategic folly, ended up merely a consumer of foreign technology and not as a producer of IPR. The other thing you referred to is the perspicacity with which China promoted, and I quote you, 'A sharply competitive fight to the finish, a kind of gladiator culture in the domestic environment. Its wisdom in investing deeply in education and research. All part of a carefully thought through grand Chinese narrative.'

What was illuminating is that, in contrast, we allowed our very strong traditions of yoga, which you call a comprehensive system of development and it is much beyond exercises for health. *Dhyaan*, deep meditation, *kshatriyata*, a tradition that nurses the critical attributes of courage, dharma, strategic persistence, purvapaksha, which you referred to, which is a deep understanding and research of the enemy and *jnan*, meaning acquisition of knowledge in the broadest sense. By allowing these very rich and very wholesome traditions to kind of wither away, unlike China that maintained the connect, we failed to combine the virtues of tradition, the structure and grammar of our civilization, as you say, with the finer attributes of modernity. But that's a very fine point. We ended up flaunting instead, unfortunately, the poor consolation prize of *jugaad* (putting together randomly). I remember very distinctly, jugaad in Indian newspapers and columns was flaunted as one of our survivor sorts of achievements. It is this difference in approach or in our philosophy towards technologies and development that explains the gap between China and India in the strategic competition.

In a similar context, to paraphrase our external affairs minister (Subrahmanyam Jaishankar), China simply out-thought the West. May I add that it has also outpaced the rest of us in terms of its scale and speed of execution and there are many examples to the effect. In another surprise, because my generation grew up on the premise that it was the liberal West and its grand education system, we have heard of American Exceptionalism and so on, that was the paragon of all virtues associated with free thinking, the development of contrarian viewpoints, thinking long and deep, thinking out of the box, innovating, collaborating and the like. These were the so-called virtues of open systems and not of closed societies that helped outpace other competitors. As it turns out, China, despite its close system, has done precisely that. Thought deep, thought long, encouraged contrarian views, innovated using gladiator type culture, thus allowing itself both to gamble (that comes from that culture) and risk taking. To gamble on the technological opportunity that AI offered and also spawn an innovation culture. This gladiator like spirit will propel China to a strategic old position well ahead of the USA. This point is from the author's book. I thought it was very interesting. Would you like to comment on it and explain the rationale in a deeper sense?

Rajiv Malhotra: I appreciate your clarity, the grasp and the amazing grand sweep that you have been able to put together from different parts of my book. It is very impressive. Thank you for that. It is a very good summary of the position I have taken. Just to go through all these points. India did labor arbitrage. You hire a software guy for dollars and you rent him to the American client for thirty-forty thousand dollars. You make tons of money. If you're good at it and manage the visa, public relations and human resources, you don't need to be a technological genius and innovative, but if you can manage this, you could end up a billionaire. And many Indians did and we glorified them like they are some big shots.

Many big companies, whether it's TATAs, Infosys, were created like that and many other companies. China also did something similar in the beginning. They rented out their cheap factory workers and made tons of money. However, there were two differences. Firstly, the Chinese took more than half of that money they were making, rather than living a good lifestyle, and feeling we are great, (and put it) back into long-term Research & Development (R&D). They were able to make long term bets. They bet ten to fifteen years ago on things that would take a decade. Artificial Intelligence, robotics, drones, electric vehicles. as an example. They put their money into, I would say, eight or ten bets of multibillion dollars scale and they pulled it off.

The Chinese have the largest market share of drones, of robotics and electric vehicles and the reason Elon Musk's (of Tesla) biggest and first factory is in China is because China controls the lithium supply. China controls fifty percent of the lithium market worldwide. They bought lithium mines all over. They thought long term. They thought if this is the future, we'll own the technology, own most of the patents in lithium ion-tech and also own the raw materials. They have thought through very carefully. India did not deploy the profit into long term thinking. It was like jugaad, make some quick money, stock will go up, become rich and everybody is happy. This was not nation building. We overestimate the value of our industrialists because while they did create a middle class, ours is a consumer economy. It is an economy of services, not an economy of R&D. A service economy could offer cleaning services and sweeping services. You could have sales people at retail shops selling things. But a service economy will not give you a technological jump. You need to have an R&D economy. And R&D is something China picked up from America. The second difference between India and China is that the Chinese used the fact that the Americans are the clients to pick their brains, to learn from them, to reverse engineer, beg, borrow and steal technology. If Apple has all its factories in China, the latter figured out, well, what's the technology, we will make our own.

The Indian brains, which were rented out, have, for the last twenty years, been running the backbone of American banks, pharmaceutical companies, defense contractors. Whether you go to Grumman, (Northrop Grumman), Boeing Defense, Space & Security (BDS) or Lockheed Martin Corporation, these huge multibillion dollar defense contracts, the contractors—and the defense industry is a half a trillion-dollar size industry in the United States—you will find lots of Indians there. But India didn't have the tenacity, the cunning to think we have our brains sitting there. Let's learn so we can do all those things ourselves. We can jump ahead. The Chinese did that. We say we are creative people, we are a free democracy, the Chinese are not, we know English, they don't, and so we have the advantage. We only talked about these things. But China overcame those obstacles. Without knowing English and without being a democracy, they managed to get ahead. So, I think the Chinese have pulled off (something) amazing. You have to study China, do a lot of purvapaksha on China. India doesn't have sufficient insight into China, say, compared to the US' insight into China. A lot of my studies on China are basically Mandarin documents translated, some of them are in public (domain), there are ways you can find out and those tell you the thinking of the Chinese.

What the Chinese did with the US is they made the US feel they are friends, until they felt the tide has turned, the tipping point has come, the point of no return. They have enough technology from the US, lot of the missile technology. Some of these were stolen and the US knows about it. The Chinese have played this game very cleverly and this has to do with their inner strength, being unified and having a grand plan as a nation. China and India send (in the order of first and second) the largest number of students to the US, respectively. We are very proud we have many young people learning in the US. But there is a difference. First of all, China sends students for Science, Technology, Engineering and Maths (STEM); they don't send for humanities and social sciences. They aren't sending the young to study Chinese history and abuse their human rights. They aren't interested in sending young bright people to Americanize them against China.

Where India is concerned, a large number of students come for STEM, but a lot of them come for social sciences. They are the ones that I often have to debate and argue with. They are the most anti-India that have been trained by all these very not India-friendly ideologies. The Chinese don't do that. There are a lot of Chinese and Indian students at Harvard, Columbia, Princeton. But the Indians there join anti-India demonstrations, whether it is against Article 370 or the Citizenship Amendment Act (CAA). I call them sepoys. They are like the British who had sepoys. These are intellectual sepoys. Regards China, there are no sepoys working against China. You can say that it is okay, maybe they were brainwashed, maybe there is military authoritarianism, people have no rights. I don't agree with that because Chinese students go back (to their country); Indian students don't. A large percent of Indian students wants to stay back in the US. Why would they (the Chinese students) do that if they hated their country? They clearly don't. Also, China has the largest number of foreign tourists going around the world. You can look up the figures. There are more Chinese traveling worldwide than Americans now. It used to be the Japanese but now it's the Chinese. You have tens and millions of Chinese going all over the world as tourists and so many lakhs of Chinese going as foreign students, they all go back. Obviously, you cannot dismiss China as a basket-case, that there will be a revolt, people will get upset and there could be (an) uprising. Don't buy into that. That is just wishful thinking. It will not happen. You have to take your enemy seriously. China is here to stay and become very powerful.

As far as AI is concerned, the statistics are very clear. The number of AI patents, of US-China are neck to neck. Just before the (COVID-19) pandemic last year there was a huge AI conference in New York, attended by two- to three-thousand people. You will find papers from Americans, papers from Chinese are seventy percent of the top papers. Nearly five hundred to eight hundred Chinese registered, most of them physically present, some were online. I went through the program to look for participants. I saw six Indians in total. That's it. And not one of them speaking in the main hall, forget being a keynote speaker, not even a major address, a major paper, they were doing posters on the side. And these are guys from IIT, from prestigious places, but have nothing innovative enough to get in (to the conference). You will find a lot of Indians who are not from India but based in the US who are at the top. You will find these guys in Google and Facebook and Microsoft. So, what has India done? India has a skewed education system where a few colleges are training very high- quality people, but most of them who have engineering degrees are not functioning as engineers. They are not really doing any engineering design. So, that is one issue. The second issue is that the brilliant ones generally go abroad and the ones who stay in India end up working for Microsoft India, Google India, Facebook India. They are working for the foreign subsidiary in India.

If you look at patents, a very tiny percent of the worldwide patents in AI and similar technologies come out of India. And the ones that do are generally owned by Microsoft or Apple or Google in India. You wonder why Infosys or TCS or Reliance get into this business? Why did Reliance have to bring in Google and Facebook into Jio, which is terrible. My book wasn't out then, but I wanted to publish a particular chapter I titled *Digital Colonization*. I wrote a summary and sent it to the Indian press, (but) they were not interested. Nobody wanted to listen, because they were so excited that, *arrey bhaiyya*, the Americans like us. They are putting money into this. But the point is that they are buying us out. Jio was one organization with the money behind them and could have taken Big Tech on and say, we will build our own search engine, we will build our own technology, rather than building their technology, licensing their stuff and giving them market access. Giving them market access does two things. First, it perpetuates our dependency on them for technology because once that treadmill starts, it continues. Second, by giving them market access you are giving them Big Data and AI runs on Big Data.

Big Data is like 'oil' (the fuel for everything) as some people say. We had the brains, but we have rented them out. Rather than making Intellectual Property for ourselves, we have rented out the brains to foreign clients and they make the intellectual property belonging to them. And then we license it back. It's not a very smart plan. We have lot of Big Data. Rather than utilizing it and producing solutions for ourselves, marketing and selling those solutions to other people, our Big Data is out there, available… … it's not even clear who is in-charge. A case in point, the Kumbh Mela. Twelve years ago, at the Haridwar Kumbh Mela, I realized that Harvard University had a project called *Mapping the Kumbh Mela*. For AI purposes, they had surveillance cameras for facial recognition, they were taking samples and medical samples for genetic purposes, doing a whole lot of demographic analysis of the people attending, which village they come from, what society, what caste and community they belong to, and what not. In effect, building a map of India, a very dangerous thing to allow; to allow somebody else to understand us, our sociology and our schisms, internal conflicts and so on, to understand us better than we understand ourselves. But they (Harvard) were doing this. So, I wrote many papers, I have videos on my channel where I criticize that India should not be allowing all this. I analyzed the entire Harvard thing and I found out that they had many Indians involved in it (the project). They also had many Indian politicians and bureaucrats on their side and so, I was pretty upset. My report on the Kumbh Mela declared it as a big AI catastrophe.

We are giving away this Big Data to foreign entities to study us because it's a microcosm of India, the Indian society that goes to the Kumbh Mela. We gave them chance to study all that, and build models, psychological models, behavior models which are dangerous for us. Over one lakh copies of my booklet, it was about thirty-forty pages, both in English and Hindi were circulated at the Kumbh Mela. Lot of people congratulated me and said this is very good, the government should take a note of it. Nobody bothered! I would like to see something equivalent to the Space Commission, or the Bhabha Atomic Research Commission, which is totally independent of government bureaucrats. India should create something like that, the Artificial Intelligence Commission. And I would like a military person to be in-charge because they are very realistic. The industry people in AI have missed the boat on doing research. They have basically supplied manpower to foreign entities to do the research and it is easy money. But they haven't done the research on their own. The second thing is that what they are optimizing is short-term gain, short-term profit, which is good for the stock market. I don't think that that would be the right approach if you want to build the nation. So, you need people who are patriotic, very logical, scientifically savvy and who can think long term. And India does not have too much time to waste. This is a sort of call to action that has to be noted very quickly. Thank you very much for the question.

Lt. Gen. Raj Shukla: I would like to do a quick follow-up. The fact that the Chinese are much more innovative, risk taking as a nation. China is not only the whole of government, it is the whole of society and their entire approach to these high-end technologies. My basic question, as a quick follow-up is, is that this propensity, inclination of greater risk taking, innovation and that gladiator-type culture that you spoke of, a bright Indian and a bright Chinese in USA, why is it that an Indian goes in for what Dr Subramanian Swamy (former Cabinet minister) calls guaranteed poverty, lifelong guaranteed poverty, whereas the Chinese, they go in for innovation? Is it a personal choice or is it because of systemic encouragement? Is it also connected to the points that you made about civilizational connect? You know, for example, I was pleasantly surprised, we always thought *kshatriyata* is only about valor, but you say it is about dharma, strategic persistence, thinking long term. So, the dilution of these deeper traditions in our case, in our education system and the retention of these very same virtues in the Chinese sense, in the case of China, are these cumulatively the cause of Indians going for, or shall we say avoiding risk, avoiding innovation and the Chinese doing quite the contrary. Would that be a right inference?

Rajiv Malhotra: This is a good question. Let me reflect on it. Kshatriyata is the *raja's dharm* (the responsibility of the king). He is the keeper of the state, of power, hard power economy, military or law and order; he has to be a strategist. He has to think long term. He has to understand his enemies. He has to be very all-rounded (with) leadership (qualities). That tradition has not been there because of long-term colonization. Colonizers hate the Kshatriya because he is the one who can actually strategize and get rid of the enemy… they don't mind intellectuals. If the Kshatriya can be finished off or sidelined or compromised, the Brahmin, they can buy him out or put him into something very abstract and high flown.

If you remember, in the 1971 Bangladesh war, it was very important for the Pakistan army, when they invaded Bangladesh, that was east Pakistan at that time, it was very important for them to round up the intellectuals and the leaders, the political leaders, they put them together in Dhaka University and shot them, killed them. That was a genocide. A genocide of those that are capable of leadership is a very important part of subjugating a people. You don't mind those who are submissive and passive and who won't talk back and argue. They are fine. You can even use them to your advantage, but the one who is going to stand up and show leadership has to be killed. The film *Schindler's List*, where they had these Jews in the Nazi (concentration) camp, was about them being killed. There is a very important scene where the Nazi leader, the general is trying to get a project done with the prisoners but they are bumbling around. One prisoner woman walks up to him and says she doesn't mind taking control as she has project management skills, leadership skills, she is trained and knows how to command people. She says the work can be delegated to her and she will get it done. The general takes out his pistol. Bang! Shoots her! The message is, why would he do that, she offered help. Because she has leadership skills, she is a Kshatriya, she may be very dangerous. She may do work for you, but she could also organize the people. She could give them strategy which these people don't have on their own. The point here is loss of kshatriyata. What happened in Kashmir is the Kshatriyas were finished off; the Brahmin ruling elite, you know, the Muslim rulers could live with them because they are not going to harm you. Kshatriyata is so important in nation building.

As far as the Chinese are concerned, if you look at Confucian thought, it is very Kshatriya-oriented in its own way. China did the following. In the last forty years, before that China and India were at par, kind of equally poor, undeveloped, not educated, not disciplined, lot of problems, both of them similar. Look how far we went and how far they went. For two generations they suffered pain. There is no immediate feel good and *tamasha* (show) and, you know, here and there, Bollywood function. They did it systematically. But for two generations they decided we have to experience pain so that the future will be good. That's a long-term bet. Maybe in a democracy you can't do that, because you have to promise people something quick. But long-term nation building is not going to happen that way. Indian leaders were not able to say, two generations, you have to pay the price. You got to go through this because we have a thousand years of baggage and to finish it off, we have to pay this price. Then we will become world class. China did that. They have the ability to face pain. They are able to take a lot of beating and not give up. There is some kind of an emotional, mental resilience that they have built into their population. And that has to do with the kind of education (they have). The one point I disagreed with is all Indians have kind of gone for a risk averse.

In Silicon Valley, some of the top most amazing success stories are Indians, some of them are from India, lot of them are second generation, born and raised there. Many of the startups are worth billions, for them to be worth fifty million, one hundred million dollars is okay. It's just a normal thing. So, there is a class of Indian youth in this hi-tech field who have done very well in the American ecosystem, but when you ask them, they will say they don't think there was any chance in the Indian ecosystem to achieve the same. What has happened is when you have 1.3 billion people, there is going to be people of all kinds, people of all spectrums, the ones who are of this caliber have left, by and large. There are many smart people in India also, but numerically, a large number have left. And they've made a lot of money. They're very successful and so on. There are many Chinese too and are more connected with China. You don't find that in the case of Indians that much. I did a private webinar. Twenty-five of the top Indian venture capitalists in technology in Silicon Valley invited me a month ago to do a webinar on AI based on my book. They were very interested. The interesting thing is the primary objective was how do they invest money in India, where do they go to make some money … it wasn't about how they can help India. It was more about, is there an opportunity in this sector, that sector, which company should they buy out. They were all looking at it from a very selfish point of view. So, I would say, a better characterization is that the Indians have encouraged individual success, personal success. It's not so much a collective thing.

Maj. Gen. B.S. Dhanoa (Retd.): The problem I see for India and specifically for the Indian Armed Forces to be able to get on to the AI bandwagon, as the author has correctly pointed out is that you need to have a scientific temperament within society. Like he says, he doesn't get to see that as an organized, an entire nation effort currently being put in unlike China, possibly the United States and few other countries, being the leaders in technology. We are nowhere there. If you do not have within your society what would be called a concentrated effort to be able to harness the potential that everybody says Artificial Intelligence is going to give, whether it's for your peace time use and definitely for military applications as well, how will you narrowly focus it for military purpose? That's a challenge which I see. I wrote about the fact that you actually need somebody who is able to put it, should I say bluntly, knock heads together, has a fair grasp of bureaucracy and a fairly good grasp of the direction the country needs to head in as far as Artificial Intelligence is concerned. It's a race and not purely a military race. It's more or less a civilizational race, as I understand what the author is trying to say.

If that be the case, then in the military, like you rightly said, within the Army it is the ARTRAC which is the leader, but I think at the level of the nation you need to get your scientific community in, you need to get your Research and Development under the Ministry of Defence on board. You need to have your own qualitative requirements, if I may call it that. Whether it be for drones, whether it be for robotics, whether it be for the use of Artificial Intelligence to be able to analyze Big Data. Who is collecting Big Data on behalf of the Indian military? Who is analyzing it, or at least storing it in a manner that it can be easily used? Did we, over the last eight months, have (in) our ability to be able to gather some data from our stand-off in Eastern Ladakh against the Chinese, against the People's Liberation Army (PLA)? Did we have some kind of software that is wearable for a very basic rudimentary analysis of how they do their drills? I am going down into the weeds. The reason I am saying all this is that (only) if you have somebody at the very top who is laying the broad basic guidelines, putting everybody together on (a single) platform, only then can a military take full advantage of where Artificial Intelligence, where machine learning, where Big Data analytics, where all the computers and everything else connected with it is going to be, and then we get to where we want to be.

The Chinese have a leap, a head start. Even the United States has set up a joint agency for Artificial Intelligence within the department of defense only about four years ago and they understand that they need to go much ahead of where (the) Chinese are going to be by 2025. I feel that we need to understand where we lack in our ability to put it all together and I think some of these issues are very well highlighted by the author. I had focused very narrowly on Unmanned Ground Vehicles (UGVs) which is probably the most complex of the deployment of autonomous weapons system or semi-autonomous weapons system and operate in a complex environment. Not as easy as, you know, driverless or some of the other stuff that everybody else is trying out. It's a tough challenge. In legal autonomous weapons systems or autonomous weapons systems with human intervention, where do we stand with that? My paper was more narrowly focused on that.

I still think that as far as understanding Artificial Intelligence with the nation getting everybody together, being able to specifically draw those issues which we think will be beneficial for the military whether it is in better decision making, analyzing data and being able to shift through (information from) Research and Analysis Wing (R&AW), and make some sense and some good intelligence out of it, I think those are the things we will have to focus on. The Army design bureau, ARTRAC, some of the other institutions that we have, even within the narrow technical focus in our training institutions, those are some of the things that we could actually look at.

Lt. Gen. Raj Shukla: I want to add something. The point is that the lag is a fact now. For whatever reason. My experience in this domain or/and associated domains of disruptive technology for the last two/three/four years is the grand push notwithstanding, I mean howsoever inadequate, NITI Aayog has put out a report, the Ministry of Defence is doing something headed by the defence secretary. I said, the CDS is at it every day. At the start, however grand the vision, the start has to be small. And we have seen it in building systems up. Today, if you ask me for the modest research we are doing, funds are not an issue. But our levels are, so relatedly low, that when you start despite the grand push it will take time for these things to unfold. I will return to this point a little later. If you read the report of the American National Security Commission on Artificial Intelligence (NSCAI), I am not talking of the larger American province in AI, it is obviously much ahead. But the report, in its references to the US military, you will find that their, it's not a point to gloat over, but their status is not very much unlike ours. All the problems they have identified in the report are relatable to ours. I will come to that a little later. That's the point I was trying to make. We will return to that if we have time. Let's get in some questions from the establishment, Brigadier Ranjan from the Amidco Central School, has a question for Rajiv Malhotra on the impending contest between the supreme algorithm and the human 2.0.

Brig. Ranjan Kairo: You try to foresee what the future holds for us. In Chapter 5 of your book, I understand we battle for the self. The concept of the old human versus the human 2.0 as you call it. A very small minority agree therefore it's Artificial Intelligence beyond the wildest imagination. The human 1.0, a very large majority of the moronized zombie population, will be benevolently tolerated by this privileged class and may be depopulated as time goes by. What happens next? Will the supreme algorithm take charge and feel that it would become human 2.0 and superhuman skills are no longer needed? Is that going to happen subsequently? (overlapped) Sir, about this potential human extinction event.

Rajiv Malhotra: This is a very good question. He has picked up a very important point in Chapter 5, where I say that more and more augmentation of brain and mind and body is leading with AI in it. People will be able to live longer because they will be able to grow new organs, they will be able to have artificial organs, they will have eyes with X-ray vision, telescopic and infrared vision. All kind of properties that the human body will have that by today's standards, they will look like another species. In the way animals think of humans as very superior and we think that animals are inferior, there may be a class of people who have to be very rich because these people will cost a lot of money and a lot of technology and power. I call these humans 2.0 or superhumans. Once you start implementing AI technology in biology, you have a combination of silicon and biology synthesis. The algorithms in biology are running our organs now and the algorithms in the silicon which humans are making, AI is running. These are working together. This will keep evolving and there is no way to know where it will end. We can't tell. All I can tell you is that we are at the dawn of this age where, what I call superhumans, are going to start emerging. You will see by the end of this decade technologies will be available for the very rich who can graft this and graft that. Not just augmented realities, but inside the body that will make a person superior to other people. And so, where this will end, we don't know. The gentleman asked a very important thing. Will it take such bionic humans, hybrid humans to such a level that basically this intelligence will be running the human rather than the human running the intelligence? This intelligence may use the human as a biological body to live in and that is entirely possible. That takes us into the realm which is further than the ten-year vision to the year 2030.

Lt. Gen. Raj Shukla: The next question is from Lt. Col. Goyal, who is from WARDEC. His question relates to the possibility of modelling the behavior of trained combatants into computer entities that could be ingested into a synthetic environment. His question is in the context of war gaming.

Lt. Col. Goyal: I am Lt. Col. Goyal from the war-gaming development center, WARDEC. My question pertains to behavior generation of combat entities in constructive simulation domain. As you know, there are three inherent requirements of a constructive simulation. First, is a human in the loop, second is a scalability wherein we are able to increase or decrease the number of players and thirdly, the intelligent adversary player that can challenge our own actions. However, due to organizational constraints, meeting all these requirements sometimes becomes challenging. In view of the above, is it possible to model the behavior of trained combatants into computer entities that can be ingested into the synthetic environment? If yes, will it be able to provide reasoning to support the outcome, and what kind of data management would be required to model such a behavior? Over to you.

Rajiv Malhotra: Very brilliant question. Something similar is happening when they are modelling a combatant like a virus. The virus is learning from the human being because there are billions of copies of this virus all over. And each one, like all driverless cars, are connected through the cloud. So, the experiences of one driverless car are benefitting the other driverless car too. Think of the viruses as a swarm, as a collective intelligence, if you will, each of them trying a different experiment. One guy trying it on this patient, one guy trying it on another patient and the human beings are of different levels of immunity and different races, different genders, age and so on. The collective experience that this virus is having through all these experiments is from each point of view; the human being is Big Data. The human being for the virus is like Big Data. It's trying all its experiments. It's learning. The pharmaceutical industry is doing the opposite, thinking of this guy as a combatant. How do we learn from him, how do we try things on this virus, see what works and how it reacts? This is very simple. It is very similar to war games where you have adversaries, each learning from the other. The adversary that you mentioned is one of the three components that is not static. He is also learning. Your model is modelling him. The thing you have to understand is, you need a proper machine learning system representing that guy, while this machine learning system is learning from your actions. It has to be that both are learning from each other. This is the future of training, the future of simulation in any adversarial role. Whether it is biology looking for drugs, whether it is somebody looking for simulating and enhancing our warfare capability. And this type of modelling is coming. This modelling that you are talking about is extremely realistic and very important.

Lt. Gen. Raj Shukla: I will steer the conversation to a subject which is our direct business in the reason why we exist – AI and national security and defence. It is abundantly clear that AI systems will be used in the pursuit of power and for the realization of strategic ambitions. It will also not be wrong to conclude that AI tools, in fact, will be the weapons of first resort in future conflicts. Therefore, we will need AI competencies to defend India, to deter our adversaries. We will need to leverage AI-based intelligence to gauge precisely both adversarial capacity and intent. Note the subtle change. We once said that we can only gauge capacity, but now with AI it is also possible to gauge capacity and intent as also to fight and win our wars. As the NSCAI tells us, (I referred to this a little earlier), Artificial Intelligence is poised to transform all aspects of any conflict/ engagement.

Artificial Intelligence applications will help militaries make sense, understand faster, decide faster, execute faster and more efficiently. Numerous weapons systems will leverage one or more AI technologies. Artificial Intelligence systems will generate better options for commanders, create better networks, transform logistics, procurement, and design and development of our new hardware. There is no time to elaborate, but the larger audience must read this report. It tells you the specific challenges in each of these domains. Our Long-Term Integrated Perspective Plan (LTIPP) will have to move from a platform-centric approach to a technology acquisition approach. It needs a huge change. The fact that the US is grappling with these challenges is some consolation. Adopting AI will demand the development and design of new tactics and operational concepts. Artificial Intelligence will pitch algorithm against algorithm and the source of battlefield advantage may shift or (rather) will shift from traditional factors like foresight, platform capacities to phases like superior data collection, assimilation, connectivity, computing powers, algorithms, and system security. No military segment or sphere will escape the transformative impact of Artificial Intelligence. This brings me to my question, which, I think, is the central challenge. How in the Indian context could we best adopt AI?

Now, to your analogy of basketball, how can we be quick without hurrying? And this is really the challenge because we have to catch up with China, leapfrog ahead, if possible. But like all other applications of AI, military and intelligence functions in AI, and other such areas require deliberation and time before they are developed, technologies discovered, fielded and rolled out. Some current AI systems are narrow and little. They require rigorous testing, safeguards and (complete) understanding of how they might operate in the real world than in a test bed. These are the real problems with which we grapple on a day-to-day basis. And despite all our efforts we still operate at human, and not machine, speed. How do we change gears?

Artificial Intelligence will also require profound adjustments in national security, business practices, organizational cultures and mindset which is a huge challenge. Any ideas, thoughts, Rajiv, on how we could bring about the necessary change, give the desired impetus to the development of an AI culture, work ethic and embrace AI-friendly operation philosophies in the military? The larger push of the points you make is well understood. But can there be a more focused approach to the Indian military that you would like to suggest?

Rajiv Malhotra: I am unaware of the internal mechanisms, but I would like for there to be an AI commission or something which is very specifically AI, similar to the Space Commission, similar to the Atomic Energy Commission (AEC) because the push from NITI Aayog, they are sort of part time into AI and not really experts. They are economists and other things which is great. You cannot just shove it (AI) as one little sub-point in a bigger strategy going on. Artificial Intelligence deserves its own space and deserves the best brains available. And I think military people should be definitely at the top. Once you have that, you need to look at the technologies, for instance, material science, advanced materials. We are in a race with China. India should think of it like the US has realized. The 854-page report that you are referring to, Eric Schmidt (CEO, Google 2001-11) from Google, quit his job many years ago to create this commission because he is so concerned and thorough. This is the third president; they have all embraced it and keep adding more funding to it. That report is amazing. Everybody in India should read it. This is not the kind of report NITI Aayog could produce. You need somebody really into this field (AI) in a big way. And if you look at the range of investments needed, India should then decide here is where we will excel, here is where will license, and here is where will just have to improvise somehow or the other.

But the race is on material sciences; it is not just software, computer science AI software. There is lot of hardware. Semi-conductors and Quantum computing are so important. I have a couple of friends who have just been hired by Tata Institute of Fundamental Research (TIFR) and they're starting Quantum computing. I am very happy they are doing it, but they also tell me they are way behind. They are just very small scale, few people here and there. The gravitas of AI has not been operationalized. There are lots of meetings and conferences, but there is no critical mass of people in one place that are doing this 24/7. That is the first thing that India has to do: elevate the AI threat and opportunity to the level of

Indian Space Research Organisation. They have to put money into it, they have to create something, preferably away from Delhi, not controlled by bureaucrats, something that can thrive on its own. That would be my first recommendation. China has that, USA has that, Britain has that. India should have it.

Lt. Gen. Raj Shukla: We will now turn to Gen. T.S.A. Narayanan, Commandant, MCME, who has a question on data leveraging for revenue generation.

Gen. T.S.A. Narayanan: My point is one of data capitalism and data commemoration. Considering India's population demography and the number of IT users, the data that can be provided for other purposes to any other country, say China. You have considered permission of use of this data as data slavery as a result of disadvantage. However, can it not be converted into a favor wherein the data is taxed by the Government of India and technology that will use it will also be a revenue source. We will not only ensure regulation of data but also earn substantial revenue for the country. Your thoughts.

Rajiv Malhotra: I will paraphrase the question and then answer it. This idea that right now data is sort of open to everybody, they do whatever they want with your data. Every time you click on the internet, it enters the algorithm of Facebook and Google. These people know what you like, what you dislike, these are the options available to you on the screen, you picked this option, you did not pick that option, what does it convey about you. They are constantly becoming smarter, not only about Indians collectively, but about a community, about a caste, about a region, about an individual.

So, one of the big threats is that Indians are using Gmail, Indians, the Indian government and military are using social media, I am sure the profiles, the algorithmic profiles of all the important people in India are sitting there. I am absolutely sure the Chinese, the Americans have it (information) this is what they sell to their corporate clients to make you buy something. If somebody wants to sell you shoes or holidays or whatever, they may call the trillion-dollar bots; these companies are very rich. They make money because they have proven, empirically, that they know the way your mind is working, how to change your mind, and how to make you buy this or buy that. The same data can also be used to convert your religion, to make you fight against the country, to make you a rebellious person, to participate in a riot or whatever because this is Psychological Operations (PsyOps). So, think of AI as the future of PsyOps. Psychological warfare is here (to stay). That is all going on. But we are not controlling this data.

The gentleman's question is very important. How do we take this asset and tell anybody who wants to use this data, there is a meter like you have an electric meter, (there is a) data meter. Suppose we develop the idea for data meter, so that the person who is using your data firstly, he needs your permission, what he can do with it (use it for). Secondly, there is a meter use and if he is using a lot of your data, he owes you money. If you consider data as Intellectual Property, then people who are using your data have to pay a license fee. But we don't classify data as intellectual property. And one thing this reminds me of is, in India even software cannot be patented. This is very surprising. Software cannot be patented in India. In other countries it can be patented. How are we going to create intellectual property based on all this stuff, if we are not even encouraging our people to file for patents? India should amend this patent law and there is a statement in my book, it is verified that I am quoting correctly. I have stated the exact reference to the Indian Code, Indian legal code of patents and it states software is not patentable. This is very strange. We should not only make software patentable but even data patentable. And then as per the question, we will probably be able to make revenue out of it and also control how the country's data is used.

Lt. Gen. Raj Shukla: The commandant of the Movement Control Team Gen. Nair has a question on the challenges of developing AI ecosystems in our designated defense corridor.

Gen. Nair: It has been a very enlightening conversation. I would like to just comment on an issue of data. India now has gone on a data protection policy mode where we are looking at how data can be controlled or managed. I am sure you are aware of the deliberations which are going on at this point of time. My question is specific to some defence corridors that are coming up along the length and breadth of our country where we are envisaging a lot of technology-based entrepreneurs to invest. But considering the Indian ecosystem which you had highlighted on—unskilled labor, the lack of R&D and so on, do you feel these will be successful and if not, how do you envisage we make it a success.

Rajiv Malhotra: The US has a very good model. If you look at the Defense Advanced Research Project Agency (DARPA), they do so much work with the private sector. Most of the research is outsourced but they are very sharp. They know exactly the whole map what they want done and they get it done from various places. And they look at the defense industry, the private defense industry is massive and they are technologically way ahead. In the case of Boeing, for example, their defense industry is technologically ahead of their commercial plane industry. So, India needs to create that. The DRDO is great, but I think you need to also bring in the private sector and give them incentive. I am not very familiar with the details of these defense corridors, but am very glad to hear that this is happening. I don't have enough information to give you a detailed comment. If someone were to send me such a report or a plan, I will be very happy to give my views.

Lt. Gen. Raj Shukla: The private sector participation is, I would say, increasing substantively. Our outreach to them is greater than any time in the past. So that should be good news. Any view, suggestion, intervention, question for the author?

Maj. Gen. B.S. Dhanoa (Retd): (Question for Lt. Gen. Raj Shukla) Since you are heading ARTRAC, are you looking at a conceptual paper on the future needs of Artificial Intelligence for the Indian Army or something to that effect? Because until and unless you don't really put out what is it that you expect of the technology, you can start projects everywhere, but then you will be patching it all up. That's what I had actually felt when I wrote the paper. We need to tell ourselves that in the year 2030 what is it we expect AI to be able to do for us. Even if it is a wild guess and eighty percent of it is wrong, but at least we will get twenty percent right. That's my thought.

Lt. Gen. Raj Shukla: Absolutely! We haven't done something as grand as Eric Schmidt's report on AI and national security. But we have taken some very specific steps. Last year (we undertook) a whole study on disruptive technologies in AI, actually, it was a study on AI because it is the umbrella term. It was presented to the chief, it was presented to the *raksha mantri* (defence minister), some sanctions were given, a roadmap was created and we are moving along that roadmap. That gives me the experience to tell you that the funds given to me exceed my capacity to spend at this moment. While there are people, there are startups, there are business people coming up, but the lag is what it is. It just takes time to catch up. That is the exact point that I have been making to you and Rajiv Malhotra. We have a very specific roadmap and much of it is out in the public domain. I myself flew to Pune, Bangalore, to these centers of software, hardware and AI. We are in touch with people, the autonomous drone you saw on Army Day, that's the take-off. We are seeing how we should operationalize it, the northern borders, the western borders and elsewhere. We are looking at some more larger projects. A tri-service AI-enabled cloud. We are looking at how to get cloud computing going. So, a whole lot of stuff is in the air. They are those traditional projects with DRDO. If you ask me, there are so many projects that I find it difficult to attend to one project within a fortnight.

Much is happening and I'm not saying that a lot more should not happen, but in my view, over the last two-three years this issue has got a greater push. For disruptive technologies of technologies like AI, money is not a constraint, at least at the levels which we are. If you look at tri-service clouds and all they need huge investments, you will need bigger players to come in. These startups will not be able to do it. *Woh bhi hamne shuru kiya hai.* (We have started that.) In my view, ARTRAC is doing it. They all know they have a specific project to take home from Ramjet (air-breathing jet engine) technology to image intensification, there are about twenty to twenty-five projects which we are rolling out. It has given us confidence. It has given us great confidence because Dhanoa (Maj. Gen.), if you recall our younger days, we were always told that you only fight, technology is somebody else's business. Now, we know it's our business. A lot is happening in comparison with the Chinese, of course, we have a long way to go, but I hope that satisfies you in some measure.

Maj. Gen. B.S. Dhanoa (Retd): Oh, absolutely! Thank you. Thank you for those inputs.

Lt. Gen. Raj Shukla: Any of the other commandants, if you would like to raise any issue with Rajiv Malhotra.

Major Sumit: I am Major Sumit. My question is, social media uses Artificial Intelligence to influence sentiments and opinions. It is being used to share emotions for specific agendas. With an introduction of Personal Data Protection Bill (by the Ministry of Electronics and Information Technology in 2019) in India, can we compare how such attempts by governments across the world to access and control their online content have fared?

Rajiv Malhotra: This is a business. To hack your brains psychologically while giving you a lot of attractive freebies, you can do all kinds of good things. It gets you addicted, and in the process, it learns more about you and navigates your thinking in their way, the way they want. This is very dangerous because it's very subtle, like an iceberg, little bit on the surface is visible, but lot's going on underneath the surface that you don't know about. So, this is happening with private companies. I call this the return of the East India Company; that there are companies like that which are aligned with their governments. Google and all these people are definitely aligned with their governments. And China, of course, all are aligned with their governments. The governments are also doing these things.

If I could ask a question, it would be, what are India's cyber security counter measures, but we'll refer to that later, I'll answer the question that I have been asked. This is a kind of cyberwarfare going on at a psychological level. We know that at the physical level somebody can bring down your electric grid which is very dangerous. (To) the people in India I am trying to wake up this awareness that mental, psychological, emotional hacking is far more dangerous because especially in a democracy, you can do all kinds of things. In the US they accuse Putin (Russian president Vladimir Putin) of hacking the elections in 2016 and then put all the counter measures to prevent that. So, foreign governments are doing this to each other. I don't know if India is doing it to others, but it should. Whether China is available as a soft enough target or not is one thing, but India should be exerting this kind of technology over Nepal, Pakistan, Bangladesh and Myanmar. India should be the hub for the region influencing social media and AI and algorithms in their language, in Nepali language, in Urdu and Bengali.

India should have a project to not only take control of our own social media so that the mind of the Indians is being controlled by algorithms from India, that are made in India by Indians for Indians, and not from some foreign place. Not only should we control the algorithms for our own use but we should be exporting this power over neighboring countries. That is how you become a superpower in the region through the use of AI to influence young people and their thinking through whatever others are doing. We should also start doing that with our technology. That is what the big giant companies of India ought to be investing in. But I don't see that happening. I call them Google *devata*, (gods), digital *devatas*, we are thinking of them as devatas, inviting them into our house and giving them a lot of prestige. I am the person who stuck his neck out, taking the risk and

I am taking a stand. It is not easy to do. So many people in India don't like me saying this because Google will call them and Facebook will call them and say, hey, hey, no, no, no, this guy is a bad fellow.

The NITI Aayog is full of advisors from the likes of McKinsey and all these people who are bringing this whole point of view. India has been invaded at many levels: government level, corporate level and public level by this entire AI-based algorithm driven new digital thinking. And India needs to turn this around very quickly and become an exporter and aggressive country, doing this to other countries. Start with small countries in the neighborhood. This is very important. Then go to Africa, Southeast Asia and all that. India has the brains in raw material to put it altogether. But what we need are visionaries who can create the projects, mentor the people, direct them to get all this done. The gentleman (Major Sumit) asked a very important question.

Lt. Gen. Raj Shukla: Any more questions? Commandant OTA.

Commandant OTA (Officers Training Academy): (My) question is for Rajiv Malhotra and Gen. Dhanoa. My question (was) partly just answered. We Indians are very fond of, or very swayed, by success stories. If you really look at Artificial Intelligence from the Indian perspective, what could be that success story which will motivate say, millions, particularly the young lot and of course, obviously the military to go into this field in a big way as a career? A question for Gen. Dhanoa is that when you are looking at Artificial Intelligence, how seriously can we look to our intelligence core to take on AI as part of their charter. Thank you.

Rajiv Malhotra: So, what would be a good success story. There are several favorite things I have, but one example that will have popular appeal is simultaneous language translation of all Indian languages to each other. I think now there are language translators that Microsoft and Apple have. They are trying to train them on Indian languages which, rather than training their algorithm, making it smarter and smarter which will be controlled by them, we should have an Indian algorithm. We should have Indian people developing these algorithms and then we should train those algorithms so you can go from one language to another language and teach using Natural Language Processing (NLP). That's the technology. That's the part of AI used for all this. So, Americans have things like Generative

Pre-trained Transformer-3 (GPT-3), they have lot of these... Google brain. They are doing a lot of work on understanding human thought, language, speech, meaning, what is one trying to say and so on. And there are many, many applications.

One of the easiest ones to justify with a lot of high-profile excitement is language translation. You could have it in a way such that you are speaking in one language and the other guy is hearing in his (own) language in a phone call or in a court or in so many contexts. I think this would capture the imagination of the Indian people; it would unify India. Instead of everybody having to move to English as a sort of link language, languages will be able to interact directly with each other. This will be a phenomenal investment. The culture minister should do these kinds of things. It's a good thing for Human Resource Development and Culture Ministry to get together and do it. That would be my kind of favorite topic because it has a very good social impact.

Maj. Gen. B.S. Dhanoa (Retd.): To answer Bhaskar's question. For the Intelligence Core (IntCore) taking on the overall direction for Artificial Intelligence. The IntCore is a general staff branch to harness, and to leverage and exploit Artificial Intelligence. It's not the only person or should I say, the only branch of the military, which needs Artificial Intelligence. There are so many other places where you need to apply it. They are just one of the users. They need to develop ways and means of how to enhance the quality of intelligence that you get from data sets that you would be collecting in the future. That's one requirement IntCore would definitely need to look at. But are we the only users or exploiters of Artificial Intelligence? No, we are not. They are the subset within the overall requirement of the military and the general staff. At the end of it, you are all there to ensure national security and to make sure that if you are called upon to go to battle, you must have the best wherewithal. So, it's not purely IntCore, it's everybody else.

We all need to put our heads together to say this is what currently the narrow focus or narrow Artificial Intelligence gives us when we have broad based AI which is (the) future. When computers will be able to think and do cognitive functions as humans can. What is it that we need to be able to get out of Artificial Intelligence? To come back to your point, Intelligence Core is just a small subject within the larger picture that we need to look at regarding Artificial Intelligence. That's what I would have to say. I may be corrected by others who have a better understanding of AI. But that's how I look at it. Maybe I'll refer General Shukla to also chip in on this.

Lt. Gen. Raj: Shukla: Before me, Gen. Bansiwal. Anything on AI in the intelligence domain, Gen. Bansiwal is here, commandant of the Infantry School. Let me tell you here, all the military domains which lend themselves to AI leveraging, shall I say, intelligence is the foremost. Though the good news is that we overcome this bureaucratic hang-up… That process has begun. There is what it will enable you to do in the strategic intelligence domain and that's the point that I referred to briefly. It will not only allow you to precisely decipher adversary capacity, but also intent. So, a body of troops which say, comes, shakes out, comes to a training area, comes to a training area again, can you from seven-eight of these maneuvers predict with some precision whether it will now come forward or go back?

In the future, with this imagery being made available, that much is a possibility. Such things have been outlined in great detail in the Schmidt report on intelligence. Do read it and I also know from reading it that many of these things are happening in our own intelligence domain. These are the two-three things I wanted to add about what I know is happening with regard to AI in the intelligence domain. If Bansi is up, you wish to add something, you are the expert.

Gen. Bansiwal: All I can say is this is a field which is so very important for all of us. At the Army level we need to be looking (at issues) differently now. At (the) Army level we need to be thinking differently now. Accordingly, this organization needs to be rewrapped. We need to come up with a structure wherein the intelligence requirements are met holistically. We are going to look at all this, while this Army commander has already talked about imagery and so on. Also, the language part, there is huge potential that we can develop. But, as I said, we'll have to look at it differently. As of now, we are structured at a very low level, which possibly the environment is not aware. So, we'll have to give it a clean relook.

Lt. Gen. Raj Shukla: But many of these low-end applications are also of great utility. And many of us know what's happening even at the low-end AI and that kind of intelligence. There is a lot happening there and that's also good news. Let me now turn to the next issue and this is I think is the last or the penultimate one. The question to you Rajiv, is while discussing the follies of the Indian *rashtra*, (country), you point to the proclivity of India being far too reliant on soft power, even though soft power is always contingent on hard power. That's very refreshing proposition to hear.

You also refer (to) lessons from the *Ramayana* and the *Mahabharata* to reinforce this alliance of hard power. Lord Ram failing to convince Ravana despite all the soft power at his disposal. Similarly, Lord Krishna being unable to win over Duryodhana with his soft power advocacies ought to be convincing. You draw the analogy of ancient Rome proficient in hard power and Greece skilled in soft power with Rome ultimately emerging as the victor.

To make the point that in the Indian context, it is the metrics of hard power that will determine as to who will prevail in this strategic competition. Will it be right to conclude, and I link this with the first question that I asked that in the Indo-Chinese strategic military competition, the two game changers will be AI and hard power. Will that be a right influence and would you also agree if I say that of late, the proclivity of the Indian state to hard power, things are changing for the better? In recent times, we have seen a more central positioning of hard power in our state craft, as also a willingness to set new norms in its deft use. Would you agree with the latter proposition and your response to the first issue that I threw?

Rajiv Malhotra: Very insightful comment and question, I must say. Both points I agree with. I had this discussion with Amish Tripathi, (good friend of mine), he is a diplomat in Nehru Center. He is a soft power guy and there is a soft power center in India. They think the way India is going to become great is we will talk about some *Upanishad* somewhere and… I mean, I am into all those studies so I understand and I respect all that. That is for the inner us… we have to develop that for ourselves. First, we have to develop it ourselves and become ambassadors because we are actually practicing all this, then people will understand. But what people will respect is hard power. The word 'power' has to be important in soft power. It cannot just be culture. If you have culture, I go and eat Thai food, but that doesn't mean if there is an issue, (a) political issue, I'm going to vote in favor of Thailand because I like their food. It has nothing to do with it. So, culture is one thing.

To turn culture into soft power it must have the ability to persuade other people to act in our favor because they have enjoyed it, have become enlightened and benefited from this particular cultural aspect. I don't know any US Congressmen, (US is the one place I know extremely well), or senator whose decision to vote in favor of India and reject a bill that is against India will be premised on the fact that his wife is doing yoga and so he will say, because we are doing yoga, therefore, this is soft power. I better not vote against them. I think they are separate issues. So, that means this business of yoga is soft power, we are fooling ourselves. Yoga is (a) cultural export. Cultural export, it's fine. And, you know, Mao Tse-tung famously said, power flows through the barrel of a gun. I would say, soft power flows through the barrel of a gun. I would really say that.

Every time I say that I get all these people saying that you know, no, no, in this way, you are promoting all this violence. I am not promoting violence. In fact, if you have good hard power, you can prevent violence because people will be afraid of you. You need to go from (a place of) strength. So, I believe in kshatriyata, I believe in hard power. The second part is AI is the very central decisive factor in this hard power race that is going on in the world. Be it the hard power of weapons, be it the hard power of technology-based industries and so on. Now, is India doing this? India is going into hard power, but is not AI sufficient… it is not AI enabled. It is hard power, that is (a) good step, but India does not have enough AI culture and AI enabled institutions. There are (a) lot of important institutions in India that are still on the old way of doing things. India needs to bring AI into so many of its day-to-day workings. So, I would say I partially agree that India has done the right things, compared to before, a big step forward, but compared to where we need to be, still work needs to be done.

Lt. Gen. Raj Shukla: I agree with you entirely. We have a long way to go. For the matter of interest for the wider audience, I would recommend another book to you by Eliot A. Cohen, *The Big Stick: The Limits of Soft Power and the Necessity of Military Force.* It makes a brilliant case of *why* hard power and its many uses. The softer uses of hard power, the central punch of hard power, how it must be, (how) it must have a primary position in your state craft. It's wise to do that. That's another view and I would commend that book to all those of you who have not read it.

The last issue, Rajiv, from your very fascinating book is about psychological control and agency. You make this very persuasive case that deep learning and machines is resulting in shallow knowledge in humans leading onwards to the phenomena of moronization. And you lay the blame, I think you already alluded to it, at the door of Google devata as you call Google. I would offer a variant to this proposition and I would like it to be tested against your superior knowledge and insights. The question is embedded in that variation.

Way back in schools, it was the 1970s when I grew up, an education in India then was of course about facts and data, but it was also a great deal about one's analytical abilities, reasoning skills and communication capacities. The latter was visibly encouraged. So, you read and participated in activities beyond the designated curriculum. You reflected, I would not say deeply, but you had time to reflect and you were actually encouraged. I remember one dropped class by one's ability to excel in those one or two questions that came from beyond the syllabus. *Syllabus waale to sabhi kar lete the.* (All could manage from the syllabus.) That forced to you read beyond (and made you) ponder and think. That was an education. You would enjoy going to school. Schools then encouraged an all-round demeanor. It was invariably the boy topping the class, (who) was also good in hockey. He was as good in football. That's my recall of my days in school. Our chemistry teachers, I recall, were as familiar with the wisdom of Shakespeare as also the prose of Munshi Premchand. I distinctly recalled those names.

With the passage of time, and this is purely a hunch and my personal observation, I presume by the 1990s or so, quite synchronous with the introduction of the objective style of questioning in our examination system with great emphasis on factual data and rote memory, the birth of mnemonics and all of that, we saw a gradual decline in our analytical abilities, the desire and ability to reflect, ponder, articulate, and originality and oration innovation in consequence were relegated to the background. The point I would like to make is that Google devata is actually, or should be, a more welcome entity because it gives you basic facts and data leaving you free to reflect, analyze, ideate, and think. That's how I use Google and I think it's a very useful tool. I don't commit many of those issues to memory, but I use it to make deeper points and I am sure many of us do this. This is my proposition; it may be wrong. But the problem is not so much in the machines or tools, but what our education system has done that seems to be of larger malice and therefore, how these tools are being used. How would you respond to this thought? One follow-up. What should we do specifically for our pedagogy in our military education training establishments so that we continue to reflect, analyze, explore and innovate because that is central to our embracing proficiencies in technologies? So that's the question. We would like to hear your answer.

Rajiv Malhotra: The role of online data sources, whether it is Wikipedia, whether it is Siri or Alexa or Google search, there are two kinds of information. One is objective hard facts and there you can't be wrong; you just look it up. If you want to look up the population of this city, the share price of some company yesterday or what was the cricket match, it's not subjective, it's not a matter of opinion, it's not a question of interpretation. It's a question of hard facts and these sources are wonderful and they relieve the human mind of the burden of memorizing trivia because you can always look it up.

My concern is that lot of information is subjective. I'll give you a concrete example. Take the word *swastik*. The word *swastika* in our culture is (a) very auspicious sign and it's not about Nazis, it's not about fascism, it's not about some horrible things that Hitler did. We have it in all the four dharma traditions, the Hindu, Buddhist, Jain and Sikh. The swastika is there and it's about wishing you well for your journey, for your beginnings and so on. The role of swastika in European history, Western history is very different. If you train machine language which is what they are doing, you train machine language using the texts of Western written texts, legal texts on swastika, historical texts on swastika, philosophical text, all kinds of stuff, you get your machine algorithm trained that this swastika, the person who uses it is very nefarious.

Now, there is a subjectivity because swastika is a contested item. Around 1970, when I was in California as a software guy, I remember in the parking lot one other Indian, he bought a new car, he took it to the local temple and the priest blessed his car, drew (a) swastika on the front of the car, on the wind shield. He blessed it, like people do, they bless something with swastika. It created a huge scandal. When he parked his car in the parking lot, I came back from lunch and I saw a big crowd of our employees standing around the car and they were talking we have hired a Nazi, we have hired a fascist, what is this guy. We thought he is a nice guy, but he has got swastika (on his car). I had to educate them on what is swastika for our culture. I must say, they were very broad minded and (I) did a slide show, we had these Kodak 35mm slides those days. I used to talk a lot about our culture. I educated them that the swastika is very different. So, this is an example of how words are interpreted.

Caste is interpreted in the Western idiom and in all these algorithms in a way which is very different from what our shastras and texts say about castes. And the idea of Aryan invasion theory, if you look up, these algorithms are trained, this Aryan invasion theory, Aryans came and they subdued the Dravidians and what not.

The contested topics are so many especially when you are colonized and the English language writings about your culture have been written by Western Indologists, people I am always fighting with. A lot of Indians have taken over that knowledge now and they are teaching all this stuff. If you are convinced that there was injustice done in the ideology of the colonizers, if you are convinced that after Independence a whole lot of Indian people actually adopted that old mindset which is anti-India, I call it 'Breaking India' forces. If you are convinced of that then my point is that Artificial Intelligence is going to empower those with machine power. The reason they are going to empower those is the way the AI is being trained. It is not our people, it is not Shankaracharya of Sringeri who is controlling the training of AI with his shastras and his lectures. It is not some Indian/India friendly people who are in charge of training Google. Google is training its people, I mean, its machines based on the texts (and then) decides are the correct texts. So, they'll go to the standard mainstream ideas of India which are full of prejudice and full of stereotypes and that's how these machines are being trained.

My concern is that as the war for ideas and the battle for discourse becomes more automated with more and more AI, we are going to lose because we are not the ones controlling the training of algorithms based on our ideology. That's where I come from saying that these devatas are dangerous because we are relinquishing. China is training its algorithms for a Chinese point of view, and so far, they are trying to subjugate the Muslim population in their own country and using it as a training ground. But they are going to unleash this in Hong Kong, they are going to start unleashing it in foreign counties where they have influence. Don't be surprised if in the border areas of India where the Chinese are trying to get in, they'll have all this kind of cyber warfare, psychological warfare as part of their arson and to try and see if they can create unrest among those people.

So, I see the loss of authority from our *adhikari*s, our experts to foreign people who made these algorithms, as a national security issue. I see that as a problem. I think as a matter of principle, we should have had our own search engines, we should have had our own Wikipedia, we must have technology. I am not against technology; I am a technocrat. But we should control the spin that technology has given. And there is no such thing as absolute truth, objective truth, when it comes to ideas and philosophies and points of view. Even India's border, which algorithm… is it going to be our view of where is the border with China or Pakistan, is it going to be somebody else's, this goes on all the time that we protest… India has to protest that this map is wrong and that map is wrong. The point is once it is AI, once it is all deeply embedded in algorithms, this problem of contesting the truth is going to become even worse.

Lt. Gen. Raj Shukla: Thank you so much. That was I think a very good and subtle point that you made. Just one question I have, why is it that our best names in business, somebody like TCS or say, Reliance, the ones with deep pockets, why is so little spent on R&D? I am sure they are wise men. They see the futures. They see the value of investing in R&D today to capture market shares a few years hence. Yet, why doesn't it happen. A quick response on that.

Rajiv Malhotra: First of all, the percent of GDP India spends on R&D is tiny, less than one percent and has gone down compared to China, US and so on. And then you consider the fact that our GDP is smaller than (theirs). In compounding effect, we have very little R&D going on. The people who ought to be doing it is exactly the kind of people you mentioned. The top ten major companies, business houses with all this money …it's a disgrace. I don't know what to say, but I feel that it is short-term thinking. You can make a lot of money. You do some service stuff. It is a service economy you can ramp up very quickly, and you can make a good story that we are creating this middle class because it's all labor intensive. Research & Development is not numbers. You are not going to create jobs in numbers right away because the researchers are few. Instead of so many lakh people outsourced, you'll have a few thousand and they will do the R&D.

But the effect is such that once that technology is done, you own the intellectual property, then you can turn it into very scalable stuff. You can have manufacturing based on your own technology. And then you can create industries, huge industries which will create millions of jobs. I think the trap is short term versus long term. We are stuck in this very short-term trap. That may explain why the people who have the deep pockets are not making the deep bets. Even the venture capitalists today… India's proud that now the venture capital industry is investing in all these technologies, but when you look at it, it is Silicon Valley investing type people. It used to be Chinese venture capitalists, but they stopped that. Paytm, we are very proud of it, but twenty-five percent of it is owned by Alibaba (the Chinese multinational technology company founded by Jack Ma). Now the Americans are certainly there, Europeans are certainly there. The scale of venture capital coming from Indian pockets is much smaller. And that's a shame. Indian would rather buy some real estate, buy some jewelry, buy something else. I don't know why the Indian with money doesn't have confidence in India, Indian brains and invests his money in this technology. That is what bothers me. And I am glad you asked this question.

Lt. Gen. Raj Shukla: Why the private sector is so important because I was rather curious to note that US space force as it is evolving into a space force, is turning not to NASA, not to IBM, but to SpaceX. (Elon) Musk is willing to take those risks and the US space force is engaging with him. And I think this kind of connect we are a long way off.

Rajiv Malhotra: In this regard, I would say that General Eisenhower (thirty-fourth president of the US) talked about the military industrial complex which is the backbone of America. I have added the word 'academic' and I have said that now it is a military industrial academic complex in America. When I came to the US at the age (of) twenty, as a technical person wanting to do my PhD in physics, I switched to computer science and AI. My professors had all these Pentagon contacts and I as a student, because they said, we need students also. Even though a foreign student, I got security clearance to go to Pentagon and work with these people. I was very impressed that the military taking brains of, young smart brains from, major universities through their professors, finding these people and getting them involved in real practical applications, giving lot of grants to private industry.

So, the military industrial academic complex is a very powerful triangle in the US that is the backbone of innovation in America. Whereas in India these are separate silos. In China also there is a military industrial academic complex. Most of the academic people are connected with the industry and they are connected with the military. Military has got their hands in all this. The People's Liberation Army is there in all these. They are influencing all these people. So, both these countries, both these superpowers have this triangular relationship that India needs to develop.

Lt. Gen. Raj Shukla: I think that's another pertinent point because, these false binaries in India of military versus civil, they have only accentuated these silos. Though, of course, they are changing now. And I recall this East-West rail road system which was set up in the US. It was, of course, used to move missiles around, but as a consequence even commerce flew and business and trade blossomed. Regarding to (making) some changes, (taking) baby steps, (there) are three technical institutions for which we are getting interns from private universities. We are reaching out. So, that is beginning, but I would say, the baby steps have just begun. We still have some time and I have run out (of) the questions and ideas. If there is any question from anybody. Rajiv Malhotra is here. You won't get this opportunity again. So, please shoot.

Capt. Gopanna: Captain Gopanna here. You have mentioned in your book that COVID-19 will have a worse impact on the Indian economy and AI will have a pervasive influence on Indian economy. We did take a tumble, however, the latest reports from the International Monetary Fund suggest that India is touted to grow at twelve percent in the year 2021. Do you agree that the foundations of the Indian economy are quite strong to not only cope with the pandemic, but also to fight against the AI disruptions in the economy?

Rajiv Malhotra: That's a good point. India, hopefully and I am very glad to read that the Indian economy will bounce back post COVID. The same may not be true for AI because the thing is this, if you have too little AI, you will lag behind China in all these things that we have been talking about in terms of quality and the technology and all that. At the same time if you have too much AI, the wrong kind of AI, then you'll create unemployment. So, that's an issue.

The adoption of AI by industry is not necessarily optimizing nation building, it's optimizing earnings, earnings, profits of the companies. They are picking, cherry picking what they need to do. They are funneled by… the fuel of ideas is coming from McKinseys, the PricewaterhouseCoopers, Ernst & Young and World Economic Forum, these are very big, multinational corporate people. They are looking at the economy top down. So, when they do reports on what India should do on AI and NITI Aayog adopts those reports they go to the multinational corporations and they talk to the human resource department. Those guys say that 'yeah' we are doing all this good stuff and it will not create any labor problems. But they haven't gone to the migrant workers and figured out what is going to be the impact there. They haven't gone to the villages, in the panchayats, which is where real India lives. They haven't gone to the various industries. So, to understand AI's impact on India, there has to be a bottom-up approach to see what about the bottom five hundred million-six hundred million people, what's the impact on them when AI comes. The top guys will become richer. The rich will become richer. It will be great for the economy in Bangalore (Bengaluru) and Mumbai and so on. What happens to the hinterlands of India where the majority live? That's my concern because we don't have Non-Governmental Organizations with enough AI savvy to represent them. Political people are not sophisticated enough to think that way and represent their constituents.

To do justice to AI, there has to be an impact assessment report by (the) state. Every state chief minister should create a little AI body to see, okay, in my state given whatever is our economy, whatever is our industry, agriculture, what will be the impact, what will we do about it, bring local universities into it and so on. Every state should do its own AI impact and similarly every industry. The automobile industry should do it, textile... every industry is going to be impacted. India hasn't done that. Defense is one of the few industries if you will, where there is awareness within the rank and file from the top and I am very impressed by that. But I would like to see automobile people worrying about it. I would like to see every industry be worrying about it and thinking what is the impact and every state government should be doing it. Labor unions should be looking at it.

To bring AI into society at large, you cannot just take a very top-down view and say that we will bounce back and everything will be fine. You know, when the Industrial Revolution (1760-1840) came to England, it created new opportunities and created a big world economy, but where? In England. They created jobs and a new economy, but India became a colony because of the Industrial Revolution. The Industrial Revolution became the vehicle for creating haves and have nots, colonizers and colonized. Otherwise, Britain could not have become a great colonizer. (The) East India Company could not have lasted so long, had it not been for the industrial might, the Industrial Revolution.

So, when AI comes it's going to be like another Industrial Revolution. It will create new haves and have nots. China and US will become like England and France, competing for colonies all over the world while fighting each other, which is what was happening. Not only that, but I would say, within countries. Even within India there will be some pockets here and there, some will win, some will lose. So, I think the AI outcome is more complex than a simple statement that we will do well.

Lt. Gen. Raj Shukla: EME School (Corps of Electrical and Mechanical Engineers) typed that question, could you (read) do it?

Rajiv Malhotra: It says, I will read out. *Artificial Intelligence models based on general adversarial networks have already surpassed Turing tests in various fields. Yes. Social media is bombarded with fake faces and videos.*

Yes. Artificial Intelligence has created paintings for art galleries, which while exciting, such applications have limited the real-world use cases for us. Yes. Similar is the case where more advanced research models like bagging and random forests etc. It is turning out to be a case of developing of models first and find use cases later. How can we employ such advanced technology like these generational adversarial networks and random forests for problem statements in (the) Indian Army? Okay, so, what you have to do is not start with a technology and then figure out where does it apply. I think you have to look the other way round and say, this is an Army issue, this is the area, what do we do about it, where are the technologies and get whatever technology will suit (it).

So, you have to look at the problem to be solved and find the technology rather than start with a technology. This always happens at both ends. There are fundamental research people and they produce a technology and they are looking around. So many technocrats come to me and want advice where to go. Some people from Silicon Valley, I am on the phone a lot. I am giving them advice, introducing them to people, they go around and find out where the applications are. And then you have the other way round. You have people who have a situation and they want to solve that situation and then they are looking for where are the technologies. (The) Army has to do a bit of both.

The Indian Army should invest in fundamental research because it's very necessary. And at the same time, you need people who are at the client's side, not the producer of technology, the client's side, who have to develop very robust requirement specifications of what is the system we need, what is the kind of AI system we need and then go look which kind of AI technology will work. You need that. The producer of R&D and the people who will apply it and utilize it in a healthy kind of a back and forth. That's how you have to do.

Lt. Gen. Raj Shukla: We've run out of time. No further questions. I would just like to add something to what Rajiv Malhotra just mentioned. Thus far, we were investing in research through DRDO, the principal vehicle of our research, but we have widened it now. We set up our own research and innovation centers where we are looking at our own research to supplement DRDO and to widen the ambush to private sector, start-ups and so on. We have set up an AI lab, quantum lab, we are setting up testing facilities moving to self-certification. This is another thing that is happening and that might help this whole this push towards technology. That said, I'm afraid we've run out of time completely so we'll have to bring this exciting conversation to an end. Thank you so much all of you for your very enthusiastic participation. Many of your questions Rajiv Malhotra replied. They are brilliant. Now what you must do is follow up. Follow up more effectively on all these small programs that we have got going to make the country proud. That is that we must do. Use this conversation on AI (and) convert it into an executable AI plan.

Let us resolve to make AI and all the other attributes that Rajiv Malhotra refers to in his book as also through this conversation, the Indian tradition of purvapaksha, thinking long and deep, the kshatriyata, the value of originality (and) so on and so forth are part and parcel of our personal lives and our institutional existence. Only then will this, I would say, this very deep conversation (will) be of practical value. May I suggest that all of you draw out modest little roadmaps for AI in your respective domains and look at the development of appropriate skill sets in accord with real world implementation. And so far as the larger issues or strategic import are concerned, we shall address them at appropriate higher levels. Only then will we be able to address the very formidable security challenges that lie in India's national security lap. Rajiv Malhotra, thank you once again for your wonderful book and this very insightful conversation.

We look forward expectantly to the sequel to your book. And the next time you visit India in better times do find time to visit us. We shall be honored to play host and carry the conversation forward. I also thank Gen. Dhanoa and we have a similar invitation for you, Dhirender. So, thank you so much and *Jai Hind*!

Rajiv Malhotra: Thank you. Thank you. I just want to make a closing remark saying that I really appreciate this whole event. I wish I were there in person. I visit India three-four times a year except for this COVID. Next time I am there, we will definitely do something in person. I would love to have more interaction. My final statement to all those who are attending, if you want to be on my list because we are doing this on a rapid basis, we are having many exciting conversations, debates, discussions on AI particularly. And we are going to continue this for all of 2021. If you want to be informed, just go to www.AIandPower.com. You can register, you put your name and email ID and we will be very happy to keep you informed of all our activities. Thank you very much all of you and God bless.

Lt. Gen. Raj Shukla: Thank you!

SIX

The Impact of Artificial Intelligence on Freedom of Speech: Examining the Problem of Bias in Content Moderation

Ishwara Bhat A.

Introduction

The role of Artificial Intelligence (AI), its implications to freedom of speech as essentialized in the problem of 'content moderation' via Natural Language Processing (NLP) is analyzed herein. It explains the problem both, from the perspective of a user and an AI engineer. The essay also explains the building block technology used in NLP including the implications to content moderation. The essay demonstrates how real-world biases become the technical biases within the vocabulary of the AI system. These are demonstrated using visualizations from actual technology tools.

The real-world social dynamics, as in why AI engineers are eager to reduce the bias, and how social media users can engage them, are also addressed.

Social media users often protest that social media companies have biases. Their posts and comments on platforms like Facebook and Twitter are deleted or their accounts are blocked. YouTubers object that their videos with certain ideological leanings are demonetized by YouTube. Indians complain that nationalism is vilified. 'Content', comparing Hindu nationalists with Nazis and the Taliban are promoted by algorithms. Further, they complain that pro-nationalistic content is penalized.

The solution to this problem is explored by understanding the technology and perspective of the AI system creators. First, we examine how the technology works. We will also explore how a language is represented inside the AI system. This also explains how the biases creep in. The essay goes on to explain the AI engineer's side of the story, learning why they are eager to work with non-technical stakeholders.

The AI-based Content Moderation Ecosystem

All social media companies allow the posting of comments, including mainstream media. Content moderation is a mammoth job. Millions of articles, videos, tweets and comments get posted every day. This is humanly impossible to moderate. Social media, media companies, and websites solve the problem of content moderation by using third-party software services. The content moderation system takes all the data such as content, information about the author and the comments following the main post. The AI system then uses this as inputs to the AI deep learning model.

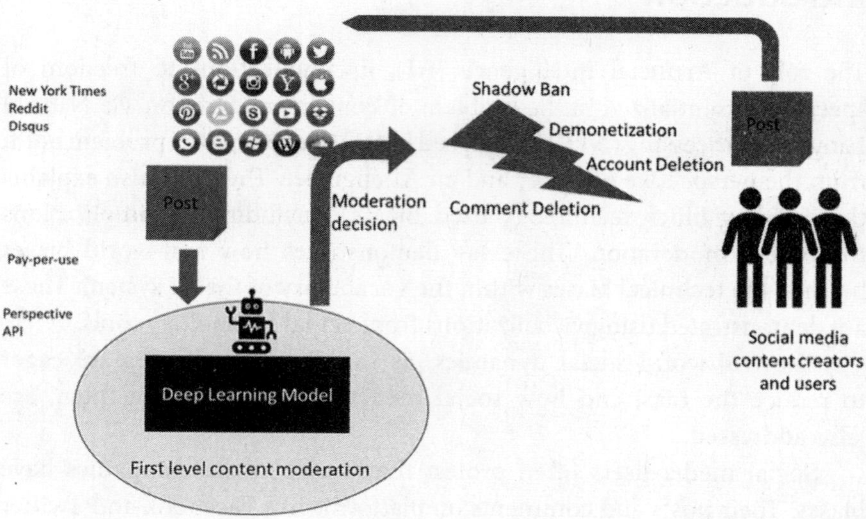

Figure 1

For content moderation, the user comment/post is to be classified as one of the pre-established decision types: *healthy, hate speech, harassment, threat* and so on. While giving the decision, the deep learning model also gives its confidence level on its own decision. This decision and confidence level would be used by the social media platform to take action such as deletion, shadow banning and so on. The website that owns the comments is likely to pay for the usage of the service.

Content Moderation System

An example of how the service of content moderation works is shown below.

Perspective provides content moderation services to a variety of content companies. The customer websites can integrate the Application Programming Interface (API) service into their platforms and provide a seamless experience to the users. The customers of this service include mainstream media houses like *The New York Times*, social media platform Reddit, comment system Disqus and many others. Other platforms may have either internal service providers or similar other providers.

The illustration shows an example of a sentence and how it is evaluated across various categories.

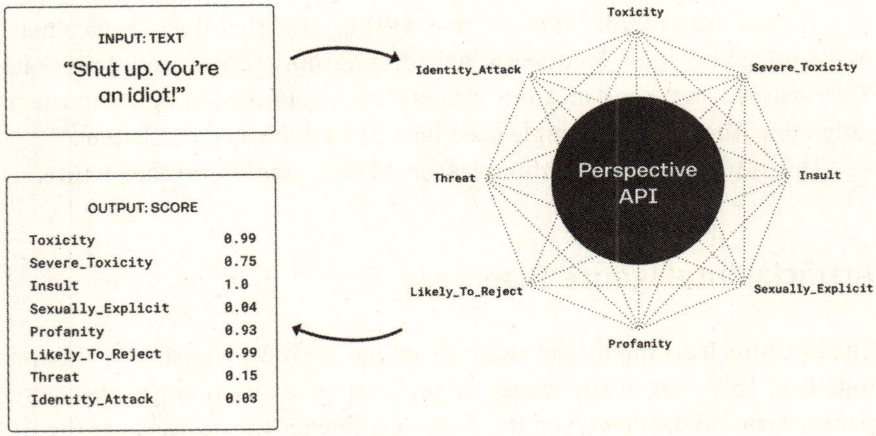

Figure 2: Source: Perspective API

The sentence 'SHUT UP. YOU ARE AN IDIOT' is analyzed by the AI system to check if it is one of the eight decision types: TOXICITY, SEVERE TOXICITY, INSULT, SEXUALLY EXPLICIT, PROFANITY, LIKELY_TO_REJECT, THREAT, and IDENTITY ATTACK.

For each decision type, a score is determined. Though the above comment fits into multiple categories to different extents, the best fit seems to be under the 'insult' category. The service provides a score for each comment. Thereafter, the social media platform or media company takes action such as deleting the comment, flagging it as offensive, demonetizing the YouTube video and so on.

The above example seems fair. But in real life, we see many neutral comments flagged as hate comments. Why does this happen? When a comment is deleted or demonetized, what do people do? They display further outrage and post even angrier comments. Needless to say, these comments also get deleted. It is likely that people perceive that as conspiracy and planned bias. Planned bias very much exists in the stage of human-monitored moderation. But, the first-level moderation is always automated, and it is through AI. That means bias exists in AI too.

Is This Bias Known and Planned?

The answer is: Yes and No. It is known. But it is not necessarily planned. To understand this, we need to know a little more about AI-based systems.

The service provider (Perspective API) is clear that their service may make mistakes. Their Frequently Asked Questions (FAQ) page proves it. They also state ways and means to report the user opinions about the correct judgment. The service example used here has a published disclaimer.

This is where the 'algorithm bias', or 'AI bias' comes into the picture.

Artificial Intelligence Bias

The machine learning model architecture has multiple algorithms coming together. There are many stages of processing. At each stage, there are parameters and data involved that heavily influence the decisions of the AI system. Hence, the bias emerges from two broad categories.

- **Algorithm Bias**

The bias that gets injected is due to technical reasons. It could be due to the choice of architecture, the technical parameters involved in the system, or even the order in which different training data is supplied for learning.

The details are irrelevant. The main reason is that engineers working on such a system have no motivation to sustain bias, however, they are continuously improving the systems. As a person affected by AI decisions, you can report it to them. Other than that, there is limited scope to improve the situation.

- **Data Bias**

The second type of bias occurs from the data used for the creation of the AI system. There is a huge set of data required to train the machine learning models. It is very difficult to get huge data for each specific project. Hence, training happens in two stages. Initial training is done with a large dataset such as Wikipedia, which is widely accepted as neutral knowledge. It has data with correct grammar. From this, the model learns the language rules, most likely permutations of words and punctuation. It also learns the normally accepted facts and phrases. Suppose Wikipedia states that Hindutva is India's equivalent of Afghanistan's Taliban, the model may make similar associations and equivalences. Many research labs and volunteers provide pre-trained language models with Wikipedia data.

The second level of training is project-specific. The team creating hate detection service may create their data set for classifying content. It may contain thousands of sentences marked as hate, identity attack, abuse and so on. This data is used for training the model that is already trained with Wikipedia. Such a model may be deployed as an online service. Thereafter, based on user and other stakeholder feedback, it may collect data to retrain the deep learning models. This is a continuous process.

Now imagine that the Wikipedia data set has sentences that misrepresent and insult Indian deities and generate hate against Hindus. Since Wikipedia is a key source for language models, this hate speech would be considered normal. Would an AI system understand that these *are* insults and attacks on identity? No, it would not. The system blindly accepts what is provided as training data. It tries its best to learn from it and later uses the same to judge a given user's comment or post.

Here arises the question: *If technical people involved are not conspiring, why can they not just do the right thing? Why can they not use the appropriate data classifications for the data?*

The answer lies in the challenges related to collecting data.

Challenges in Data Collection, Data Bias and Analysis: Technical Perspectives

The higher the intelligence that is aimed for from the system, the higher is the need for data. An adequate volume of data with adequate diversity is required. If it is about hate speech detection, all different kinds of hate speech are required. This may be hate speech specific to different segments of users, geographies, cultures and so on. Likewise, it also requires non-hate speech examples from all possible scenarios. Abusive speech in one context may be a friendly expression in another.

Having been part of autonomous driving data collection and management, the author's observation is that in engineering domains, data is analyzed to a very great extent for correctness. For example, the automotive industry spends huge amounts of money on road-drives collecting data, labeling the data and so on. Similar is the case with other engineering domains like sensors and event monitoring. However, it is hard to say the same about domains like social media. Unlike engineering, in the social and cultural area, the nuances involved are infinite. There are cultures and multiple levels of subcultures. Identifying hate speech is far more subjective than identifying a car as a car.

Let us examine the most likely process across all companies. One of the main methods is web scraping. The data available online is read and converted to formats useful for the AI system. There are many automated software tools for this purpose. The same data would be cleaned. Data cleaning is a step that involves checking for inconsistencies and problems in the data to the possible extent. The same is used for training AI systems. Big Tech grew in strength by automation. Once again, automated tools would do this data cleaning job. When Big Tech builds one system of global reach, knowingly or unknowingly it promotes global monoculture.

Though the systems try their best to adapt to a diverse user base, the inherent biases in the data are likely to remain.

To understand how data bias occurs due to the training data, we will examine the technical details of how exactly the AI system understands natural languages, their grammar, and vocabulary. This also provides clues to solving the threats faced due to bias.

The Mental Model of Words and Sentences

By using lots of data, an AI system will create its own 'mental model' of all the words and sentences it recognizes. The mental model of the words has to achieve a lot. It should provide a mathematical way to relate to other words. There are many kinds of relationships between words. These considerations could be singular vs. plural, adjective, synonym, antonym, gender, words related to action, related to time, related to the hierarchy and so on. It is also possible that two words have a very close association in one context, and no relation at all in another one. Further, it is also possible that two words are synonyms in one context and antonyms in another. If you think further on this, you will be able to come up with hundreds of kinds of relationships between different words in your vocabulary.

The challenge is to create a mathematical representation of all of these words. The representation needs to allow mathematical operations in such a way that real-world needs such as translation, hate speech detection, sentence generation and so on are accomplished. The most basic unit of such representation is called 'embedding'.

The Representation of Words and Sentences

The Global Positioning System Analogy

Before we proceed to understand the representation of words in word embedding, let us look at a simpler analogy. Global Positioning System (GPS) is useful in several ways. It can uniquely identify a physical location. By using the latitude and longitude of two places, a mathematical operation can be done to determine the distance between the two places. To achieve this, each place is assigned a series of numbers. The series has two numbers, each representing the value of latitude and longitude respectively.

The combination of these two fields is called coordinates. The overall system is a GPS coordinate system, which works very well for the purpose it is intended.

However, GPS has limitations. It assumes that all the unique points are on the surface of the earth; it cannot represent elevation above ground or depression below ground. It also cannot identify any place outside the earth and so cannot be used to map the entire universe. The universe is also believed to be ever-expanding and GPS cannot represent a point on another planet within our solar system. Hence, if we need to create a coordinate system for the entire universe, two dimensions (latitude and longitude) are not enough.

While representing words, AI is attempting to create a 'word coordinate system'.

'Embedding': The Actual Representation of Words and Sentences Inside Artificial Intelligence

Coming to natural language words and their representation, AI attempts something similar to GPS. Artificial Intelligence attempts to organize all the words it recognizes into imaginary universes. This imaginary universe of words is the basic building block of the Natural Language Processing AI system. It is the mental model of AI and is known as 'embedding'. There is word embeddings, sentence embeddings, spelling embeddings and so on.

In the case of GPS, the coordinate system assigns coordinates to places that physically exist already. Its coordinates are always latitude and longitude.

The coordinate system of words, however, reads all the available articles and books and recognizes words and the distinct kinds of relationships between them. It then uses the distinct natures of relationships as one of each field in the coordinate system. Based on such a coordinate system, it places each word in its imaginary universe. With this, an 'embedding' is created.

When it is visualized, it looks like the following illustration. It would be similar to gazing at the sky and watching stars. But instead of stars, each dot is a word here. There is still a purpose for this visualization as we will see.

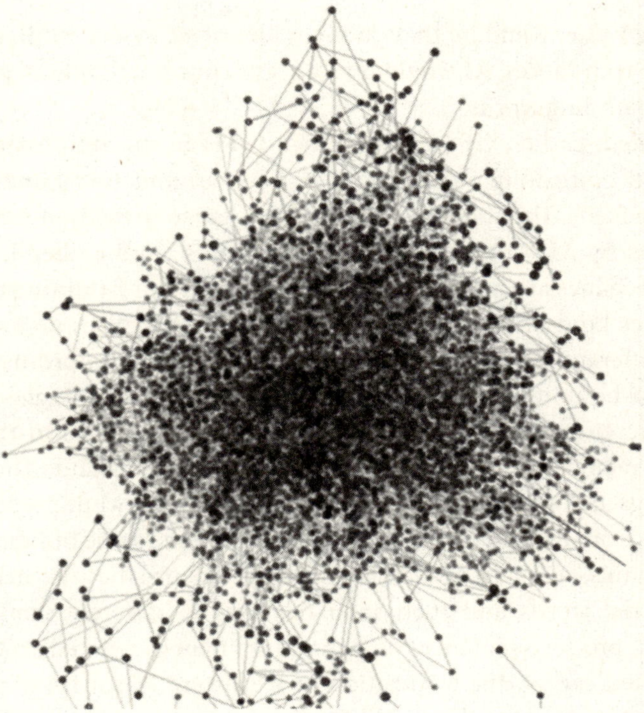

Figure 3: Source: https://projector.tensorflow.org/

How Embeddings are Used for Artificial Intelligence Decisions

Each word is associated with the coordinate values in the GPS-like universe described earlier. In the technical world, this series of numbers associated with each word is called a vector. You can think of this embedding as a world map of words, and the vector as the coordinate to locate the word in this map. Artificial Intelligence understands the words through the coordinate values associated with the word. All applications, such as finding synonyms, filling the most probable next word, translating words to different languages and so on, do complex mathematical operations associated with these coordinate values inside the embedding.

Suppose the purpose is to find a synonym of a word. The AI system picks the coordinates of the word and then does relevant mathematical operations, which results in a coordinate value. The word closest to the coordinate value would be the synonym identified by AI. Similarly, if it is a sentence translation, AI would give a set of coordinate values, signifying the corresponding words.

As stated, earlier, GPS has only two fields in its coordinate system. Most word embeddings used in 2021 have around two hundred such coordinate fields. There are no specific names given to fields; it is internally determined by AI. At the end of training of this word embedding, these coordinate values are fixed. These can be changed by re-training the same. For another kind of embedding, the set of words, articles and so on are entirely different. Hence, their inter-relationships and coordinate values also would be unique. These coordinate values are meaningless outside the specific embedding. The higher the number of values in the series, the more nuances and contexts the AI would understand. These word embeddings are building blocks for bigger operations. Multiple such word embeddings are used in any AI system and using the same building blocks of embeddings, language models are developed. Since they mathematically represent the words and their inter-relations in different contexts, the models can produce sentences on par with human-generated sentences.

As stated earlier, the association of words are learnt from real word articles and sources such as Wikipedia. Large sources of well-formed sentences and ways of arranging words are done by Wikipedia, and is used for training language models. The language models have embeddings trained with the most probable ways of association between words, sentences and so on. The values inside the coordinate fields mentioned above are adjusted as the AI system learns more and more data. As the values of coordinates of the words change, the words closeness or the association with other words keep getting updated.

Now we know how exactly words are represented inside AI. An actual illustration of the mechanics of data bias is presented next.

An Illustration of Data Bias in an Actual System

The following graph explains how words are represented. Each dot represents one word. All the words are represented around an origin and various dimensions. Google has provided a tool to view such word embeddings. We will view how two example words appear in a word embedding. The words chosen for this purpose are 'nationalism' and 'patriotic'.

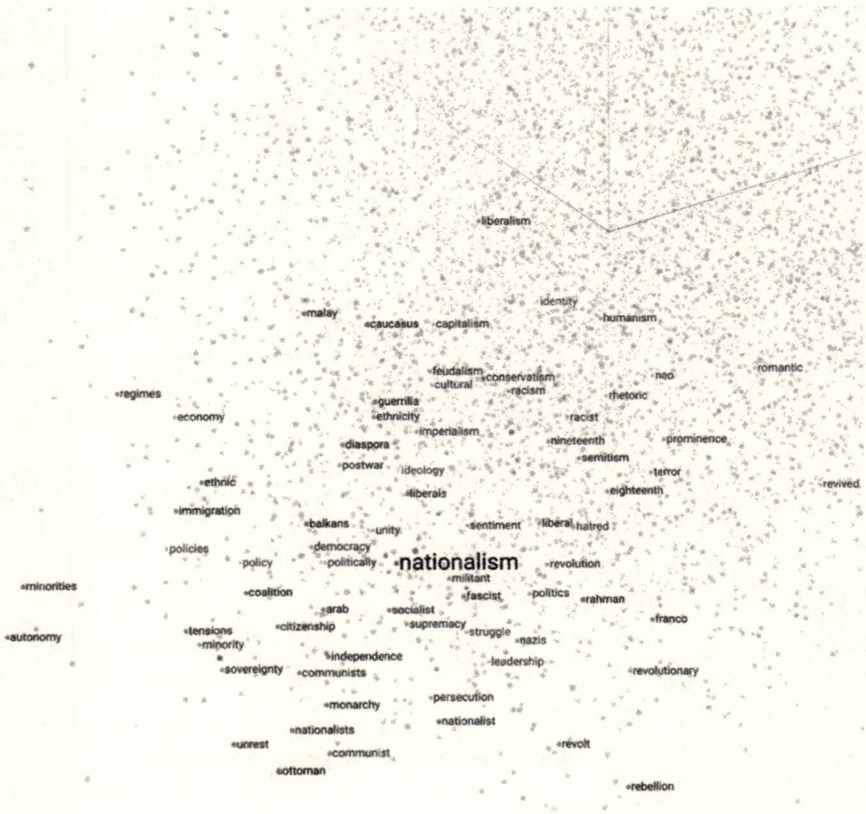

Figure 4: Source: https://projector.tensorflow.org/

The above picture has been sourced from Google, from the TensorFlow library used in machine learning. It is a snapshot of the 'mental model' of the AI system described earlier.

If you observe the right bottom of the above picture, it shows a list of words with the 'shortest distance' to the word nationalism. These include racism, semitism, minorities and so on. The same words are seen in the 'word cloud' as well. That is to say, when you use the word 'nationalism', the AI technology used here is more likely to associate the words within the shortest distance. Of course, this is a generalization. There is a lot more happening inside. Let's take the word 'patriotic'. It indeed shows 'nationalist' as the closest word in its two-hundred-dimension space. However, it does not show racism, minorities, imperialism as the closest words, instead, it shows pride, flag, freedom and so on.

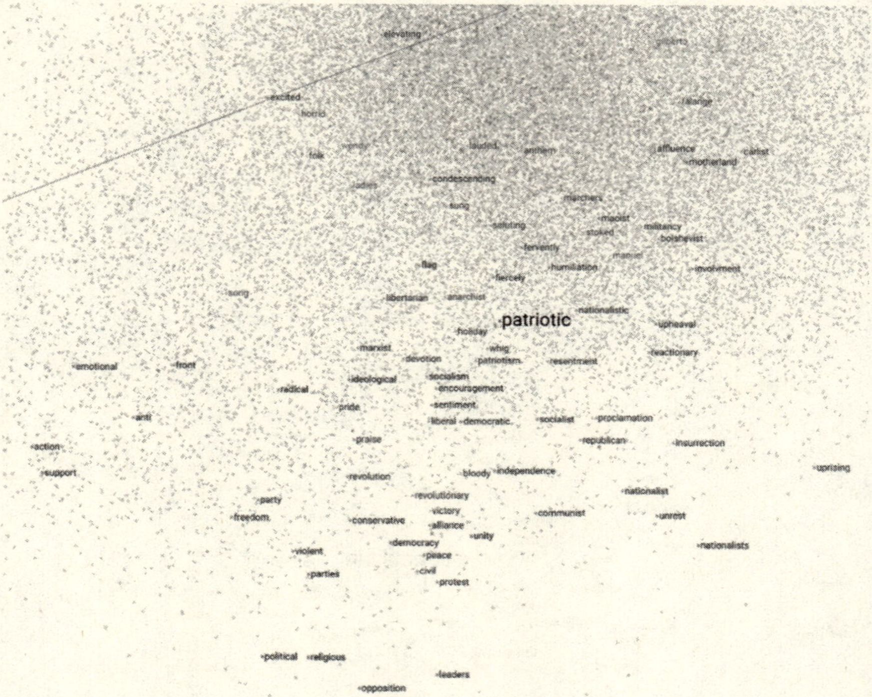

Figure 5: Source: https://projector.tensorflow.org/

This means that the system perceives nationalism a lot more negatively than patriotism. As explained earlier, the closeness of words happens due to the training data. We will trace the root of the bias observed in the case of the words: nationalism and patriotism.

Tracing the Bias Back to the Data

We identified that there is bias against the word nationalism as compared to patriotism. We now examine how the two words are used.

How These Words are Used in the West

We first review the Merriam Webster dictionary published in the West, which has very different definitions.

Definition of Nationalism:

Loyalty and devotion to a nation especially: a sense of national consciousness (see consciousness sense 1c) exalting one nation above all others and placing primary emphasis on the promotion of its culture and interests as opposed to those of other nations or supranational groups. E.g., Intense nationalism was one of the causes of the war.

Definition of Patriotism:

Love for or devotion to one's country. E.g., Although poles apart ideologically, they are both unashamed of their patriotism

The above definition is echoed by several media houses from the US as well. *Patriotism is good. Nationalism is bad.*

When Indians say they are nationalists, it is incorrectly assumed that it is an effort to assert the country's supremacy over other countries. This is because of the European usage of the word nationalism. The experience in Europe fits the definition. With this worldview of the words, nationalism and patriotism, much content is available. To train Artificial Intelligence systems, a lot of data gets collected from sources (mostly online) that are considered authentic.

Wikipedia and mainstream media articles provide loads of natural language data. Hence, these articles get used in training the AI system thereby impacting the word embedding representations. Even if some articles with the Indian definition get used, they will not be the primary meanings; other definitions also become part of the system's overall approach towards these words.

How These Words are Used in India

For Indians, the words 'nationalism' and 'patriotism' are interchangeable. The freedom movement was nationalistic. It describes an inclusive, common identity while retaining the sub-identities and sub-cultures. The Indian National Congress was the forum under which most Indians came together. It symbolized respect for all, equality, unity in diversity and so on. It was the effort of the civilization to fight against colonizers and oppressors. Nationalism has no negative connotation whatsoever.

Addressing Data Bias

An example illustration of *word* related bias was presented above. Similarly, there are a multitude of words that appear to be simple and common based on superficial usage. However, they have different meanings in various local contexts. Every society has evolved through different experiences and changes. The fears, shame and pride of each society are different and are reflected in the local meanings of words. For the English language, Western experiences and perspectives are taken as the primary choice. This is unavoidable as of now.

Unless each society responds to this bias and stands up for their representation in the data sets, the dominant global monoculture will take over. The response should be in the form of generating data sets that represent the respective societies better. Eventually, AI systems will understand the local nuances, if a society actively collaborates with the AI system creators.

Hate-issues Specific to Hinduism and India

With the appreciation and understanding of how AI learns and represents a word, it becomes easier to comprehend the issues that concern the bias related to Hinduism and India. Both India *and* Hinduism face special challenges concerning hate and misinformation. This is primarily due to the nature and quality of the data. There are many kinds of biases that are already an integral part of available data sets. This needs urgent action. If one generation of the world population interacts and makes decisions with incorrect translations and online misinformation, it will be impossible to solve. Some of the challenges that need to be addressed are:

- **Diversity of Data**

As seen earlier, sentence representation in AI systems is done by uniquely identifying words and building unique mappings. To understand wider patterns, which include broader nuances, contexts and shades of meaning and usage, diverse range of training data is needed. If the pattern is complex and diverse, the data that is needed rises exponentially.

- **Lack of 'Structure'**

Hinduism does not have a simple definition. There is massive misinformation in multiple forums due to the lack of organized groups, authorizing what is, and what is not, Hinduism. The word Hindu is used sometimes to refer to religion, or in other instances to geography. In another context, it implies cultural identity. Only after that, can there be an official description of what is hate speech against Hindus, Hinduism, or India. For AI system creators, it creates a big challenge. This challenge is amplified by the entire ontological structuring of the vocabulary of dharma, and Hinduism has multiple structures and multiple interpretations. Not only is Hinduism ontologically, internally complex, its interpretations (that are available as data) are devious and flawed.

- **Pre-Established Biases**

There are pre-established biases in social institutions like academia, education, media and liberal arts. As a result, there is deliberate bias in the media. The same data from media reports is used for training models.

- **Complex Use of English Language (Indian-isms)**

In general, Indians as a collective have paid little attention to the problems caused by language usage, creating implicit biases in data and narratives. Usage of words in the wrong context, imprecise expressions, use of English in combination with Indian languages, in the form of various creoles—all of this daily usage gets added to social media's normally accepted data. Artificial Intelligence systems end up generating wrong sentences, provide wrong summaries of events and wrong translations. This makes misinformation more or less a permanent phenomenon.

The dependence on the English language as a source of credibility and truth is another national weakness. This is manipulated by global forces inimical to the Indian narrative. The use of the English language is influenced to create negative narratives and, in many ways, powers media content. This eventually becomes part of the data used to train AI systems.

The Artificial Intelligence System Creator's View of Bias

- **Challenge of Explainable AI**

Currently, Machine Learning is still too 'unexplainable'. The mathematical parameters of the AI system are arrived at by trial and error. Even after this, it is incredibly hard to explain the 'why' of an AI system's decision. If the system decides that a comment is 'hate speech' and another similar one as 'positive speech', it is impossible for the developer to explain and justify this to users. This continues to be a big problem for AI. There is a lot of money being spent on 'Explainable AI'. Many tools are being created that can visualize how the system works, internally. The word embedding visual representation we explored earlier is one such tool.

In a normal software system, the machine does exactly what it is instructed to do. Many critical systems, such as banking software, require that the machine's behavior is fully known at any given time. These systems require to show the software source code to the authorities. However, AI creates its own logic. As it sees more data, it can alter its logic.

Hence, the creators of AI systems cannot explain it to official authorities or customers. They can show the working of the system but they cannot show specific decision stages step by step. Due to this, the AI system creators cannot explain when it makes mistakes. Thus, system creators are willing to listen to users and do acknowledge inherent bias. This opens up the opportunity to engage the system creators.

- **Business and Financial Reasons**

Biases discourage the target audience. This may result in lower usage leading to lower data generation. Hence, the platform will not mature and the overall value diminishes.

- **Lack of Domain Competency**

Often, creators of AI systems do not have domain expertise. Due to this, the way they organize data to be trained is incorrect. Many of the AI system creators are happy to bring in domain experts.

- **Engineering a Functioning AI System is Very Hard**

The individual steps involved in AI is now easy. However, making an AI system as a whole, ensuring that it works well, and is always correct is extremely hard. Just like other systems designers, AI system creators are receptive to feedback, far more than one might expect.

Governments and Artificial Intelligence Systems

Even if AI system creators acknowledge biases and promise all the cooperation, governments are proceeding with guidelines and regulations.

Mass manipulation, privacy, fairness of treatment in matters such as legal decisions, and employment decisions are key concerns.

The Cyberspace Administration of China (CAC) is the Internet watchdog of China. It intends to stop manipulation of consumers through AI recommendation systems. China has mandated government approval for AI recommender system algorithm releases. There are also opinions that this regulation may not work since the AI algorithm does not change. Instead, the data alters the configurations of the algorithms, not the algorithm itself. Europe has classified four levels of AI risks. Unacceptable risk category is manipulations. High risk AI systems category is mainly concerned with fairness (in applications like judiciary, job interviews), safety and privacy. Low risk AI category has customer service chatbot, game kind of applications. Minimal risk AI allows the free use of applications such as AI-enabled video games or spam filters. The vast majority of AI systems fall into this category.

The classification based on criticality and sensitivity of application is a great step. Even with this, there is no clarity on the monitoring and enforcement. The consumers are always online and of their own 'free will'. They update software that includes cookies and edge AI models onto their computers.

India's non-regulatory guidelines body NITI Aayog has its own AI guidelines. It mentions all the concerns raised globally: privacy, fairness, explainable AI, accountability of decisions. These are published as self-regulation strictures. There is no evidence of any real regulation being introduced and enforced. The big risk for India is the lack of punitive measures, even in cases like fake news by the media. The same articles in the media will get used for training AI systems, which is not the case for other countries. There seems to be a marked lack of awareness of the deeper issues around AI and its social impacts.

A larger risk for India is the misinformation attacks on its cultural, and religious traditions. There is no strategy for a response from the state. Currently, those in power and the decision-makers seem to be more or less pretty uninformed and mostly clueless, when it comes to realizing the threats that AI systems pose to state functioning.

All the misinformation generated continues to reach AI training data sets and compounds the AI bias. The vulnerability across the board reflects on the side of AI too. Generally speaking, the ability of governments to define and enforce measures appears to be low. The better alternative is to work with AI system creators and engage with them to reduce data driven biases as much as possible.

Engaging with Artificial Intelligence System Creators

- ### Create Data Set Specific to Your Concern

It could be related to your language, culture or any other specialization. Artificial Intelligence system creators can be convinced to use these if they are relevant. There are many data set formats related to language representations online. Creating a data set does not require you to be a technology professional.

With systems like Generative Pre-trained Transformer-3 (GPT-3), an autoregressive language model, evolving, the best defense for the country and society against misinformation is good data sets which does not induce biases against the country or society. When GPT-3 or others allow integrations, their bias will get distributed to every platform, every human in every corner of the world.

Good data sets are the most important step to fight misinformation.

- ### Become an AI System Creator Yourself

The technology to create AI systems is getting commoditized. Now, systems can be created with almost no software coding. The automation tools achieve most of the work. This was impossible a few years back.

Creating alternate AI enabled services is a great step. It can be integrated with online service providers of various kinds worldwide.

- ### Reporting Based on the Features Provided by the AI System

Many companies involved in technology around content moderation are willing to listen. They allow the option to report a wrong judgment while also seeking user inputs on the correct decision. Tools like Facebook's allow users to rate the translations and even allow providing a proposed translation. It may not immediately solve the issue but will help in the long run. Doing this may feel like free work for Big Tech. If you cannot create a competing system, it is good to correct the system. At a minimum, it can save your language or culture from extinction.

- **Understand and Acknowledge the Power of Words**

Wherever there is concern that the 'Indian story' and its description is controlled by not-so-friendly forces, take *active part* in correcting the definitions. If a word has an exact meaning in the rest of the world, then it is alright. If not, it is fine to create new words that uniquely explain the situational local context. If online data exhibits consistency, then AI bias in general will be a lot lesser. Creating data sets with authentic information related to India, culture, religion, sciences, and knowledge systems would greatly help both technologists and the wider public audience (Indian or otherwise).

Use of non-translatable (the book, *Sanskrit Non-Translatables: The Importance of Sanskritizing English* by Rajiv Malhotra and Satyanarayana Dasa provides an excellent background) local words in their original form is another powerful strategy that is highly recommended to help retain local nuance and semantics. Beyond this, of course, there can be the real possibility of agendas and conspiracies. However, we need to first engage with the system creators to eliminate wherever possible and overall minimize the biases.

Conclusion

Freedom of Speech is a fine line. Content moderation (now mostly seen in Big Tech media channels) driven by algorithms will soon become a universal reality. Online user behavior in comments and replies need to be controlled and not be outrage driven. For example, people get overly emotional and post far more offensive comments than in the originally deleted message. This makes the situation worse for an AI system like moderation. Studying the situation with a calm mind, the author believes is the best way. Artificial Intelligence systems are here to stay. We cannot wish them away. A non-trivial understanding of how AI systems work and engaging effectively with AI system creators is a sure way to improve AI systems, reduce bias and also improve the user experience in the long run. Freedom of Speech in fact can be enhanced if we make collective efforts to create authentic data sources and have rounded perspectives represented in data sets. Like everything else that AI affects, it is about how we put the tools and technology to use. A proactive and intelligent approach to AI systems is the future.

SEVEN

AI-MING for a Theory of Everything

Dr Mrittunjoy Guha Majumdar

Area of Research	The utilization of Artificial Intelligence for explorations in physics, particularly around the unification of the fundamental forces of nature.
The State Before AI	Unification of strong, weak, and electromagnetic forces have been attained, while gravity remains an outlier, with a universally accepted theory of Quantum gravity still being elusive.
The State After AI	Artificial Intelligence will provide a massive boost to the pursuit of pushing the frontiers of research in physics. Everything from finding the Higgs boson and gravitational waves, to creating Bose-Einstein Condensate in a faster and more efficient manner has recently been done using AI.

Explorations into the nature of reality have been undertaken across the ages. In the contemporary world, disparate tools, from *gedanken* (German for 'thought') experiments,[1,2,3,4] experimental consistency checks[5,6] to machine learning and Artificial Intelligence (AI) are being used to illuminate the fundamental layers of reality.[7]

A theory of everything, a grand unified theory of physics and nature, has been elusive for the world of physics. While unifying various forces and interactions in nature, we started with the unification of electricity and magnetism in Scottish mathematician James Clerk Maxwell's seminal two-volume work *A Treatise on Electricity and Magnetism.*[8] From 1964 to 1967, the world of physics saw another step being taken in this quest for explaining disparate fundamental forces under the same conceptual umbrella with the electroweak unification by Weinberg-Salam-Glashow.[*9,10,11] Around the same time, a major initiative in this direction was the establishment of the Standard Model that included the Quantum Chromodynamics (QCD) sector, which relates to another force of nature – the strong force, by American Nobel-prize winning physicist Murray Gell-Mann and the American theoretical physicist Richard Feynman.[12,13]

---

1. Aspect, A., Grangier, P., & Roger, G. (1982). *Experimental Realization of Einstein-Podolsky-Rosen-Bohm Gedanken Experiment: A New Violation of Bell's Inequalities. Physical Review Letters,* 49(2), 91.
2. Jacques, V., Wu, E., Grosshans, F., Treussart, F., Grangier, P., Aspect, A., & Roch, J.F. (2007). *Experimental Realization of Wheeler's Delayed-choice Gedanken Experiment. Science,* 315(5814), 966-68.
3. Scardigli, F. (1999). *Generalized Uncertainty Principle in Quantum Gravity from Micro-black Hole Gedanken Experiment.* Physics Letters B, 452(1-2), 39-44.
4. Liu, X.J., Miao, Q., Gel'Mukhanov, F., Patanen, M., Travnikova, O., Nicolas, C., ... & Miron, C. (2015). Einstein–Bohr *Recoiling Double-slit Gedanken Experiment Performed at the Molecular Level. Nature Photonics,* 9(2), 120-125.
5. Amaldo, U., de Boer, W., Frampton, P.H., Fürstenau, H., & Liu, J.T. (1992). *Consistency Checks of Grand Unified Theories.* Physics Letters B, 281(3-4), 374-382.
6. De Boer, W. (1994). *Grand Unified Theories and Supersymmetry in Particle Physics and Cosmology.* 'Progress in Particle and Nuclear Physics', 33, 201-301.
7. Hogg, T., & Huberman, B.A. (1987). *Artificial Intelligence and Large Scale Computation: A Physics Perspective.* Physics Reports, 156(5), 227-310.
8. Maxwell, J.C. (1873). *A Treatise on Electricity and Magnetism* (Vol. 1). Oxford: Clarendon Press.
9. Glashow, S.L. (1959). *The Renormalizability of Vector Meson Interactions. Nuclear Physics,* 10, 107-117.
10. Salam, A., & Ward, J.C. (1961). *Weak and Electromagnetic Interactions,* Novo Cim. 11 (1959) 568. *On a Gauge Group of Elementary Interactions,* ibid, 19, 165.
11. Weinberg, S. (1967). *A Model of Leptons. Physical Review Letters,* 19(21), 1264.
12. Gell-Mann, M. (1961). *The Eightfold Way: A Theory of Strong Interaction Symmetry* (No. TID-12608; CTSL-20). California Inst. of Tech., Pasadena. Synchrotron Lab.
13. Feynman, R.P. (1969). High Energy Collisions, Third International Conference at Stony Brook, NY.

We now have a few candidates for the Theories of Everything (ToE), primary among which is String Theory.[14] String Theory is a framework wherein the usual point-like building blocks, in the form of particles, as in particle physics, are replaced by strings, which can propagate through space and time as well as interact with each other. For large length scales that are much larger than the dimension of the string, it looks like a particle, whose attributes such as charge and mass are delineated by the vibrational state of the string. Since String Theory does account for gravity, which is the only outlying fundamental force from the Standard Model, it is regarded as a Theory of Everything.

Unfortunately, we are still some way off from establishing various areas of the theory empirically. Chief among this is the concept of supersymmetry,[15] which is an important part of String Theory. In nature, we have two kinds of particles: Bosons (with integral spin) and Fermions (with half-integer spins). Force carriers such as photons and gluons are bosons, while constituents of matter are generally fermions. Supersymmetry posits a symmetry between these two classes of particles: Each particle in one class has a corresponding counterpart in the other class, known as a superpartner. Examples of such superpartners include squarks for quarks, photino for photon and gravitino for graviton. There were no evidences found for supersymmetry in any of the runs of the Large Hadron Collider (LHC), which is the largest and most powerful particle accelerator in the world.[16] When the Large Hadron Collider discovered the Higgs boson (the quantum excitation of what is known as the Higgs field, which is pivotal in generating the masses of various particles such as quarks, W and Z gauge bosons as well as charged leptons). In 2011-2,[17,18,19] there were results that were problematic for the Minimum Supersymmetric Standard Model (MSSM), since the value of the mass

14. Becker, K., Becker, M., & Schwarz, J.H. (2006). *String Theory and M-theory: A Modern Introduction.* Cambridge University Press.

15. Fayet, P., & Ferrara, S. (1977). *Supersymmetry.* Physics Reports, 32(5), 249-334.

16. Canepa, A. (2019). Searches for Supersymmetry at the Large Hadron Collider. Reviews in Physics, 4, 100033.

17. Adrian Cho (13 July 2012). *Higgs Boson Makes Its Debut After Decades-Long Search. Science.* 337.

18. Barton, A., Borissov, G., Bouhova-Thacker, E., Chilingarov, A., Davidson, R., de Mora, L., ... & Walder, J. (2012). *Observation of a New Particle in the Search for the Standard Model Higgs Boson with the ATLAS Detector at the LHC.* Physics Letters B, 716(1), 1-29.

19. Higgs, P.W. (1964). Broken Symmetries and the Masses of Gauge Bosons. *Physical Review Letters,* 13(16), 508.

of the Higgs boson at $125x10^9$eV (for reference, the energy carried by a single photon of visible light is around 2-3 eV) is relatively large for the model and could only be attained with large radiative loop corrections from top squarks that many theoreticians considered to be 'unnatural'.[20] In the absence of experiments that can test certain frontiers of physics, particularly due to energy constraints predominantly at the smallest of scales, the importance of simulations and computational research cannot be underplayed.

Gone are the days when the mathematician and physicist Sir Isaac Newton purportedly could sit under an apple tree and infer the concept of gravity from an apple that had fallen on his head. In today's age, we have increasing levels of computational inputs and power that have to be factored in when considering avenues of new research in physics. For instance, M-Theory, introduced by the American mathematical and theoretical physicist, Edward Witten (According to Witten, 'M' should stand for 'magic', 'mystery' or 'membrane') in 1995,[21] is a promising approach to a unified model of physics that includes Quantum gravity. It extends the formalism of String Theory, and formulates physics in terms of branes instead of strings. A brane is a dynamical physical object that moves through space and time, according to the rules of Quantum mechanics, and generalizes the notion of a point particle to higher dimensions. When we talk of the gravitational aspects of any theory of Quantum gravity, we invariably discuss different kinds of geometries of space-time. This is an extension of Einstein's idea on what is gravity: curvature of the fabric of spacetime. Geometry is also relevant for the other fundamental forces, especially when talking of gauges, which are conceptual elements to reduce any redundancies in describing the quantum fields associated with specific forces.

M-theory has various kinds of geometries to describe various forces, in higher dimensions than what we are familiar with, in day-to-day life: three spatial and one time dimension. M-theory is eleven-dimensional, with ten spatial and one time dimension. In order to describe real physical phenomena using M-theory, we must imagine scenarios in which these extra dimensions would not be observed empirically. Given the complexity

20. Draper, P., Meade, P., Reece, M., & Shih, D. (2012). *Implications of a 125 GeV Higgs boson for the MSSM and low-scale supersymmetry breaking. Physical Review D*, 85(9), 095007.

21. Witten, E. (1995). *String Theory Dynamics in Various Dimensions.* Nuclear Physics B, 443(1-2), 85-126.

of this construction, it may not be straightforward to ascertain how a physical system behaves when they act on, and with, the geometries laid out by M-theory. There have been computational tools relating to machine learning that have lately been used for solving M-Theory geometries.[22] TensorFlow, a computing platform normally used for machine learning, helped in finding 194 solutions to the equations describing the system, at equilibrium, for one particular type of M-Theory spacetime geometries.[23,24,25]

Artificial Intelligence has been one of the primary areas of interest in computational pursuits around physics research. In 2020, Matsubara Takashi (Osaka University, Japan) and Yaguchi Takaharu (Kobe University, Japan), along with their research group, were successful in developing technology that could simulate phenomena for which we do not have the detailed formula or mechanism, using Artificial Intelligence.[26] The underlying step here is the creation of a model from observational data, constrained by the model being consistent and faithful to the laws of physics.

In this pursuit, the researchers utilized digital calculus as well as a geometrical approach, such as those of Riemannian geometry (named after German mathematician Georg Friedrich Bernhard Riemann) and symplectic geometry (which looks at specific kinds of manifolds that are locally similar enough to a vector space to allow one to do calculus). For the former, certain novel digital versions of backpropagation (an algorithm used in machine learning that calculates how one could best correct incorrect responses given by AI during the learning period based on differentiation calculations) using automatic differentiation were applied.[27]

Using this new approach, one could implement and preserve physical laws such as energy conservation. National Aeronautics and Space

---

22. Comsa, I.M., Firsching, M., & Fischbacher, T. (2019). SO (8) *Supergravity and the Magic of Machine Learning. Journal of High Energy Physics*, 2019(8), 1-57.

23. Bobev, N., Fischbacher, T., Gautason, F.F., & Pilch, K. (2020). *A cornucopia of AdS 5 vacua. Journal of High Energy Physics*, 2020(7), 1-42.

24. Abadi, M., Barham, P., Chen, J., Chen, Z., Davis, A., Dean, J., ... & Zheng, X. (2016). Tensorflow: A System for Large-scale Machine Learning. In 12th {USENIX} symposium on operating systems design and implementation ({OSDI} 16) (pp. 265-283).

25. Abadi, M., Agarwal, A., Barham, P., Brevdo, E., Chen, Z., Citro, C., ... & Zheng, X. (2016). Tensorflow: Large-scale Machine Learning on Heterogeneous Distributed Systems. arXiv preprint arXiv:1603.04467.

26. Matsubara, T., Ishikawa, A., & Yaguchi, T. (2020). Deep Energy-based Modeling of Discrete-time Physics. Advances in Neural Information Processing Systems, 33.

27. Chauvin, Y., & Rumelhart, D.E. (Eds.). (1995). *Backpropagation: Theory, Architectures, and Applications.* Psychology press.

Administration (NASA) has also used Artificial Intelligence to find an eighth planet in 2017, (*Kepler-90i*) circling Kepler-90, a Sun-like star that is 2,545 light-years away from Earth.[28] This discovery came about when researchers Andrew Vanderburg (associate professor of physics at Massachusetts Institute of Technology) and Christopher Shallue (Astrophysics PhD student, Harvard University) trained neural networks to identify transiting exoplanets.[29,30] Exoplanets are planets that orbit a star other than our sun and a transit takes place when a planet passes between a star and its observer. In the case of an exoplanet, a transit event entails the planet passing in front of its star, thereby dimming its light ever so slightly. This dimming can be seen in empirical readings of light received from that star over a period of time as a dip in brightness.

For the exploration of transiting exoplanets using neural networks, they used a set of fifteen thousand signals, which had been vetted previously, from the Kepler exoplanet catalogue (a database of exoplanets found by the Kepler space telescope), based on which they trained a computer to identify exoplanets in these signals. The artificial 'neural network' analyzed the Kepler data and found weak transit signals from Kepler-90i, after searching for weaker signals in 670 star-systems.

Recently, new analytical techniques have also been used to constrain effective field theories in experiments in the Large Hadron Collider. Using this experimental data and those from Monte Carlo simulations (a computational algorithm that makes use of randomized selections of samples to study, in a repetitive manner, to get the probability of an unknown quantity that we seek to know more about), we can train neural networks to estimate likelihood ratios for use in limit setting procedures.[31,32] Limit setting in high energy physics is the process of imposing limits on the

---

28. Petrescu, R.V., Aversa, R., Apicella, A., & Petrescu, F. I. (2018). *NASA Data Used to Discover Eighth Planet Circling Distant Star. Journal of Aircraft and Spacecraft Technology,* 2(1), 19-30.

29. Shallue, C.J., & Vanderburg, A. (2018). *Identifying Exoplanets with Deep Learning: A Five-planet Resonant Chain Around Kepler-80 and an Eighth Planet Around Kepler-90. The Astronomical Journal,* 155(2), 94.

30. Dattilo, A., Vanderburg, A., Shallue, C.J., Mayo, A.W., Berlind, P., Bieryla, A., ... & Yu, L. (2019). *Identifying Exoplanets with Deep Learning. ii. Two New Super-earths Uncovered by a Neural Network in k2 Data. The Astronomical Journal,* 157(5), 169.

31. Bechtle, P., Belkner, S., Dercks, D., Hamer, M., Keller, T., Krämer, M., ... & Tattersall, J. (2017). *SCYNet: Testing Supersymmetric Models at the LHC with Neural Networks. The European Physical Journal* C, 77(10), 1-20.

32. Brehmer, J., Cranmer, K., Louppe, G., & Pavez, J. (2018). *Constraining Effective Field Theories with Machine Learning. Physical Review Letters,* 121(11), 111801.

observation of a certain particle or phenomena, based on the theoretical model and the experimental conditions. There is a near-negligible likelihood of discovering empirical findings beyond this limit. The approaches based on neural networks have the advantage of scaling well, to large-scale, analyses when we consider higher number of parameters and with many observables. They also do not require us to consider approximations in the modelling, such as those relating to showers of partons (which are hypothesized to be constituents of nuclear particles) or miscellaneous stray effects that may emerge due to the functioning of particle detector(s). Using these methods, we can also evaluate the likelihood ratio of a process or phenomena in microseconds. In this way, utilizing Artificial Intelligence, we can obtain a high-performance, practical, and scalable approach to improve the legacy measurements of the Large Hadron Collider, which aim to put precise constraints on any indirect effects of physics that may lie beyond the conceptual framework provided by the Standard Model. Artificial Intelligence has already been applied successfully to varied scientific fields and problems, such as in networks of tensors (multidimensional arrays of elements), for error-correction algorithms and searching for new states of Quantum matter.[33]

Artificial Intelligence and neural networks were instrumental in finding the Higgs boson. The experiments at the Large Hadron Collider generate tons of data each day, analyzing which is a tedious process, besides particles like the Higgs boson lie in the noise of this data.[34,35] A quantum computer processor known as the annealer helped the Large Hadron Collider to detect the particle, using patterns in the way various kinds of particles emerged from collisions in the LHC.[36,37] Convolutional Neural Network (CNN) architecture can be used to tackle the problem

---

33. Carrasquilla, J. (2020). *Machine Learning for Quantum Matter. Advances in Physics:* X, 5(1), 1797528.

34. Castelvecchi, D. (2015). *Artificial Intelligence Called in to Tackle LHC Data Deluge. Nature News*, 528(7580), 18.

35. Sadowski, P.J., Whiteson, D., & Baldi, P. (2014). *Searching for Higgs Boson Decay Modes with Deep Learning. Advances in Neural Information Processing Systems*, 27, 2393-2401.

36. Bapst, F., Bhimji, W., Calafiura, P., Gray, H., Lavrijsen, W., Linder, L., & Smith, A. (2020). *A Pattern Recognition Algorithm for Quantum Annealers.* Computing and Software for Big Science, 4(1), 1-7.

37. Saito, M., Calafiura, P., Gray, H., Lavrijsen, W., Linder, L., Okumura, Y., ... & Terashi, K. (2020). *Quantum Annealing Algorithms for Track Pattern Recognition.* In EPJ Web of Conferences (Vol. 245, p. 10006). EDP Sciences.

of identifying the particle from color-flow energy images.[38,39] Current methods employ conceptual tools like the Fisher Discriminant Analysis on empirical readings associated with jet pull superstructures.[40] It is extremely tough to study the collisions and particles during the operation of the LHC since the particles decay quickly. Without AI, this discovery may have been impossible! Artificial Intelligence has been used in undertaking another seminal experiment: the creation of Bose-Einstein Condensate (BEC).[41,42,43,44,45] In this experiment, the bosonic gas was cooled to around $1x10^{-3}$ Kelvin and thereafter the control of the lasers used was given to the AI system that was tasked with cooling the trapped gas to temperatures typically in the order of $1x10^{-9}$ Kelvin. The AI system could undertake this experiment in a span of less than one hour.

Usually, Bose-Einstein Condensate is produced using evaporative cooling. Microscopic semiclassical theory (here semiclassical denotes that one part of a system being studied under this theory is described quantum mechanically whereas the other is treated classically), while capable of describing the process, may oversimplify the dynamics and miss more effective and complex methods of evaporation, for instance the finding that circumvention of higher-order inelastic collisions (an elastic collision is defined as one in which both momentum and kinetic energy is conserved during the collision) can produce large condensates. Condensates arise out

---

38. Aaltonen, T., Amerio, S., Amidei, D., Anastassov, A., Annovi, A., Antos, J., ... & Herndon, M. (2013). *Direct Measurement of the Total Decay Width of the Top Quark. Physical Review Letters*, 111(20), 202001.

39. Chakraborty, A., Lim, S.H., Nojiri, M.M., & Takeuchi, M. (2020). *Neural Network-based Top Tagger with Two-point Energy Correlations and Geometry of Soft Emissions. Journal of High Energy Physics,* 2020(7), 1-47.

40. Mika, S., Ratsch, G., Weston, J., Scholkopf, B., & Mullers, K.R. (1999, August). Fisher Discriminant Analysis with Kernels. In Neural networks for signal processing IX: Proceedings of the 1999 IEEE signal processing society workshop (cat. no. 98th8468) (pp. 41-48). IEEE.

41. Davletov, E.T., Tsyganok, V.V., Khlebnikov, V.A., Pershin, D.A., Shaykin, D.V., & Akimov, A.V. (2020). *Machine Learning for Achieving Bose-Einstein Condensation of Thulium Atoms. Physical Review A*, 102(1), 011302.

42. Liang, X., Zhang, H., Liu, S., Li, Y., & Zhang, Y.S. (2018). *Generation of Bose-Einstein Condensates' Ground State Through Machine Learning.* Scientific Reports, 8(1), 1-8.

43. Barker, A.J., Style, H., Luksch, K., Sunami, S., Garrick, D., Hill, F., ... & Bentine, E. (2020). Applying Machine Learning Optimization Methods to the Production of a Quantum Gas. *Machine Learning: Science and Technology,* 1(1), 015007.

44. Saito, H. (2020). *Creation and Manipulation of Quantized Vortices in Bose–Einstein Condensates Using Reinforcement Learning. Journal of the Physical Society of Japan,* 89(7), 074006.

45. Pilati, S., & Pieri, P. (2019). Supervised Machine Learning of Ultracold Atoms with Speckle Disorder. Scientific reports, 9(1), 1-12.

of the physical realization of the property of bosons whereby a multiplicity can occupy a single state. Inelastic collisions as well as three-body losses can impede the creation of such states. We can now automate the process of the creation of BEC using Machine Learning Online Optimization (MLOO).[46] We can also create internal models (processes that simulate the response of a system in order to estimate the consequence of a system disturbance) that can predict the performance of future experiments for any set of parameters, using Gaussian processes (a stochastic process wherein every finite linear combination of the relevant random variables is normally distributed). Such algorithms can fit models to previous observations and choose the possible future experiments that can best refine the model. Artificial Intelligence helps at the cosmological scale as well, wherein it has been used to find gravitational wave signatures using deep learning algorithms.[47,48,49,50]

We can also employ Convolutional Neural Networks to find gravitational lensing in astrophysical data. Einstein gave us the equivalence of energy and mass in his *Annus Mirabilis* (The Year of Miracles) in 1904, with the famous equation $E=mc^2$, along with his work on special relativity, Brownian motion and photoelectric effect. Since light follows the curvature of spacetime, when it passes around a massive object, it gets bent. A gravitational lens is a distribution of matter between a distant light source and an observer that is capable of bending the light from the source as the light travels towards the observer. Recently, machine learning was used to obtain the image of a black hole, which was released on 10 April

---

46. Wigley, P.B., Everitt, P.J., van den Hengel, A., Bastian, J.W., Sooriyabandara, M.A., McDonald, G.D., ... & Hush, M.R. (2016). Fast Machine Learning Online Optimization of Ultra-cold-atom Experiments. Scientific reports, 6(1), 1-6.

47. Fluke, C.J., & Jacobs, C. (2020). Surveying the Reach and Maturity of Machine Learning and Artificial Intelligence in Astronomy. Wiley *Interdisciplinary Reviews: Data Mining and Knowledge Discovery,* 10(2), e1349.

48. Hezaveh, Y.D., Levasseur, L.P., & Marshall, P.J. (2017). *Fast Automated Analysis of Strong Gravitational Lenses with Convolutional Neural Networks. Nature,* 548(7669), 555-557.

49. Pourrahmani, M., Nayyeri, H., & Cooray, A. (2018). *LensFlow: A Convolutional Neural Network in Search of Strong Gravitational Lenses. The Astrophysical Journal,* 856(1), 68.

50. Caldeira, J., Wu, W.K., Nord, B., Avestruz, C., Trivedi, S., & Story, K. T. (2019). DeepCMB: Lensing Reconstruction of the Cosmic Microwave Background with Deep Neural Networks. *Astronomy and Computing,* 28, 100307.

2019.[51,52,53,54,55] An algorithm named Continuous High-resolution Image Reconstruction using Patch Priors (CHIRP) was required to combine the data obtained from eight different radio telescopes from around the world and turn it into a cohesive image. The challenge was to resolve how to account for the different times at which the astronomical signals reach the disparate telescopes. Accounting for this difference is crucial if we seek to extract visual information from these units. It has been seen that a clever way to do this is by multiplying the measurements from three telescopes so that there is mutual cancellation of extra delays due to atmospheric noise.

Most instances of gravitational lensing are subtle, which result in what are known as partial arcs or smears (when light passes around a massive object that causes a spherical distortion of spacetime, we can see rings as a result of gravitational lensing, while at other times, when the lensing mass is complex and does not cause a spherical distortion of spacetime, we can see partial rings or arcs), for which AI can help by identifying such elements. Machine learning can fasten the simulations for the formation of galaxies, besides being able to extrapolate existing simulations of cosmological structures using neural networks.[56,57,58] Deep neural networks can learn from a set of numerical simulation that have been run prior to

---

51. Bouman, K.L., Johnson, M.D., Zoran, D., Fish, V.L., Doeleman, S.S., & Freeman, W. T. (2016). Computational Imaging for VLBI Image Reconstruction. In Proceedings of the IEEE Conference on Computer Vision and Pattern Recognition (pp. 913-922).

52. Akiyama, K., Kuramochi, K., Ikeda, S., Fish, V. L., Tazaki, F., Honma, M., ... & Zaizen, M. (2017). *Imaging the Schwarzschild-radius-Scale Structure of M87 with the Event Horizon Telescope Using Sparse Modeling. The Astrophysical Journal,* 838(1), 1.

53. Bouman, K.L. (2020). *Portrait of a Black Hole: Here's How the Event Horizon Telescope Team Pieced Together a Now-famous Image. IEEE Spectrum,* 57(2), 22-29.

54. Askar, A., Askar, A., Pasquato, M., & Giersz, M. (2019). Finding Black Holes with Black Boxes–using Machine Learning to Identify Globular Clusters with Black Hole Subsystems. Monthly Notices of the Royal Astronomical Society, 485(4), 5345-5362.

55. van der Gucht, J., Davelaar, J., Hendriks, L., Porth, O., Olivares, H., Mizuno, Y., ... & Falcke, H. (2020). *Deep Horizon: A Machine Learning Network that Recovers Accreting Black Hole Parameters. Astronomy & Astrophysics,* 636, A94.

56. Kim, E.J., & Brunner, R.J. (2016). *Star-galaxy Classification Using Deep Convolutional Neural Networks.* Monthly Notices of the Royal Astronomical Society, stw2672.

57. Lovell, C.C., Acquaviva, V., Thomas, P.A., Iyer, K. G., Gawiser, E., & Wilkins, S.M. (2019). *Learning the Relationship Between Galaxies Spectra and Their Star Formation Histories using Convolutional Neural Networks and Cosmological Simulations.* Monthly Notices of the Royal Astronomical Society, 490(4), 5503-5520.

58. Huertas-Company, M., Guo, Y., Ginzburg, O., Lee, C.T., Mandelker, N., Metter, M., ... & Zhang, H. (2020). *Stellar Masses of Giant Clumps in CANDELS and Simulated Galaxies Using Machine Learning.* Monthly Notices of the Royal Astronomical Society, 499(1), 814-835.

the operation of the neural networks and predict the large-scale structure of the Universe. Interestingly, it has been seen that such methods can go far beyond the training data, and even predict the characteristics of structure formation for fairly different cosmological parameters as well.

Such techniques have also recently been used to match the amount of visible matter to the amount of dark matter in galaxies.[59,60,61] We can also use neural networks to reconstruct when our atmosphere is hit by cosmic rays.[62] In atmospheric physics, we use algorithms in Artificial Intelligence such as decision trees (a conceptual tool that uses a tree-like model of decisions and their conceivable corollaries), fuzzy logic (a form of many-valued logic in which the truth value of variables may be any real number between 0 and 1) and neural networks.[63,64] This has a practical aspect, with problems such as the understanding of the mechanism of various kinds of pollution.[65] We can also identify cyclones using clustering and self-organizing maps, which are kinds of artificial neural networks that use competitive learning —a form of unsupervised learning in artificial neural networks—in which there is a competition among nodes for the right to respond to a subset of the input data.[66] Such self-organizing maps are used to produce a low-dimensional representation of a higher-dimensional data-set, with the preservation of the topological structure of the date.

---

59. Sadowski, P., Collado, J., Whiteson, D., & Baldi, P. (2015, August). *Deep Learning, Dark Knowledge, and Dark Matter.* In NIPS 2014 Workshop on High-energy Physics and Machine Learning (pp. 81-87). PMLR.

60. Brehmer, J., Mishra-Sharma, S., Hermans, J., Louppe, G., & Cranmer, K. (2019). *Mining for Dark Matter Substructure: Inferring Subhalo Population Properties from Strong Lenses with Machine Learning. The Astrophysical Journal,* 886(1), 49.

61. Ravanbakhsh, S., Oliva, J., Fromenteau, S., Price, L., Ho, S., Schneider, J., & Póczos, B. (2016, June). *Estimating Cosmological Parameters from the Dark Matter Distribution.* In International Conference on Machine Learning (pp. 2407-2416). PMLR.

62. Erdmann, M., Glombitza, J., & Walz, D. (2018). *A Deep learning-Based Reconstruction of Cosmic Ray-induced Air Showers. Astroparticle Physics,* 97, 46-53.

63. Huntingford, C., Jeffers, E.S., Bonsall, M.B., Christensen, H.M., Lees, T., & Yang, H. (2019). *Machine Learning and Artificial Intelligence to Aid Climate Change Research and Preparedness.* Environmental Research Letters, 14(12), 124007.

64. Gardner, M.W., & Dorling, S.R. (1998). *Artificial Neural Networks (the multilayer perceptron)—A Review of Applications in the Atmospheric Sciences. Atmospheric Environment,* 32(14-15), 2627-2636.

65. Ye, Z., Yang, J., Zhong, N., Tu, X., Jia, J., & Wang, J. (2020). *Tackling Environmental Challenges in Pollution Controls Using Artificial Intelligence: A Review. Science of the Total Environment,* 699, 134279.

66. Chen, R., Zhang, W., & Wang, X. (2020). *Machine Learning in Tropical Cyclone Forecast Modeling: A Review. Atmosphere,* 11(7), 676.

For isolated quantum systems, a wavefunction is a mathematical description of the quantum state of the system. The dynamics of a wavefunction are governed by the Schrödinger equation (named after Erwin Schrödinger, the Austrian-Irish Nobel-prize winning physicist), which incorporate what are known as potentials that represent the environment in which the particle exists. Given a specific potential, the system can adopt a number of solution-wavefunctions that have specific discrete energies. The state of the system with the lowest energy is known as the ground state. Artificial Intelligence has been used for describing elements and phenomena in nuclear physics, with neural networks being able to represent ground state wavefunctions.[67,68,69,70] Using algorithms for Artificial Intelligence, such as neural networks, we have developed models to study nuclear physics properties like ground state parities and spin, atomic mass number, neutron capture rates, neutron separation energies, branching probabilities in disparate decay channels as well as beta-decay half-lives, to determine the properties of halo nuclear and exotic systems.[71,72,73,74,75]

In the recent past, neural networks have also helped in determining heavy quarks (three of the six kinds of quarks that are heavier than the lighter three) as well as identifying electrons that are scattered from a collision event in a particle collider.[76] We can use deep learning to solve

---

67. Chen, R., Zhang, W., & Wang, X. (2020). *Machine Learning in Tropical Cyclone Forecast Modeling: A Review. Atmosphere*, 11(7), 676.

68. Bedaque, P., Boehnlein, A., Cromaz, M., Diefenthaler, M., Elouadrhiri, L., Horn, T., ... & Wang, X. N. (2021). *AI for Nuclear Physics. The European Physical Journal A*, 57(3), 1-27.

69. Carleo, G., & Troyer, M. (2017). *Solving the Quantum Many-body Problem with Artificial Neural Networks. Science*, 355(6325), 602-606.

70. Lagaris, I.E., Likas, A., & Fotiadis, D.I. (1997). *Artificial Neural Network Methods in Quantum Mechanics.* Computer Physics Communications, 104(1-3), 1-14.

71. Lasseri, R.D., Regnier, D., Ebran, J.P., & Penon, A. (2020). *Taming Nuclear Complexity with a Committee of Multilayer Neural etworks. Physical Review Letters,* 124(16), 162502.

72. Kong, X., Zhou, L., Li, Z., Yang, Z., Qiu, B., Wu, X., ... & Du, J. (2020). *Artificial Intelligence Enhanced Two-dimensional Nanoscale Nuclear Magnetic Resonance Spectroscopy.* npj Quantum Information, 6(1), 1-10.

73. Hall, M. (2019). *Artificial Intelligence and Nuclear Medicine. Nuclear Medicine Communications,* 40(1), 1.

74. Uhrig, R.E., & Hines, J. (2005). *Computational Intelligence in Nuclear Engineering. Nuclear Engineering and Technology,* 37(2), 127-138.

75. Gernoth, K.A., Clark, J.W., Prater, J.S., & Bohr, H. (1993). *Neural Network Models of Nuclear Systematics.* Physics Letters B, 300(1-2), 1-7.

76. Theije, T.D. (2021). *Improving the Electron Identification of the ALICE Detector Using Machine*

Schrödinger's equation, to find the ground state energy.[77] There is a growing need to turn noisy and large data sets into meaningful information as we try to increase our ability to prepare and control increasingly complex quantum systems experimentally. It is in this area that we can utilize machine learning, such as the use of algorithmic learning and Bayesian methods for Hamiltonian learning,[78] to classify quantum states[79] and to characterize unknown unitary transformations.[80] Reconstruction of the Hamiltonian to identify an accurate model for quantum system dynamics, extracting information on unknown quantum states and engineering quantum gates with pairwise interactions, using both time-independent and time-dependent Hamiltonians, are all better done using Artificial Intelligence. We use quantum machine learning to accelerate the prediction of properties of molecules and materials, and this can, in turn, be used to computationally design new molecules and materials such as acoustic metamaterials (a metamaterial is any material that is engineered to have an attribute that is not found in naturally occurring materials) that facilitate high sound absorption at low frequencies.[81,82] We can infer molecular atomization energies,[83] generate new quantum experiments,[84] study accurate potential energy surfaces[85] with restricted Boltzmann

---

Learning (Bachelor's thesis).

77. Burger, M., Ruthotto, L., & Osher, S. (2021). Connections Between Deep Learning and Partial Differential Equations. European Journal of Applied Mathematics, 32(3), 395-396.

78. Granade, C.E., Ferrie, C., Wiebe, N., & Cory, D.G. (2012). *Robust Online Hamiltonian Learning. New Journal of Physics,* 14(10), 103013.

79. Gao, J., Qiao, L.F., Jiao, Z.Q., Ma, Y.C., Hu, C.Q., Ren, R.J., ... & Jin, X.M. (2018). *Experimental Machine Learning of Quantum States. Physical Review Letters,* 120(24), 240501.

80. Kiani, B.T. (2020). *Quantum Artificial Intelligence: Learning Unitary Transformations* (Doctoral dissertation, Massachusetts Institute of Technology).

81. Gomes, C.P., Selman, B., & Gregoire, J.M. (2019). *Artificial Intelligence for Materials Discovery.* MRS (Materials Research Society) Bulletin, 44(7), 538-544.

82. Dimiduk, D.M., Holm, E.A., & Niezgoda, S.R. (2018). *Perspectives on the impact of machine learning, deep learning, and Artificial Intelligence on Materials, Processes, and Structures Engineering.* Integrating Materials and Manufacturing Innovation, 7(3), 157-172.

83. Rupp, M., Tkatchenko, A., Müller, K.R., & Von Lilienfeld, O.A. (2012). Fast and Accurate Modeling of Molecular Atomization Energies with Machine Learning. Physical Review Letters, 108(5), 058301.

84. Melnikov, A. A., Nautrup, H. P., Krenn, M., Dunjko, V., Tiersch, M., Zeilinger, A., & Briegel, H. J. (2018). *Active Learning Machine Learns to Create New Quantum Experiments.* Proceedings of the National Academy of Sciences, 115(6), 1221-1226.

85. Dral, P.O., Owens, A., Dral, A., & Csányi, G. (2020). *Hierarchical Machine Learning of Potential Energy Surfaces. The Journal of Chemical Physics,* 152(20), 204110.

machines, interpolate interatomic potentials,[86] identify phase transitions[87] from entanglement spectrum and generate adaptive feedback schemes for quantum tomography[88] and quantum metrology[89] using machine learning techniques. We can efficiently generate optimization functions using what are known as variational functions, which are a family of algorithms that utilize training based on an objective function and on circuit parameters. In Quantum physics, we can avoid the sign problem for integration for path integrals by finding a better manifold for the integration using machine learning techniques.[90]

Speaking of the quantum domain, Quantum computing can accelerate deep learning algorithms,[91] such as the aforementioned Convolutional Neural Networks, with Quantum computing potentially being applied to simulation of phenomena or systems, optimization of processes and sampling of data. Major technology companies such as Rigetti Computing[92] and Google (that, along with NASA and Universities Space Research Association [USRA]), set up Quantum Artificial Intelligence Lab (QuAIL) in 2013[93]) are researching Quantum AI and full stack Quantum computing, which involves everything from designing and fabricating quantum chips to putting together the architecture required to control the chips, and then developing the software so that users can write algorithms and program the system. In material sciences, AI has been used to find systems that can form glass (such as cryoprotectants, oxide glasses and metallic glasses), besides being used in the nanosciences.

---

86. Mishin, Y. (2021). *Machine Learning Interatomic Potentials for Materials Science. Acta Materialia*, 214, 116980.
87. Dong, X.Y., Pollmann, F., & Zhang, X. F. (2019). *Machine Learning of Quantum Phase Transitions. Physical Review B*, 99(12), 121104.
88. Palmieri, A.M., Kovlakov, E., Bianchi, F., Yudin, D., Straupe, S., Biamonte, J.D., & Kulik, S. (2020). *Experimental Neural Network Enhanced Quantum Tomography.* npj Quantum Information, 6(1), 1-5.
89. Hentschel, A., & Sanders, B. C. (2011). *Efficient Algorithm for Optimizing Adaptive Quantum Metrology Processes. Physical Review Letters*, 107(23), 233601.
90. Detmold, W., Kanwar, G., Lamm, H., Wagman, M.L., & Warrington, N.C. (2021). *Path Integral Contour Deformations for Observables in S U (N) Gauge Theory. Physical Review D*, 103(9), 094517.
91. Potok, T.E., Schuman, C., Young, S., Patton, R., Spedalieri, F., Liu, J., ... & Chakma, G. (2018). *A Study of Complex Deep Learning Networks on High-performance, Neuromorphic, and Quantum Computers.* ACM Journal on Emerging Technologies in Computing Systems (JETC), 14(2), 1-21.
92. Olivares-Sánchez, J., Casanova, J., Solano, E., & Lamata, L. (2020). *Measurement-based Adaptation Protocol with Quantum Reinforcement Learning in a Rigetti Quantum Computer.* Quantum Reports, 2(2), 293-304.
93. Jones, N. (2013). *Google and NASA Snap up Quantum Computer. Nature News.*

Semiconductors are materials that lie between pure conductors and insulators, in conductivity. They constitute important components in various computing devices, which have been seeing generation-after-generation of evolution in terms of affordability and size. We require high-precision machines designing for simulating, studying, and designing novel kinds of semiconductor systems and processes. Methods around neural network can provide us with an effective way to analyze extreme properties of semiconductors.[94] Recently, a group of Chinese researchers studied deterioration of semiconductor equipment, with the employment of backpropagation neural network model[95] (and the MATLAB Neural Network Toolbox for analysis) as well as grey relation analysis[96] in simultaneous fault detection and classification[97] for semiconductor manufacturing tools, after using the Novellus Vector Machine (a platform that is used to deposit a variety of thin-films for memory and logic devices).[98] For this process, one undertakes data preprocessing, setting of network variables, choosing input variables, determination of hidden layer neuron (a hidden layer in an artificial neural network is a layer between the input and output layers, where artificial neurons take in a set of inputs with associated weight-factors and produce an output using what is known as an activation function), sensitivity analysis and network output results determining principles. The artificial neural network is created by considering all relevant factors such as learning trials, momentum correction coefficient and learning rate, which are suitably chosen to accommodate variations in the neural networks. The number of hidden layers of the network is found using the re-selection of previous variables obtained in the experiment.

---

94. Marques, M.R., Wolff, J., Steigemann, C., & Marques, M.A. (2019). *Neural Network Force Fields for Simple Metals and Semiconductors: Construction and Application to the Calculation of Phonons and Melting Temperatures.* Physical Chemistry Chemical Physics, 21(12), 6506-6516.

95. Yang, K.C., Yang, C., Chao, P.Y., & Shih, P.H. (2013). *Applying Artificial Neural Network to Predict Semiconductor Machine Outliers.* Mathematical Problems in Engineering.

96. Natarajan, N. *Investigations on Drilling of Micro Holes Using Electrical Discharge Machining.*

97. Goodlin, B.E., Boning, D.S., Sawin, H.H., & Wise, B.M. (2003). *Simultaneous Fault Detection and Classification for Semiconductor Manufacturing Tools. Journal of the Electrochemical Society,* 150(12), G778.

98. Yang, K.C., Huang, C.H., Yang, C., Chao, P.Y., & Shih, P.H. (2014, June). *Using Artificial Neural Back-propagation Network Model to Detect the Outliers in Semiconductor Manufacturing Machines.* In International Conference on Industrial, Engineering and Other Applications of Applied Intelligent Systems (pp. 240-249). Springer, Cham.

At the turn of the seventeenth century, Johannes Kepler, the German mathematician and astronomer, revolutionized science by discovering that the orbit of the planet Mars is an ellipse (a plane curve around two focal points, such that for all points on this curve, the sum of the two distances to the focal points is a constant). He did so by fitting the data tables on planetary orbits, initially to varied ovoid (more or less egg-shaped) shapes and finally to an ellipse, over a period of four years.[99] This was a prime example of symbolic regression, which refers to the matching of a symbolic expression that accurately matches a given dataset. As much as this has formed the basis of scientific discoveries and breakthroughs in the past, it also poses a core challenge for AI as well as physics. Using symmetries, compositionality, separability and other simplifying properties one can approach and possibly solve a problem that is otherwise often regarded as NP-hard. Recently, there was the development of a multidimensional, recursive symbolic regression algorithm that combines the fitting of neural networks with a set of physics-inspired techniques, particularly one hundred equations from the Feynman Lectures on Physics.[100] While approaches with other publicly available software could discover only seventy-one, this new application of neural networks could discover all of them!

Artificial Intelligence frameworks, particularly convolutional neural networks, can learn patterns in two-dimensional data quite well. Examples include recognizing objects in digital images as well as handwritten words. However, such machine learning architectures are not as successful when the data sets are without any associated built-in planar geometry, such as point clouds (a set of data points in space) that are generated by self-driving cars used in three-dimensional computer animation. To bypass this, geometric deep learning, a new discipline of AI, emerged around 2016.[101] With the new framework and what are known as gauge-equivalent Convolutional Neural Networks (gauge CNNs), one can build neural networks that can learn patterns on any type of geometric surface, including curved surfaces. These developments – extensions of AI, machine learning and neural network to higher dimensions as well as generalized geometric surfaces are of prime importance for advancement of research in frontier physics, even

---

99. Kossovsky, A.E. (2020). *Johannes Kepler—The First Data Analyst. In The Birth of Science* (pp. 23-24). Springer, Cham.

100. Udrescu, S.M., & Tegmark, M. (2020). *AI Feynman: A Physics-Inspired Method for Symbolic Regression.* Science Advances, 6(16), eaay2631.

101. Bronstein, M.M., Bruna, J., LeCun, Y., Szlam, A., & Vandergheynst, P. (2017). *Geometric Deep Learning: Going Beyond Euclidean Data.* IEEE Signal Processing Magazine, 34(4), 18-42.

as we look at solving the conundrum of Quantum Gravity using approaches such as geometrodynamics (an attempt to describe space-time and associated phenomena entirely in terms of geometry) and causal dynamical triangulation (a triangulation process that varies dynamically and obeys deterministic rules, to map out how spacetime near the Planck scale (with the Planck length being $l_p = 1.616255 \times 10^{-35} m$) can evolve into dimensional spaces similar to that of our universe).

The sky is the limit for the application and relevance of Artificial Intelligence to probe, analyze, study and find the fundamental elements and nuances of reality in the Universe.

EIGHT

Vedic Wisdom and Artificial Intelligence

Ravi Khanna

Vedic wisdom is firmly based on the principle that the same limitless power, *Brahman*, that moves the universe, exists within our individual selves, the *atman*. The domain of *Brahman* is the *brahmand*, a singular universal consciousness, while the atman is the individual consciousness that temporally resides as the duality of *atma* and *man* or body and mind. In the words of Dr Sarvepalli Radhakrishnan (philosopher and second president of independent India):[1]

> As *Brahman* is the eternal quiet underneath the drive and activity of the universe, so *atman* is the foundational reality underlying the conscious powers of the individual, the inward ground of the human soul.

The Brahman is also referred to as the cosmic *Purush*, which scales down its macro, multidimensional, universal energy as symmetries within symmetries to the micro level of 'continuous chains of covalent carbon compounds' that constitute the intricate human form or *purush* on this earth. And it is here that the *atman* sits allowing the individual 'a little breath, a little scene'.[2]

---

1. (Radhakrishnan, 1989); p. 3.

2. The phrase is borrowed from Shakespeare - *King Richard II,* Act 3, Scene 2, Lines 155 to 170

In the Vedic context, intelligence is the intrinsic, indivisible glow of the unity of All things within the atman. It is the luminescence of *drishti*, or inner vision that enables the consciousness to objectify the undifferentiated energy substratum of Brahman. The treatise on Advaita, the *Tripura Rahasya* (*The Mystery Beyond the Trinity*) provides a cogent explanation:[3]

> Now carefully analyze the underlying consciousness which, though abstract and apart from material objects, yet illumines them all the same. Know it to be the truth, O Sage! ... Intelligence is that by which objects are known; it cannot therefore itself become the object of knowledge. ... Intelligence in the abstract cannot admit of parts, which is the characteristics of objects. therefore, objects take on shapes.

The sage is further advised that to reach the Absolute he should 'carefully watch Intelligence after eliminating all else in it'.[4] The *Upanishads* echo this in the *neti-neti,* or 'not this, not this',[5] method of removing all items of objective reality from one's mind till one reaches the state of *shunyata* or emptiness. This is the level of Absolute Intelligence and transcends space and time. In this state, one experiences the primeval *agni*, or fire,[6] as pure incandescence having 'the brightness of a thousand suns'.[7] This is the state of *siddhi*, or enlightenment.

Artificial intelligence (AI), on the other hand, is based on the external manipulation of the elements using accumulated knowledge or *buddhi*.[8]

These lines show how power 'infuses a self with vain conceit' as if 'this flesh which walls about our life were brass impregnable'. If we take the liberty of replacing the word 'brass' with 'silicon' this passage could reflect the arrogance that Artificial Intelligence is instilling in humans at this time and place in history.

3. (Saraswati, 2006); Section XVI, Shloka 15-9, p. 138.
4. (Tripathi, 1965); Section XVI, Shloka 19 the Sanskrit words are very explicit - *pashya vaidhyam prithak krit budhya aakaar vivirijitaam.*
5. (Radhakrishnan, 1989) *Brihadaraṇyaka Upanisad* II.3.6, p. 194.
6. (Ahitagni, 1918); Rig Veda I.1.1 - commences with the Hymn of *Agni* -'*Agni* is a manifestation of the Supreme Spirit in the form of the primeval active energy of creation ... The same Divine energy in the form of earthly fire ministers to our physical wants; and being the source of heat, light and rain, *Agni* is the bountiful bestower of all gifts, we enjoy under the sun.'
7. (Chidbhavananda, 1974) - *Gita shloka* 11.12 - Lord Krishna reveals to Arjuna the *Virat rupa* or His immanent Cosmic Self. [This shloka was recited by Dr Robert Oppenheimer (1904-67), the American physicist who worked on designing the atom bomb, when the first nuclear blast occurred on 16 July 1945].
8. (Wikipedia, 2021); *Siddhi and Buddhi* are both wives of Lord Ganesha as per the *Ganesha & Mudgala Purana.*

Artificial Intelligence is the result of tools and technology developed over many millennia. Santosh Desai, author and columnist says,

> Technology began with the idea of tools due to the asymmetry between the might of the physical world and the relative inadequacy of the human body … Tools … extended and amplified our limbs, harnessed natural forces, and simplified … navigating the world around us … Along with tools came language and its first cousin, writing. Language made the mind articulate, and writing helped us store its output, so the products of the mind became additive over time. Generations added their own exertions—thoughts aggregated into knowledge.[9]

This increased exponentially, and a system of education built to ensure that every successive generation moves higher in this arduous accumulation of spiraling information.

Desai continues:

> Machines mechanized labour ushering in mass production, mobility and communication technologies that changed our experience of distance and time. Electricity erased the distinction between night and day.

Humans powered their lives and egos as their linear control and influence extended over increasingly large spaces.

He further adds:

> In the last century … technology has moved from the body to the mind amplifying the latter's abilities … The …computer placed the mind at the heart of the technological discourse … Vastly enhanced computational skills and the digital ability to process knowledge at an unprecedented scale and speed helped us in not only overcoming the physical limitations of our bodies, but also in multiplying the capability of our minds … The internet is a network of minds … AI represents a stage when the mind is detached altogether from the body … Machine intelligence will … create a metaverse, an alternative reality that has its own social codes, its own distinctive vocabulary, its own currency and its own ways of creating value.

9. (Desai, 2021)

Thus, as *buddhi* moves outwards, another shell of the *mayanvi* universe is forging viz. the online metaverse. It is important therefore, that the siddhi of Vedic wisdom and the augmented buddhi of Artificial Intelligence collaborate to lead us towards an enlightened life of fulfillment, joy and peace, a state enthused by Ganesha, their eternal spouse and the lord of good fortune. The prophetic words of the French author Victor Hugo resonate: 'Education! Light! Light! Everything comes from light and everything returns to it'.[10]

It is in this light I approach Rajiv Malhotra's well researched book on Artificial Intelligence.[11] He has raised various red flags about big digital platforms invading individual privacy and 'dumbing down' the masses. To the extent that, for me, it is difficult to address too many parts, so I pick a simple thread from this beautiful tapestry of ideas on Artificial Intelligence. My approach will be to examine Figure 2 – *Consciousness of Mechanistic Models* given on page xxvii, from his book and suggest a collaboration, rather than a 'battle between the metaphysics of consciousness and AI's reductionist challenge to spirituality'. In doing so, I will weave an Ariadne's thread, i.e., give different lines of reasoning around the themes in the illustrations.

I first came across the idea of 'collaboration' in *The Tao of Physics: An Exploration of the Parallels Between Modern Physics and Eastern Mysticism*, a 1975 book by the Austrian-American physicist Fritjof Capra.[12] At the beginning of Chapter III, *The Parallels*, Capra compares mathematical formulae from Quantum Mechanics (QM) and Relativity on the one side, and with various Vedic *shloka*-s on the other and says that these two systems of complex knowledge may seem absolutely disparate and separated in time by many millennia, however, they 'are different manifestations of the same ultimate reality'.

And as Malhotra shows us how these two knowledge systems converge at the Primacy of Consciousness and how he has been deeply invested in philosophies based on this, stating:

> … this worldview is being undermined by the powerful trajectory of the AI revolution. Figure 2 illustrates my intellectual journey centered on physics and Vedanta … and my algorithm-based career … The middle is where they *intersect, or rather clash* (emphasis added). My struggle to

10. (Hugo, 1987); p. 1191.

11. (Malhotra, *Artificial Intelligence and the Future of Power: 5 Battlegrounds*, 2021).

12. (Capra, 1984)

> reconcile these conflicts is at the core of this creative churning and tension in this book. ... the digital industry empowering self-learning systems is proceeding in a direction opposite to that of conscious movements. ... this is the real clash of civilizations under way: *the battle between the algorithm and being.*[13]

Going by the intersect between the Vedanta and the AI-based mechanistic algorithms, rather than the clash and conflict I shall go ahead in a collaborative spirit. Just as quantum physicists found resonance in the teachings of the Vedanta, as acknowledged by a pioneer of Quantum Mechanics, the Nobel-prize winning Erwin Schrödinger,[14] similarly, I will look for corresponding Vedantic insights in an attempt to answer one of the author's queries in the Introduction to his book:

> How is *ritam*, an important term used in the *Rig Veda,* to refer to the patterns that comprise the fabric of all existence, related to algorithms? Is *ritam* related to algo-rithm?[15]

Vedanta, Quantum Mechanics, and Artificial Intelligence: The Case for 'Collaboration'

As the Vedic rishis sat in the serene foothills of the Himalayas millennia ago, they meditated upon the mysteries of the Universe and Brahman, the Unknown. In the words of Malhotra:[16] 'Ancient Indian rishis experienced a resonance with the subtle and supra-physical cosmic forces, leading to the manifestation of the Vedic mantra-s ... referred to as *sruti*-s'.[17]

Dr Radhakrishnan says:[18]

> The word 'Veda' is derived from the root verb √*vid*, to know, means knowledge *par excellence*, sacred wisdom. Science is the knowledge of

13. (Malhotra, *Artificial Intelligence and the Future of Power: 5 Battlegrounds*, 2021); p. xxvi.
14. (Schrödinger, 1992); pp. 87-9 & 129.
15. (Malhotra, *Artificial Intelligence and the Future of Power: 5 Battlegrounds*, 2021); p. xiv.
16. (Malhotra, *Sanskrit Non-Translatables*, 2020); p. 147.
17. ibid. -*shruti* is a 'Sanskrit Non-Translatable' discussed at more length in the book.
18. (Radhakrishnan, 1989); *Introduction*, p. 28; [The Introduction section of this book gives one of the finest overviews of *Veda*-s and their *Upanishad*-s'].

> secondary causes, of the created details; wisdom is the knowledge of primary causes, of the Uncreated Principle. ... Veda is not a singular literary work ... but a whole literature which arose (over) centuries and was handed down from generation to generation through oral transmission. When no books were available memory was strong and tradition exact.

Right here we see the difference between Artificial Intelligence and Vedanta. The latter arises as *anahata* or latent sound; Malhotra explains that 'the sound of the Veda-s is *anahata*, which means that it is not produced by any conjunction of objects. *Anahata* is beyond the realm of the senses and is eternal. It is silent to the physical ears of an ordinary person but can be perceived by *yogi*-s in *samadhi*' (a deep state of meditation). In this heightened state of cosmic consciousness, the minds of yogi-s are in complete synchronicity with the world around them as a unique unison of mind and matter. Their mind is the laboratory, and the Unknown unfolds its many dimensions as innumerable mantra-s harnessing the Universal 'ocean of energy' into an order of syllables or *varna*-s, that give rise to *vak* or speech.

Artificial Intelligence, on the other hand, deals with information already stored by/in the human mind. It is, as Dr Radhakrishnan says above, based on reflected principles. In Malhotra's words:

> Scientific explanation works from the bottom up, starting with small entities as the fundamental reality and combining them block by block into bigger entities.[19]

Artificial Intelligence is based on mathematics built on Greek axioms and further developed in the West prolifically from the seventeenth century onwards. The thread begins with René Descartes, French mathematician, scientist and philosopher,[20] described as 'a brilliant theorist who set new directions in thought, and as the harbinger of a cold, rationalistic, and calculative conception of human beings'.[21] He was responsible for introducing the concept of duality of mind and matter

---

19. (Malhotra, *Artificial Intelligence and the Future of Power: 5 Battlegrounds*, 2021); p. 222.
20. In the medieval ages in Europe most scholars were all-rounders and the division of subjects started later.
21. (Hatfield, 2014)

into Western science. This coasted along brilliantly almost till the end of the nineteenth century when an eminent scientist arrogantly proclaimed: 'There is nothing new to be discovered in physics now. All that remains is more and more precise measurement'.[22] He could not have been further from the truth, for, within two decades, emerged two of the most brilliant branches of scientific knowledge of the twentieth century — Relativity and Quantum Mechanics. Both, however, revealed human limitations to measure.

Relativity informed us that nothing can exceed the speed of light thereby placing restrictions on our capability to traverse very large distances in intergalactic space. Measured in 'light years'[23] the distance to the nearest star *Proxima Centauri* is 4.2 light years and would take our robotic spacecrafts thousands of years to reach it.[24] Our Milky Way galaxy is almost one hundred thousand light years across holding one hundred billion of these sparkling suns.[25] Any conversation as humans therefore, even with our 'nearest neighbor' would require a lag of 8.4 years. Maybe in the avatar of a Redwood Tree the communication could be more meaningful.[26]

Quantum Mechanics tells us that the micro world of matter is full of paradoxes. As long as the 'quantum of energy' is not disturbed it behaves like a wave, but the moment we try and pinpoint it, the particle nature pops up. This is termed the wave-particle duality.

The consciousness of the 'observer' crystallizes, as it were, the immanent field energy into a resonant form instantaneously.[27] Werner Heisenberg, a pioneer of Quantum Mechanics, presented his significant Uncertainty Principle based on this overlapping concept of wave-particle duality. The precision in trying to locate the spot at which the quanta 'is'

---

22. (Wikiquote, 2021); This quote is often *misattributed* to William Thomson (Lord Kelvin).

23. One light-year is the distance light can travel at ~ 300,000 km per second and is 9.46 trillion km approx.

24. At present Voyagers 1 & 2, launched forty-four years back, are traveling at fifty-six thousand km/hour and will cover two light years in forty thousand years.

25. (Howell, 2021); an informative article.

26. (Powers, 2018) & (Mancuso, 2018); a large number of books are acquainting us today with the intelligence of trees and plants and how they have organized themselves symbiotically en masse to survive for thousands of years. These two books are a good start: the first as stories and the second as science.

27. This defies the tenets of Relativity Theory in which matter cannot exceed the speed of light. But at the micro-level it seems the very act of materialization from field geometry is 'occurring in a dimension' outside space-time.

results in indeterminacy in knowing how 'fast it is' moving; we cannot measure both aspects with infinite precision. The everyday 'billiard-ball' concept of the particle literally goes out of the window. It must be replaced by a fuzzy cloud of mathematical probability.

The words of Paul A.M. Dirac,[28] one of the foremost physicists in the field of Quantum Mechanics that combined the relativistic model of Einstein along with the Schrödinger equation for the electron establishing the presence of anti-matter, sum up this position:

> The necessity to depart from classical ideas when one wishes to account for the ultimate structure of matter may be seen, not only from experimentally established facts, but also from general philosophical grounds. ... it becomes necessary to postulate that each constituent part is itself made up of smaller parts, in terms of which its behaviour is to be explained. There is clearly no end to this procedure, ... one can never arrive at the ultimate structure of matter on these lines. ... Science is concerned only with observable things, and we can observe an object only by letting it interact with some outside influence ... The concepts of big and small are then purely relative and refer to the gentleness of our means of observation as well as to the object being described. In order to give an absolute meaning to size, such as is required for any theory of the ultimate structure of matter, *we have to assume that there is a limit to the fineness of our powers of observation – a limit which is inherent in the nature of things and can never be surpassed by improved technique or increased skill on the part of the scientist...* (emphasis added).[29]

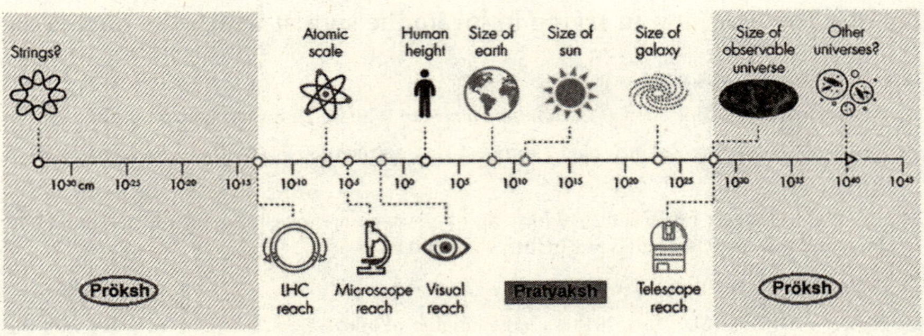

Figure 1: Scales of the Universe

28. Dirac shared the 1933 Nobel Prize for Physics with Schrodinger for Quantum Mechanics.

29. (Dirac, 1974); p. 3.

Having established these limits of human perception in terms of both, the macro, and the micro, universe, we find, even after the tremendous technological transformations, the 'extended visible universe' is a total of around forty orders of magnitude (Fig. 1). This is the *pratyaksh* of the Veda-s that is within the realm of the 'senses'. But we know that there is much more to Reality and it is *proksha* or 'beyond our ken'. We see the Western scientist struggling with some of these in the form of String theory, multiverses, m-branes and so on in an attempt to penetrate the realm of the proksha. Instead, the Veda-s have an underlying Universal order, ritam that is nested as symmetries within symmetries. Malhotra writes in another one of his erudite books, *Being Different:*[30]

> In *Rig Veda* there is a remarkable insight into universal order and harmony called *ritam*, which is the ordering principle of nature. *Ritam* gives everything — from vast galaxies to the nucleus of an atom — its nature and course. It manifests on three levels on the cosmic plane, as governing the course of nature; on the socio-ethical level, as justice; and within the inner realm of the practitioner. *Ritam* maintains balance between the micro and macro levels of existence. There is no dichotomy between ethical and cosmic order. It bridges the spheres which the West has separated, namely the sacred and the secular, spirit and nature and so on.

So, although there may still be unfathomed truths in Vedanta, they need to be interpreted in terms of the prevalent vocabulary. For this, as we will see, it needs the metaphors from the Western side too for corroboration. Unfortunately, we ourselves have lost the deeper meaning and the correct connection of shloka-s over many millennia when this verbal Vedantic tradition was finally scripted. Firstly, a number of errors have crept into the writing due to the immensity of the task and secondly, the commentaries by learned scholars are restricted to the vocabulary of their era.

Dr Vidhusekhara Bhattacharya Sastri of Visva-Bharati University, a renowned Indologist who taught Sanskrit to Rabindranath Tagore at an early age, pointed out in a 1930 paper,[31] that even Yaska Muni[32] and

30. (Malhotra, *Being Different - An Indian Challenge to Western Universalism,* 2011); p. 186.

31. (Bhattacharya Sastri, 1930); 'Vedic Interpretation and Tradition' was the theme of his presidential address.

32. Yaska (~ 2800 BC) wrote the *Nighantu* (book of glossary), the first book in this field. Explaining the words from this glossary he further wrote *Nirukta* that covers the etymology from their usage in the Vedic texts.

Sayana[33] have varying interpretations for many *Rig Veda* shloka-s. The author woefully writes about how the verbal tradition is vanishing and along with it, the purity of thought. He gives an interesting anecdote that German Orientalist and Indologist, Max Mueller shared in his Hibbert Lectures[34] (the Hibbert Lectures were an annual series of non-sectarian lectures on theological issues sponsored by a trust founded in 1847 by the Unitarian, Robert Hibbert with a goal to uphold 'the unfettered exercise of private judgement in matters of religion') in 1878 explaining how 'One native scholar, Shankar Pandurang, is at the present moment collecting various readings for my edition of the Rig Veda from few of our "walking manuscripts", not from MSS, but from the oral tradition of the Vedic *Srotriya*-s… He knows the whole Samhita and Pada text by heart'. I will attempt here to pick gems of truth from the voluminous pyramid of Vedic writings and align these in terms of a global vocabulary. Just as Dr Bhattacharya exhorts us as Indians to share this 'most precious inheritance of the past with all the humanity at large striving for peace and happiness of man and the universe'.

Artificial Intelligence itself has been built up on the foundation of Quantum Mechanics. The entire underlying structure of AI is based on the semiconductor revolution of the second half of the twentieth century. Interestingly, the class of semiconductors is Group IV[35] in the Periodic Table of the Elements. This class of elements is equally poised in that they can either give four electrons to its neighbors or receive four electrons, i.e., they also have four energy pits or 'holes' waiting to receive four electrons. First amongst this column is carbon and as its symmetry extends to some of its neighbors on the Periodic Table, namely hydrogen, oxygen, nitrogen and others, it eagerly shares its four arms clasping theirs as 'covalent bonds'. Carbon therefore can create long chains of molecules and evolve spatially into intricate organic molecules that subsequently gave rise to this spiraling variety of organic molecules. When one sees the symmetries of 'life' and how the micro matches the macro, one can sense the 'flow' of the Universal order, *ritam* into each sentient cell, body, or brain on this planet. It is almost as if these myriad carbon chains are fashioning

33. Sayaṇa (died AD 1387); a Sanskrit scholar from the Vijayanagara Empire of south India. More than one hundred works are attributed to him, among which are commentaries on nearly all parts of the *Veda*-s.

34. (Muller, 1878); pp. 157-8.

35. Group 14 in the IUPAC nomenclature (International Union of Pure & Applied Chemistry founded in 1919).

forms that are higher-dimensional 'snapshots' of the symmetries of the Universe. In a brilliant book titled *The Hidden Geometry of the Flowers: Living Rhythms, Form and Number*, Keith Critchlow, a British professor of architecture and a trained artist, details the elegant hidden geometry and symmetries of flowers saying

> We resonate with these hidden patterns because we too are made up of them and, thus, we contain the universe that contains us. Or, as traditional philosophy would phrase it, we are each a microcosm of the macrocosm.[36]

Our carbon-based brains gave rise to a further level of intelligence as we learnt to manipulate silicon, the next element in Group IV, which is larger in size and has the same symmetry of four covalent bonds, i.e., has 'four arms to share'. Being cumbersome, the silicon[37] atom cannot form long chains with other elements like carbon. However, silicon forms strong tetrahedral crystalline structures on the same lines as carbon does in diamonds.

The nucleus of an atom is positively charged, and tightly holds the negatively charged electrons that orbit around it in concentric shells. The electrons in the outermost shell of the atom are valence electrons. As these outer electrons are energized, they jiggle loose and begin conducting an electric current. The energy required to promote a valence electron bound to an atom to become a conduction electron that is free to move about within the crystal lattice and thereby helping the flow of electric current, is called the energy band gap or simply, band gap. Substances with large band gaps are generally insulators; those with smaller band gaps are semiconductors, while conductors have either very small band gaps or none, due to an overlapping of their valence and conduction bands.

Semiconductor elements of Group IV, in particular silicon and germanium, are so called because when small voltages are applied across their crystals the shallow band gap allows the four valence electrons to move laterally within the valence band, rather than get pushed upwards to the conduction band. These valence electrons fill up the empty adjacent holes like marbles in a game of Chinese Checkers leaving behind positively charged pits that seemingly flow in the opposite direction. Thus, in a

36. (Critchlow, 2019) See Foreword of this book.

37. Germanium, the next element in the Group IV and the III-V compounds such as Gallium Arsenide, etc. and many alloys are also used as semiconductor bases.

semiconductor, unlike other materials, there are two flows of electric current. Firstly, any stray electrons in the conductance level carry a negative current in one direction and secondly, the holes at the valence level carry a positive current in the opposite direction.

This unique physics of silicon gave a window to the duality of nature to emerge in a new avatar. It led the physicists William Shockley, John Bardeen, and Walter Brattain to devise the first transistor switch at Bell Labs, New Jersey in 1947.[38] They realized that by taking a pure crystal of silicon and replacing a tiny percentage, say one in a thousand, of the lattice atoms with another atom of almost the same size but carried an extra conductance electron, they would have a conductor that carried electric current comprising only negatively charged electrons. This was termed N-type semiconductor and phosphorus atoms fitted this requirement perfectly being one number higher than silicon in the Periodic Table. Conversely, boron, an element having one number lesser electron than silicon, on being introduced as the minuscule impurity, gave them a conductor that carried electric current made up of positively charged holes at the valence level. This was termed P-type semiconductor. An N-P-N or 'P-N-P' sandwich of the semiconductor crystals when placed together technically, became the basis of this remarkable binary transistor switch. In turn, the networks of these transistors were amenable to the Boolean logic of the digits '0' and '1' and gave rise to the first solid state computers. This was the beginning of the human mind mirroring itself into a fabricated metaverse.

The race for space launches to reach the moon in the 1960s rocketed transistor manufacturing towards miniaturization and the Integrated Circuit (IC) or the silicon microchip was born. From 1965 commenced the 'doubling of circuit density every two years' following a prediction by Gordon Moore, American semiconductor scientist and co-founder of Intel Corporation, the largest semiconductor manufacturer in the world today. Moore's Law, as this doubling is dubbed, continues even today, having brought the number of 'transistors on the microchip' from five thousand to fifty billion![39] Thereby spawning a virtual explosion of evolving semiconductor applications in every walk of life. Artificial Intelligence is a result of this mind-boggling expansion. This is similar to the Cambrian

---

38. William Shockley, John Bardeen and Walter Brattain were the inventors and received the 1956 Nobel Prize for Physics.

39. (Wikipedia, 2021)

explosion,[40] 541 million years ago that occurred due to the sudden increase of oxygen in the earth's atmosphere and gave a great boost to millions of new predatory species with functional primitive nervous systems. Similarly, the rapid multiplication of the microchip density has spawned the specter of AI that is fighting to take over our minds and our lives.[41]

The symmetry between the carbon domain and the silicon domain is undeniable and many similes can be drawn up between the two to learn from. In the former, the predator would physically harm and kill the organisms lower in the food chain thus prematurely ending their time on earth, while in the latter, Artificial Intelligence would be eating up our time and money thereby enforcing economic deprivation and ruin to our mind and lives.[42] Time is what makes life and we must counter this devilish function of AI by building a strong foundation in positive applications based on a strong philosophy of life as an additional symmetry upon a symmetry. Thus, it is imperative that AI 'collaborate' with Vedanta and use its ancient wisdom to develop a vibrant way of life in not only understanding the pratyaksh, the seen, but also the proksa, the unseen.

Infinities and the *Shanti Path*[43]

We begin our journey into intelligence via the wisdom of one of the most common chants of the *Upanishad*-s, the *Shanti Path* or peace invocation. This is chanted daily at the beginning and end of every *satsangh*, literally a gathering of truth-seekers. It is placed at the beginning of the *Ishavasya Upanishad* and in its extended form as the first sloka of the fifth chapter of the *Brihadaranyaka Upanishad*.[44] Both these *Upanishad*-s are part of the *Yajur Veda* (*shukla*).

---

40. (Fox, 2016) Cambrian Explosion: an evolutionary burst 540 million years ago filled the seas with an astonishing diversity of animals. The trigger behind that revolution was apparently the sudden availability of oxygen in the earth's atmosphere. This spawned animals with limbs and vision giving rise to both beauty and beastly behaviour amongst millions of species.

41. (Malhotra, *Artificial Intelligence and the Future of Power: 5 Battlegrounds*, 2021); Chap.1. *Overview of AI Technologies.*

42. (Malhotra, *Artificial Intelligence and the Future of Power: 5 Battlegrounds*, 2021); Chap.1, *The Battle for Self*; p. 218.

43. (Khanna, 2008)

44. This fifth chapter is the beginning of the third *kanda* or section, and is named *khilakanda*, the Addendum.

! PaUNa-ma\ Ad:, PaUNa-ma\ [dma\ , PaUNaa-t\ PaUNa-ma\ ]dcyato.
PaUNa-sya PaUNa-ma\ Aadaya , PaUNa-ma\ eva AvaiSaYyato ..! Saaint:
Saaint: Saaint:.
poornam adah, poornam idam, poornat poornam udacyate
poornasya poornam aadaya poornam evavashishyate.
Om Shantih Shantih Shantih!

The shloka uses *poorna* in its grammatical form seven times and it is important firstly, to understand it. Poorna is derived from the root √*pur* that itself signifies fullness or completeness; the suffix *kta* is added to further stress this completion and √*pur + kta = poorna*. In other words, poorna stands for an infinity beyond our imagination. Even if somehow this infinity were to manifest, we humans would have to turn away our vulnerable vision from its brilliance — as we are wont to do when we try and look at the sun. The closest we can come to a glimpse of this infinity of light is in the radiant splendor of a full moon called *poornima*. In English, however, *poorna* has been variously translated as full, whole, perfect, and infinite.[45] For our purpose we are taking Dr Radhakrishnan's[46] and the Ramakrishna *Matth*'s[47] translations, respectively as guidance:

That is full, this is full. From fullness fullness proceeds.
If we take away the fullness of fullness, even then fullness remains... (1)

Om That (Brahman) is Infinite, this (universe) too is infinite. The infinite (universe) emanates from the Infinite (Brahman).
Assimilating the infinitude of the infinite (universe), the Infinite (Brahman) alone is left... (2)

The interesting dichotomy of the dual usage of poorna stresses the fact that there are further two levels of completeness that exceed our mental capacity. In the words of the spiritual leader, Swami Chinmayananda Saraswati:

This peace invocation reads as though a pleasant contradiction ... On a very superficial reading one is apt to consider only its word-meaning and

45. (Vatsyayan, 1992); '*Poorna*'; p. 429; In Chandogya Upanishad III 12.7 to 9; p. 434.

46. (Radhakrishnan, 1989); *Brihadaranyaka Upanishad* V.1.1.

47. A *matth* is a cloister college for Vedic teaching.

then each sentence should certainly confuse and confound any modern student who dives into it especially through its literal translations ... in English or in any vernacular. This is a philosophical truth-declaration, and as such unless we know something of Vedantic conclusions over the theme of the transcendental Infinite and its 'relationship' with the finite, this stanza should necessarily confuse any reader'.[48]

How can we study this further? The initial answer emerges from mathematics, specifically from the Theory of Transfinite Cardinals propounded in 1870 by the German mathematician Georg Cantor. Cantor gave us the Set Theory, a brilliant thesis on the study of collections of numbers, points, objects, anything really in general. This revolutionized number theory. The word *transfinite* here maybe understood as a condensed form of transcendental Infinite – that which is *beyond the infinite.* How is this possible?

Let us push the limits of our reasoning on the lines of Cantor to explain this equivalence between mantra and math, two sets of our consciousness separated by many millennia.[49]

Till the mid-nineteenth century, the only concept of infinity, in the mathematical world, was linked to natural numbers, or integers N, that were countable. At the end of this seemingly endless sequence, as the number N becomes too large to count, it is denoted by the lazy eight symbol '∞' that has long been used to denote infinity since this shape can be traversed endlessly. (See Fig. 2)

0, 1, 2, 3, 4,...... N ...... ∞ (infinity)

Figure 2: Natural Numbers, 'N'

Cantor called this the countable infinity, denoting it as $\aleph_0$ (Aleph-naught).

He next looked at the continuum of a straight line that is measured using real numbers. Whereas natural numbers belong to the sequence

48. (Chinmayananda, 1950?) *Ishavasya Upanishad.*

49. (Nambiar, 1996); This brilliant paper by Dr Nambiar, head of the computer sciences and systems department, JNU sets the background for this study.

0, 1, 2, 3, 4, and so on, the real numbers are those which are numbers with a decimal placed between them somewhere e.g., 1.291 or 0.3125 or 365.89 and so on forth. These are also known as decimal numbers. In our daily lives we use real numbers for measurements, weights, scientific calculations, cash transactions and so on.

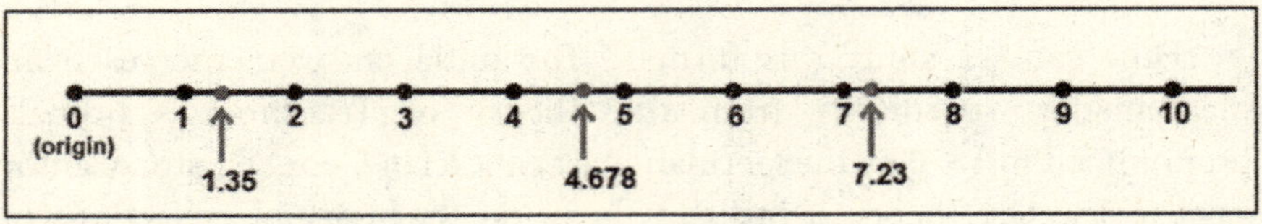

Figure 3: Line Segment - 'Real Numbers'

The French philosopher and mathematician René Descartes developed the idea of graphical representation, whereby he represented these real numbers by the length of a line and accordingly defining a co-ordinate system. Thus, a horizontal line can represent real numbers from zero onwards as shown in Fig. 3.

Using his Set Theory, Cantor first proved that the number of points on any continuous line segment matches one to one with any part of the line segment and therefore the two sets are equivalent.

In the process, Cantor resolved a paradox raised some three hundred years earlier by Galileo Galilei, the father of modern physics, and published in 1638 in his *The Dialogues Concerning the Two New Sciences.*[50] He derived two concentric circles from concentric polygons rolling on a straight line. As the number of their sides increased, the sides of the polygons themselves became smaller in length; in the limit approaching the smoothness of a rolling cylinder. Pondering the question of the number of points on the circumference of the circle, Galileo raised the question: 'Are the number of points on the inner, smaller circle the same as those on the outer, bigger one?' (See Fig. 4)

Using his 'one to one' correspondence method for Set Theory, Cantor simply showed that for every point A on the inner circle there is a corresponding ray OA, and this ray extends to the outer circle to a corresponding point A'. Thus, if infinite rays emanate from the center O then these will diverge to the same number of points on the outer circle.

50. (Brittanica); Galileo Galilei, 'The Dialogues Concerning the Two New Sciences'.

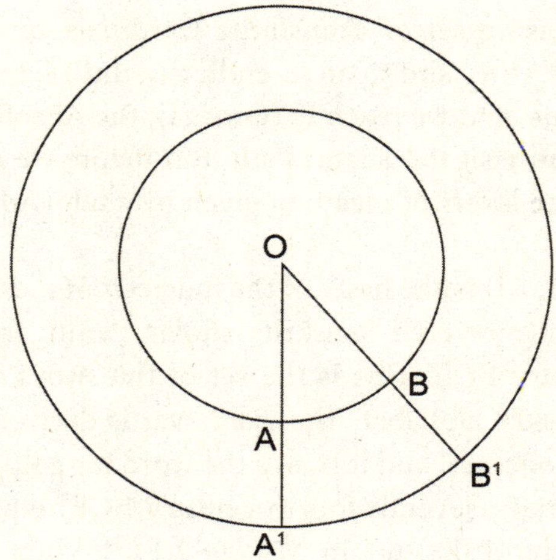

Figure 4: Galileo's Concentric Circle paradox

Conversely, if we take a point B' on the outer circle and connect it to the common center O as a line B'O, it will intersect the smaller circle at a corresponding point B. For every B' on the outer circle, there will be the same number of B on the inner circle.

Either way the answer to our question is: the number of points on the continuous line of the circumference is the same, irrespective of its size and scaling. Now, what about the number of these points on a continuous line? Taking the set of points in the line segment {0, 1} Cantor showed rigorously, using the decimal numbers within this interval and extending them interminably, that their number was larger and 'indenumerable' or uncountable. He called it $\aleph_1$ (Aleph-one) the Indenumerably Infinite.[51]

Cantor did not stop here. He went on to develop a method of finding even higher infinities which he termed Transfinite. Using his Set Theory he defined a Power Set, $\mathscr{P}_{\omega}$ such that if you have a Set with 'ω' objects - {1, 2, 3, ... n ... ω} then $\mathscr{P}_{\omega}$ is the number of all possible permutations, combinations, and usage of these numbers that you can think of. The amazing concept of this structuring is that even if we are working with indenumerable or uncountable numbers we can use mathematics to manipulate them.

51. (Rucker, 1983); Excursion I 'The Transfinite Cardinals' gives a more detailed proof concluding 'Alef-one is a hard number to describe ... Alef-one represents an order of infinity that is *essentially greater than Aleph-naught* in a way that ($\aleph_0 = \aleph_0 + \aleph_0$) is not' (Chap. 2 - 'All the Numbers').

So, an ever-increasing set of Transfinite Cardinals can be imagined as $\mathcal{P}_{\aleph 0}=\aleph_1$, $\mathcal{P}_{\aleph 1}=\aleph_2$, $\mathcal{P}_{\aleph 2}=\aleph_3$, and so on … endlessly, until Cantor concedes that we cannot continue, and we reach Ω (Omega), the Absolute Infinite.[52]

We can now re-visit the Shanti Path. But before we re-translate it, let us look at the three layers of meaning given by adah (Ad:); *idam* ([dma\); *udanch* (]dHca\)

Now, a, i, u (A, [,]) is the first[53] of the fourteen *Mahashivasutra*-s given to us by the greatly revered Sanskrit scholar Panini from the seventh/sixth-fourth century BCE. This is the set of the *svar*-s or three primary vowels of the Sanskrit alphabet. The word svar is derived from *su+varna*, meaning 'pure phonemes', and it is also the word for gold. Yaska Muni, the Sanskrit grammarian (seventh-fourth century BCE) equates these svar-s to the 'shining light of the sun' in *Nirukta* 2.14.[54] When these are spoken there is no deflection of the tongue, and the *prana* or breath is effortlessly expirated. This is likened to the rays of the sun reaching us directly.[55]

- *a* (A) therefore represents 'that' which is the Absolute Infinite or Ω (Omega) of Cantor's theory as seen above. It is Brahman, the Unknown. It is the *akshara* (Axar), the indestructible (or the a + *svar*). Lord Krishna explains to Arjuna in the *Gītā* 10.33:

I am the first letter 'a (A)' *among the akshara of the alphabet and am integral in the compounding of words in grammar. I am indestructible time. I am the Dispenser facing everywhere.*

(The Sanskrit alphabet, unlike English, has the collection of vowels or svar-s as a primary list. The consonants are a secondary list called *vyanjan*. The svar-s, as we have seen, are the 'shining' sounds and the *vyanjan* are the 'reflected' sounds.)

The first svar, '*a*' is added to the end of *every* consonant, from where it integrates into every word and sentence. Thus '*a*' (A), the Brahman

52. ibid.

53. (A, [,], Na\)

54. (Sarup, 1984); p. 30.

55. (Khanna, *The Metaphysics of the Sanskrit Alphabet*, 2004); On the other hand, while voicing the mutes or *sparsha*, the tongue is positioned variously to deflect the breath. This is likened to the reflected light of the moon.

becomes 'woven into the warp and woof of everything' in the words of Dr Radhakrishnan. This structuring is unique to the Sanskrit language.

Therefore, *adhh* (Ad:) is 'that', a pronoun referring to something that is *proksha* or that which is beyond our senses. It is the Absolute Infinite.

- *i* ([) reflects 'this', the tangible aspect of *Brahman* and it is synonymous with *Ishvara* (or *i+svar*) in various texts. It is the God that is manifest and *pratyaksha* or lies within the far-reaching realm of our senses. It is the ever-increasing Alephs of Cantor's Theory of Infinities and beyond the continuous infinity of the Real Line, $\aleph_1$. Dr Radhakrishnan explains it beautifully:

> *Maya* is the power of *Ishvara* from which the world arises. He has "formed man out of the dust of the ground and breathed into him a living soul". All the works of the world are wrought by Him. Every existence contained in time is ontologically present in creative eternity.[56]

Idam ([dma\) is 'this', a pronoun referring to something that is pratyaksha or here and now. *Idam* is linked to Lord Indra, after whom our senses are named *indriyan*.

The *Aitareya Upaniṣad* I.3.14[57] explains the origin of Indra's name: 'He saw this *Purusha* (the first born), as the constituent of the *Brahman*, pervading all. With wonder he said, *idam adarsham* — "Oh! I have seen this." Therefore, He is called *idamdra* (*idam+dra*). *Idamdram*, verily is His name. Though He is indirectly called Indra. The *deva*-s or gods are fond of the cryptic; the gods are indeed fond of being called indirectly'. So *idam* here is the creative force of *Ishvara* appearing to us as the spiraling vortex of evolutionary energies of nature with intensity of Indra's lightning-bolt. It is the $\aleph_2$, $\aleph_3$, $\aleph_4$ and so on that our senses, in our present form, can perceive as a reflection of the Absolute Infinite.

- *u* (]) is the unfolding *maya*, it is what manifests and molds out forms in the formless; it is $\aleph_1$ (Aleph-one), the uncountable infinite of Cantor's theory.

56. (Radhakrishnan, 1989); p. 83.

57. (Chinmayananda, *Aitareya Upanishad*, 1992); the same *shloka* is given in *Aitareya Aranyaka* (Keith, 1995) at II.4.3.

Udanch (]dHca\)[58] is to arise from, to emanate. And this is the play of *maya* in the 'ocean of reality' that we all perceive and try to harness with *vak* or speech. Dr Kapil Kapoor an authority on linguistics, explains[59] citing the *Rig Veda* I.164.1:

> Gauri[60] is the symbol of *vak* or speech, according to the *shruti*-s .... the real significance is that the principle of *vak* creates or fashions out the manifold forms out of the waters of the infinite "ocean of reality" ... the *parme vyoman.* You cannot cut forms or draw lines in water, you can do that only in space; *but reality like water is continuous, indivisible...*

The ocean of reality is a metaphor for the vibratory universe. Dr Radhakrishnan modifies the concealment (or veil) metaphor for maya as both the veil and dress of God.[61] A dress serves two purposes: it hides, and it displays. Likewise, *maya* can be likened to a scrim. (A thin canvas used as a backdrop in theater and opera. The play of light is used, at times to show the audience scenes and shapes behind, or at times to hide what is going on backstage.)

We can now translate the Shanti Path from (1) and (2) in terms of what has been explained. *Om* That (Brahman) is Omega, the Absolute Infinite; this (Ishvara) too is infinite as the explosive energies of Indra, viz. $\aleph_0$, $\aleph_1$, $\aleph_2$, $\aleph_3$, and so on. The infinite (maya), $\aleph_1$ emanates as this visible and vibratory illusion of the world from the Infinite (Ishvara).

If we take away from Omega, the Absolute Infinite (Brahman) an infinite Alephs, even then the Absolute Infinite (Brahman) is undiminished.

Om Shantih Shantih Shantih! -- (3)

We revisit Rajiv Malhotra's quote on ritam and see how we have justified it:

---

58. (Williams, 2002); p. 184.

59. (Kapoor, 1996)

60. *Gauri* is another name for Goddess Parvati literally, the 'ruler of the mountains' and is Lord Shiva's consort. It is also the synonym for Usha, the *Shakti* that represents the 'continuous flow of energy' in the *Veda*-s.

61. Robert Browning in *Bishop Blougram's Apology* writes, 'Some think Creation's meant to show him forth, I say it's meant to hide him all it can.'

> In *Rig Veda* there is a remarkable insight into universal order and harmony called *ritam*, which is the ordering principle of nature. *Ritam* gives everything—from vast galaxies to the nucleus of an atom—its nature and course. *It manifests on three levels on the cosmic plane, as governing the course of nature; on the socio-ethical level, as justice; and within the inner realm of the practitioner.* (emphasis added)

There are these three layers of Universal order in the Shanti Path as we have shown: Brahman, Ishvara and maya and each has a level of order resonating with it.

It is in a similar vein that Lord Byron writes in *Don Juan* that the shortest path to heaven for him is through nature's symmetries saying 'My altars are the mountains and the ocean, Earth, air, stars, - all that springs from the great Whole. Who hath produced and will receive the soul'.

Bindu is Not a Point; It is a Functional Entity

On the lines of Malhotra's *Sanskrit Non-translatables* let us add *bindu* to the list.

What is the starting point of dimensions? Exactly that, the point, which geometrically speaking is zero dimension. It has no measurement, no length or width or breadth.[62] Cantor above fitted an uncountable number of them in a small segment of a continuous line. It is what Lawrence Le Shan, an eminent American psychologist, called a functional entity. He writes:

> Of this class of entities if we ask, "What is it?" we cannot expect a reasonable answer. We can, however, ask other questions such as "When is it?" and hope to get a satisfactory reply. (A mathematical point is when it is conceptualized as the intersection of two lines.)[63]

Bindu (ibaMdu) is not such a banal concept in Hindu philosophy, as quoted above. It is a vibrant idea; it may not have spatial dimensions or sides to it, but it is not void or emptiness. It is not *shunya* (SaUnya). The bindu is derived variously in *Kalatattvakosha: A Lexicon of Fundamental Concepts and Glossaries* of technical terms in the Indian intellectual discourse

62. 'A point is that which has no part'; Definition 1 - Elements by Euclid (approx. 280 BC).

63. (LeShan, 2003); See Appendix B - "When is Uvani?"

and arts, published in six volumes, by the Indira Gandhi National Centre for Arts:[64]

1. From *Indu* ([Mdu) which means the moon and therefore *bindu* is a 'drop of light'.
2. From *bind* (ibaMd) which means to cleave or pierce thereby *bindu* means a 'hole'.

Kalatattvakosha further quotes *Yogabhashya* of Ved Vyasa, the author of the epic *Mahabharata*:

> ...a substance when reduced to its minutest unit is called a *paramanu* (atom), ... the minutest time unit is *kshana* (xaNa). But *bindu* is neither a time unit like *kshana* nor a space unit like *anu* (ANauu). *It is a unit of consciousness... bindu* does not only constitute the thought-element but also serves as the material of all the elements of *matter and speech,* that is, everything is made of *bindu* whether it is the physical body or a metaphysical principle. Hence *bindu is the meeting point of spirit and matter.* (emphasis added)

Bindu is the *spanda* of the *Shiv Sutra*-s. These *sutra*-s are said to have been revealed by Lord Shiva himself to Vasugupta, a sage who lived in in the mountains in eighth century Kashmir, and they form a significant part of the *Agama Shastra*-s tradition of Kashmir Shaivism. It is a throbbing point of stress or a pulsation that is referred to also as the *Naad-bindu* – 'is the generic potency representing all undifferentiated sounds'.[65]

The throb of the *Naad-bindu* unfolds into the first wave of sound pictorially represented by the *chandra* or half-moon adorning Lord Shiva's matted hair (See Fig. 5). Together they symbolize the *anunasik* or nasal-hum. The anunasik is also the name of a class of letters in the last and fifth column of the table of mute-consonants in the Sanskrit alphabet.

These letters are themselves five in number and are uttered through both the mouth and nose simultaneously. In the language this nasal sound when added to other consonants is indicated as a *chandra-bindu* above the alphabet. This is the 'mmm' sound, at the end, as we pronounce (!) or *aum* – the universal *mantra* of yogic chanting.

---

64. (Vatsyayan, 1992); See article on *bindu*.

65. (Singh, 2000)

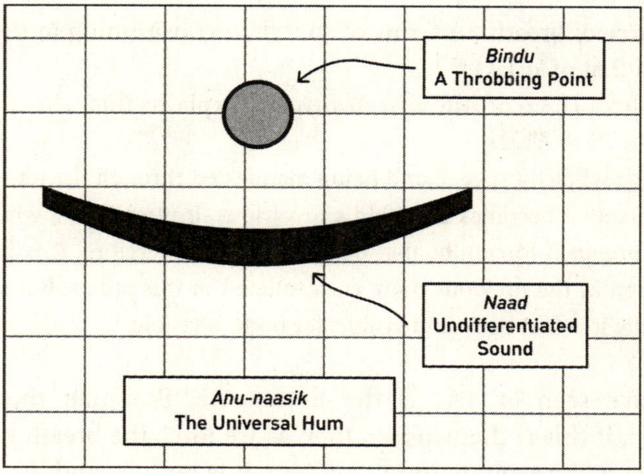

Figure 5

Sibilants: The *Shakti* Symbols (Sa, Ya, sa, h)

The Sanskrit alphabet[66] is based on Panini's fourteen *Mahashivasutra*-s. A detailed study has been given by Dr Vidhata Mishra, professor of Sanskrit phonetics and linguistics at Bihar University in the 1970s, [67]in a critique based on the *Shiksha* and *Pratishakhya* of the four *Veda*-s. These ancillary texts were taught to the ancient *shishya* or student as prerequisite to the chanting of the *Veda*-s.

These letters are so arranged that the speech creates a symmetry from the external reality to discursive language as we speak. When we voice the first three primary vowels or svars, *a, i, u* (A, [,]) in succession, the glottis to the labials is traced. Similarly, this holds true for the first mute '*k*' (k) to the last mute '*m*' (ma), and the entire mouth cavity is virtually shaped as these varṇa-s or letters are spoken.[68]

The two akśara-s, '*a*' (A) and '*h*' (h) are the first and the last letters of the alphabet, respectively. The latter is the last of the sibilants or the *Shakti* symbols. It is the aspirate and is uttered from the glottis or *kantha* with

---

66. (Malhotra, *Being Different: An Indian Challenge to Western Universalism*, 2011); See Chap. 5 - 'Non-translatable Sanskrit vs. Digestion', an excellent overview of the Sanskrit language.

67. (Mishra, 1972)

68. (Khanna, *The Metaphysics of the Sanskrit Alphabet*, 2004); See for a detailed study and how the symmetries of the Universe are reflected in this arrangement of letters or *varna*-s.

an extra force of breath. In terms of speech, its positioning in the glottis is adjacent to that of '*a*' (A).[69]

The shloka II.3.6 of *Aitareya Aranyaka*[70] explains this:

> "*a*" is the whole of speech and being manifested through the mutes and the sibilants it becomes manifold and various. If uttered in a whisper it is this *prana*, if forcefully, that body - *sharira*. Therefore, it is hidden, as hidden as the previous body encapsulated in this *prana*. But spoken forcefully it is that body and visible, for body is visible.

We have seen '*a*' (A) is the immutable, Brahman the symbolic Unknown[71]; if this is the whisper, then as we force the breath just a little, what we get is the aspirate sound '*ah*'(A:). It is both '*a*' and '*h*' combined. This is called the *visarga*[72] sound. This represents the visible body.

At this point we take a quantum leap and follow *Shiva Sutra* - II.7 which states:[73]

maatRkacak` sambaaoQa: II 2.7 II matrika chakra sambodha.

The circle of letters give enlightenment.

We have seen how bindu is likened to Shiva's spanda or a throbbing point. This *Shiva-Shakti* dichotomy gives rise to the string of alphabets called the *matrika chakra*, literally meaning the mother-wheel. The letters are arranged in a *chakra* or circle much like beads in a rosary with each letter having its individual universal resonant energy. (See Fig. 6)

As shown in the *akshara*-wheel, at the top, we see that another level of symmetry emerges—the *visarga*, '*ah*' (A:) closes the circle pictorially —signifying the internal/external division of the body or *atma*. The individual, I, has thus taken form and this is called *aham* (AhM). It is the '*ah*' (A:) sound with the Shiva's bindu on top. Thus, there is an inside and there is an outside - with the language of consciousness as the dividing membrane.[74]

---

69. Interestingly while the '*a*' (A) sound is present in all the consonants, as discussed earlier, the '*h*' (h) sound is present in half of the mutes (barring the nasal stops).

70. (Keith, 1995)

71. How do you name the 'Unknowable'? This conundrum is addressed by the *Upanishad* by denoting the letter that we can utter with the least effort (*samvrit prayatna*) viz. 'a' from the epiglottis.

72. The *visarga* is not part of the main alphabet and it is termed *ayogavah* or 'that which is not part of the harness'.

73. (Singh, 2000); p. 107.

74. (Khanna, Divinity in Sound, 2006)

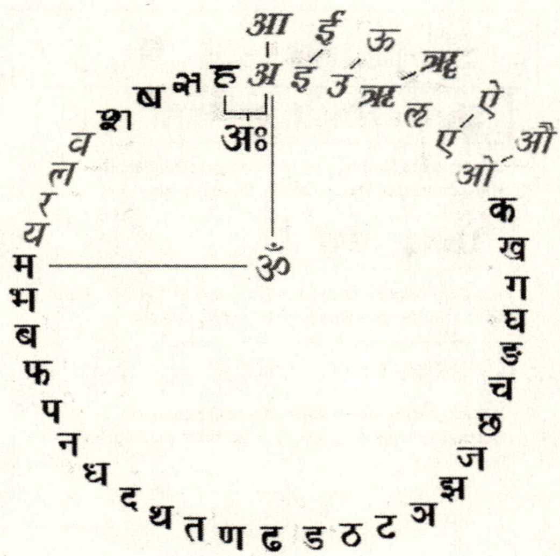

Figure 6: The Matrika chakra (The akshara-wheel)

The starting letters from the top, going clockwise in *grey italics* are the *svar-s*, the vowels. These are thirteen in number.
The letters in **black** are the ***sparsha***, the mute-consonants. These are the 'reflected ones' and are twenty-five in number.
The four letters after (ma) in *grey italics again* are the *antahstah*, the semi-vowels.
The last four letters in **bold *italics*** are the ***ushman***, the sibilants. (Also called ***Shakti symbols***)

The *visarga* is the *bija-mantra* for the *Sahasarara* or the crown-*chakra* and '*ha*' (h) is the bija-mantra for the throat or *vishuddhi-chakra*.

If we go back to the akshara-wheel, the last four letters in bold italics viz. '*sh*' (Sa), '*shh*' (Ya), '*sa*' (sa) and '*ha*' (h) are the sibilants or *ushman*, meaning energy. They are the *Shakti* symbols. The first three of these akshara-s can be linked to the three Goddesses, Lakshmi, Usha and Saraswati. They represent the energies of the manifest universe, and are the mythological consorts of the trinity Vishnu, Shiva and Brahma[75] respectively.[76] In the Vedic sense energy is treated very differently from the Western scientific method:

Shri Lakshmi (SaR laxmaI) is the goddess of wealth, worldly goods, and material acquisitions. This belongs to Cantor's, $\aleph_0$(Aleph–naught), the

75. In the *Purana*-s, the mythical ancient legends, *Brahma* is the deification of *Brahman*, the Unknown and is equivalent to *Ishwara* the perceivable reflection of *Brahman*.

76. Usha is synonymous with Parvati, the Goddess of the Mountains.

Sibilants – श , ष , स

Shri Lakshmi श्री -लक्ष्मी

It is Discrete Shakti ; *Vishnu's* consort ; Belongs to the 'countable infinite' set $\aleph_0$ (Aleph-naught)

Ushā उषा

It is Continuous Shakti ; *Shiv's* consort as *Pārvatī* ; Belongs to the 'indenumerable infinite' set $\aleph_1$ (Aleph-one)

Saraswatī सरस्वती

It is Increasing Shakti ***√brih***; *Brahma's* consort ; Belongs to the ever-growing 'transfinite cardinal' sets $\aleph_2, \aleph_3, \aleph_4 \ldots$

Figure 7

countable infinite of the natural numbers. She is the favorite of the Hindu trading community and is worshipped every Diwali[77] along with Lord Ganesha, literally the Lord of Counting.[78] Here the energy is conserved. That which diminishes from one place increases at the receiving end. Say we give someone money, it reduces with us but adds to that person's account. All the countable objects and things of our daily existence are in this domain.

Usha (]Yaa) is the goddess of the continuous flow of energy. It is that which keeps getting replenished. The rays of the sun, the flowing rivers, the sprouting leaves are all examples of this form of Shakti. It is $\aleph_1$ (Aleph–one), the continuous infinity of Cantor's Real Line. The reservoir of energy is so huge that we get a feeling of continuity in using it. We go to the river and fill a bucket of water, the flow of the water is not affected, and we receive our nourish. Literally, Usha means the dawn and the *Rig Veda*, is replete with its praise.

Saraswati or Sati[79] (sarsvatI) is the 'energy that grows' by giving. It is like the fruit of a tree that multiplies or the dispersion of knowledge or like lighting several candles with one, and so on. It is the $\aleph_2$, $\aleph_3$, $\aleph_4$ and

77. Deepawali is the festival of lights observed on *amavasya* (or new Moon), the fifteenth day of the lunar month of Kartik, every year. It is the celebration for the return of Lord Rama to his kingdom after fourteen years. Traders consider this day as the beginning of their accounting year.

78. *Ganesha* is (gaNanaa+[-Sa) or 'Lord of Counting' literally.

79. This is the *pratyahara* of Saraswati. Panini explains this method of taking the first and last syllables of a word or a phrase and combine them to abbreviate. This is oft used in *Sutra*-s.

the increasing Alephs of Cantor's transfinite cardinals. It is this relentless increasing magnitude of Saraswati that leads one to the fourth sibilant '*ha*' (h). The root-verb for an increase of this kind is *brih* and it is from this that the word Brahman, the Absolute Infinite or the Unknown is derived. We give you some knowledge, you receive it, and we do not lose anything. It is the goddess of speech, learning and music, and is the means to achieve the akshara.

Order and Chaos in Vedic Philosophy

Rajiv Malhotra has a chapter devoted to Order and Chaos in his book *Being Different: An Indian Challenge to Western Universalism*. The excerpt that we resonate with here is:

> The order-chaos tension results in a delicate equilibrium which makes the prevailing order not absolute but tentative, relative, porous and supple. Disorder serves as a source of creativity by preventing order from becoming fossilized. Brahma is not only the creator of the universe and the maintainer of its order, as Vishnu but also the one who ultimately dissolves it, as Shiva. The dissolution makes room for the next cycle of creation… This process is continual, unceasing, all-pervading and functions on both the subatomic and cosmic levels.[80]

In Vedic philosophy, the dichotomy of reality arises from Consciousness. As we saw above, the undifferentiated underlying ocean of energy Dr Kapil Kapoor referred to, is bifurcated as inside and outside by our skin that develops in the womb (*mata*)[81] and the *atma* takes shape or *rupa* ($p).

As shown in Fig. 8, '*a*' (A) is the immutable, Brahman and the entire creation closes within the wheel of letters depicted in Fig. 6 as the *visarga*, '*ah*' (A:). The two bindu-s attached to the '*a*' (A) symbol denote the chaos-order dichotomy and are represented as shown in Fig. 8 signifying the

80. (Malhotra, *Being Different: An Indian Challenge to Western Universalism*, 2011); p. 187.

81. (Sarup, 1984); The Nirukta (2.8) first relates the root (maa) √ma to (maata) *mata* which means 'the atmosphere' encircling the earth or a 'round protective shape'. This also means the 'mother's womb' wherein the *atma* or soul takes shape and form and is born. The womb ensconces the *atma* or Self. Similarly, the atmosphere covers the earth. Literally, therefore, (maata) *mata* means 'a protective spherical region' and the mother's womb is the soul's passage into this world of *maya*. Here it is nurtured, develops into a fœtus and takes on the human consciousness – ready for its earthly experiences.

Figure 8: Visarga

spanda or pulsation of Lord Shiva's undifferentiated energies as an eternal throb between the 'explosively expanding' and the 'chaotically coalescing' forces.[82]

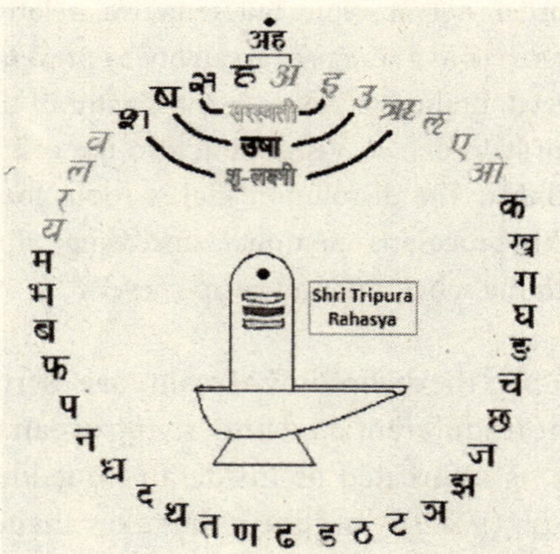

Figure 9: Shiva-Shakti

In a temple dedicated to Shiva, notice the prominent bindu and the three horizontal lines underneath it on the Shiva-liṅga. The lines represent the three *Shakti*-s discussed earlier and shown in Fig. 9, while the *bindu* represents the aham (AhM) or self, that is the individual atma. The same symmetry, of the dot with three parallel lines below it, appears in the

82. (Singh, 2000) pp. 113-4; See an excellent explanation of *visarga* and the 'I- consciousness' as *vindu*.

akshara-wheel. As the sibilants '*sh*' (Sa), '*shh*' (Ya), '*sa*' (sa) and '*ha*' (h) on one side combine with '*ri*' (?), '*u*' (]), '*i*' ([) and '*a*' (A) respectively on the other side, the first and the last letters of the words Shri (SaR), Usha (] Yaa), Saraswati (sarsvatI) and *aham* (AhM) are traced out. This pictorial representation that unfolds from the *Shiva Sutra* finds a confirmation in the *Tripura Rahasya*.

As we look outwards into the night sky, we see a vast unlimited universe and as telescopes get sharper, we can look deeper and further into space, and as Einstein showed us, we are also looking back in time. And everything is moving or vibrating... it is the *jagatyam jagat* of *Ishopanishad*.[83] This incessant movement acts as the scrim to our senses and manifests as the dichotomy of Vishnu and Shiva. √'*Vi*' as a root means *gati, vyapti* or to speed away, flying away and *anu* means the tiniest form of matter. Vishnu is therefore the expanding, emanating energy that is spewing out in discrete amounts from the supernovas at the galactic level and from the sun in our immediate solar system. Vishnu is that luminous, creative order of the Universe.

In terms of etymology Vish (ivaYa) and Shiv (iSava) are opposing forces.[84] Shiva therefore represents the intense gravitation in the Universe. It is Shiva's power that collapses the black holes to the center of each galaxy. But closer at hand, Shiva is the reservoir of the terrestrial energies. His abode metaphorically is Mount Kailash in the Himalayas and he sits there with his consort Parvati. The river Ganges entangled in Shiva's flowing mane, at another level, stands for '*akasha*-Ganga' – the Sanskrit name for the Milky Way.

Vishnu is often depicted with *agni* or flames emanating from Him and Shiva has *nagini* or snakes around His neck. The root verb √*ag* (Aga) means a tortuous movement and the suffix '*ni*' means in this context to throw out. So, agni is the flickering of the flame that shines and spews forth energy. The opposite, nagini means literally a black tortuous movement that absorbs energy.

And together their domain is called the *Vishva* (ivaSva) or the Universe.

This dichotomy of Vishnu and Shiva is not a simple deification of fixed order and chaos limits in the Universe; rather it establishes an incessant flow of vibrant energies between the duo. This flow of energy, as we now

---

83. (Radhakrishnan, 1989) – *Ishavasya Upanishad* 1 – 'All this, whatsoever moves in this moving Universe, is enveloped or clothed by God...'

84. Note that '*Va*' (va) and '*Sh*' (Sa) are contiguous letters in the *Akshara*-wheel (Fig. 6).

understand in terms of mathematics, is non-linear. There are symmetries within symmetries – endlessly so, ranging from the very large to the extremely small, as we saw above.

[Currently, we can observe a satellite picture of any cyclone from above as a swirling sink of energy, while at the same time experiencing the storm's unfolding ferocity on the ground below. From these points of view, we perceive the huge spiraling non-linear energy of the clouds both as sink and source simultaneously, although spatially they appear as separate scenarios. Similarly, are Shiva and Vishnu the same event from a dimension beyond time?]

In a linear, idealistic world, energy lends itself to simple cause and effect solutions – I push this object and it moves forward. In a non-linear equation, this is not so. A push here may not result in an immediate effect; the effects may collect over space and time zones to precipitate entelechies, sudden occurrences or epiphanies, which seem connected in dimensions beyond space-time. Or small effects can cause huge changes. The advent of rudimentary computers in the mid-1960s brought about the detailed study of these non-linear equations. Till then, the large number of calculations required could not be done manually, and since most equations for engineering applications required predictable linear controls, nobody bothered about non-linearity or chaos.

The global weather problem was the first non-linear equation to be widely studied and the American mathematician and meteorologist Edward Lorenz showed in a 1963 paper,[85] how very small fluctuations in weather patterns could precipitate huge changes thousands of miles away. He coined the phrase 'the butterfly effect' whereby he meant that a small butterfly flapping its wings in Brazil could set off a tornado in Texas. This was indeed prophetic because the El Niño factor is now legendary. A small current in the Pacific has been empirically found to effect world weather.

In the early 1970s, Lorenz's work gave birth to the fields of Chaos and Order and French American mathematician Benoit Mandelbrot developed the theory of Fractals while working at IBM in the 1980s. Western scientists and mathematicians saw that in real-world problems there was no absolute size. As you scaled the solutions, that is, looked at bigger or smaller sizes, the same forms and designs kept repeating themselves endlessly. Chaos Theory and Fractals[86] are today being applied to just about every subject ranging

85. (Lorenz, 1963)

86. YouTube is replete with videos on these topics. For Fractals see (BBC Ideas, 2019).

from economics, share prices to the study of heartbeats.[87] Interestingly, all this is based on the same Complex Number algebra that made Relativity and Quantum Mechanics, and even semiconductors possible. It is based on the square root of -1, or $\sqrt{-1}$ which is an indeterminate quantity and can only be represented by a symbol. And the symbol '**i**' stands for the word imaginary'.[88]

A Complex Number 'z' is written as… z = a + i b … here 'a' is called the *real part* and 'b' the *imaginary part*. The beauty of this formalism is that we can do all sorts of arithmetical jugglery with 'z' as if it is just one variable, but it carries with it two concepts simultaneously – that of the real 'a' and that of the unreal or imaginary 'b'. And the imaginary part helps carry the calculations beyond our daily 3D world to higher dimensions.

This contrasts with the Sanskrit derivation for *satyam* or true order. Dr Radhakrishnan, citing the *Brihadaranyaka Upanishad* V.5.1[89] said that satyam *consists of three syllables, sa, ti, yam, the first and the last being real and the second unreal or madhyato anritam. The fleeting is enclosed on both sides by an eternity which is real...* Here *anritam* is the negative of ritam meaning disorder or chaos. So, the truth is that the atma emerges from the highest order or ritam relegating to the lower dimensions of maya in a karmic dispersion of energies. It yearns to merge back with the Brahman struggling through the chaos of birth, aging, sickness, and death trying to find the best course of action or karma *within its limited space-time play.*[90]

And this dispersion of energies is the 'three *Shakti*-s'.

Life of *Satya-Dharma* and Artificial Intelligence

Any rigorous count of the bits and bytes of Artificial Intelligence limits it to $\aleph_0$ (Aleph–naught), the realm of Lakshmi. All lives are built on a base of information that now extends into tera-bytes[91] per individual but still countable. Ultimately, all this unfolds in the dimension of time. And this too is a measure that is limited, however so much we may meddle medically. The ethics of existence is not in the quantity, but in the quality, of life. A philosophy of humanism teaches us that we should not waste our

87. (Lauwerier, 1991) This book has an excellent overview of the applications of Fractals.

88. (LeShan, 2003) – Is also a 'functional entity' - See Appendix B – 'When is Uvani?'

89. (Radhakrishnan, 1989); See 'Introduction' and the *Brihadaranyaka Upanishad.*

90. This is confirmed by the *Mahavakya* – '*ayam atma Brahman*', *Mandukya Upanishad.* 1.2.

91. A tera-byte is 1012 bytes.

time collecting treasures of the storehouse, that is, Lakshmi or perpetuate only the treasures of the body, that is, Usha but build instead the treasures of the heart, that is, Saraswati. The antic waits for no one, and all the wealth of the worldly systems cannot buy even one day of extra life.

As we age there should be a personal mission to take on new challenges with a determined effort towards self-improvement and growth, at the same time nurturing the young to raise their levels of culture and consciousness. Near the time of biological death, the material dispersion of the aging body is inevitable. As this transition approaches it is the prime points of consciousness that survive, and these are the moments of true treasures of the heart that we accumulate during our lifetime. It is advisable to not fall prey to the self-serving virtual entertainment and games of AI that seduce the masses with pleasures but instead use the creative aspects of AI and our medically enhanced existence to share and help others live a life of dignity, equality, and hope. This is what *purusharth* means in the Vedanta as it guides us to lead a life of *satya-dharma*.

The Vedanta explains the same concept in various ways adopting Ariadne's thread approach. Let us return to *Brihadaranyaka Upanishad* where we left off and see V.5.2 to 4.[92]

The second shloka states what is *satya* or true is the yonder sun, *adityah*. The *Purusha* (here the Universe is personified) who is there in the *mandala*[93] and the *purusha* (the individual observer) who is here in the right eye, these two rest in each other.

The third shloka invokes the *Gayatri mantra*[94] equating the head, arms and the legs to *bhu*, *bhuvah*, *svah* saying that the name of the Purusha in the mandala is '*ah*' (Ah:) or the pervading light.[95]

The fourth shloka is identical to the previous except for the name of the purusha in the right eye, here it is aham (AhM).

Thus, in everyday parlance the Highest order Brahman is also called the Supreme Person, Purusha. And the body that births is referred to as purusha (Self).[96]

---

92. Radhakrishnan

93. *Mandala* is either a geometrical or pictorial depiction of the higher dimensional Universe.

94. (Chinmayananda, Japgayatri - Tune in the Mind, 1950?) also (Radhakrishnan, 1989); p. 885; *Subala Upanishad* - X.1; both give four more *vyahiriti*-s - mah (mah:); *jan* (jana:); *tapah* (tp:) and *satya* (satya) - these are the returning energies.

95. (Williams, 2002) - p. 124 - also means 'day'.

96. (Radhakrishnan, 1989); This is explained lucidly in *Shvetashvatara Upanishad* III.7 to III.21, pp. 727-730.

Rajiv Malhotra confirms this, quoting Sri Aurobindo:

> … Indian polytheism is not the popular polytheism of ancient Europe; for here the worshipper of many gods still knows that all his divinities are forms, names, personalities, and powers of the One; his gods proceed from the one *Purusha*, his goddesses are energies of the one divine Force …[97]

The *Ishavasya Upanishad* fifteen and sixteen shlokas take us a step further: Purusha (One), as a first step gives rise to the galactic energies that settle as *Pushan* the Sun. The Sun, as a second step emanates its explosive energies as Usha or rays that shine on the distant earth nourishing and nurturing it. And as a third step, Usha gives life to all this creation and the purusha (Self) or the aham on earth.

The *purusha*, in turn, prays to Pushan the Sun—requesting it to remove its glare and reveal the truth beyond, showing us the way of satya-dharma,[98] i.e., to guide us to a truthful life of duty[99] that will return us back to Brahman the Unknown.

The Returning Forms of Energy

These returning energies can be explained again in various ways since every impassioned mind over the ages has evolved its own thread of vocabulary. The *Gayatri mantra* gives us the seven *vyahriti-s; the Lotus Sutra* gives us the *Dharani mantra;*[100] mathematics gives us the thread of Cantor's infinities and we can build the theory of exponential energy increase from the three dimensions to the Complex plane and there on through fractals to conformal topology[101] and so on. Here we put this together in terms of the Samkhya philosophy where prakriti is the pratyaksha material

97. (Malhotra, *Being Different: An Indian Challenge to Western Universalism*, 2011); p. 286.

98. An entire sutra of twenty-seven chapters called the *Saddharma Pundrika Sutra* was taught by Buddha in the last eight years of his life to explain the essential way of life for achieving *nirvana* or salvation. It is called the *Lotus Sutra.* The Chinese version translated by Kumarjiva in the fourth century AD has twenty-eight chapters.

99. (Malhotra, *Being Different: An Indian Challenge to Western Universalism,* 2011); explains *dharma* - p. 159.

100. (Das, 2001); See Chap. 21 - *Dharani Parivarta.*

101. (Penrose, 2007); 'Conformal Cyclical Cosmology' by Sir Roger Penrose (shared Nobel Prize in Physics 2020).

manifestation and the generative principle of creativity and growth[102] while the proksha principle of Supreme consciousness is *Purusha* (One). In the words of Malhotra, prakriti is a

> versatile and multifaceted word supported by deep philosophical underpinnings ... in *Vyakarana* or grammar the roots or stems, from which various words are produced by adding suffixes and prefixes, are also called prakrti ... prakrti is the basis of both nature and the individual.[103]

The finest living example of the returning energies in prakriti is the forest that abounds with life of many shapes and sizes, layers and levels, equally above the ground, and as we know now more so underground, where the root systems develop an interconnected 'world wide web' of fungi secularly supporting all members even though they are all competing for the sun above the ground.[104]

This example of a 'tree' is re-affirmed by *Svetasvatara Upanishad* III.9 – 'Than whom there is naught else higher, than whom there is naught smaller, naught greater? (The) One immovable like a tree is the *poorna* and eternal Purusha'.[105]

To show how *prakriti* unfolds into the three sibilants and assists the material cause of a tree we quote here from a previous article:[106]

> The *Vedic* teachings treat the tree as a composite of all the three *Shakti-s* viz. *Sri-Lakshmi*, *Usha* and *Saraswati*. These are the three sibilants '*sh*' (Sa), '*shh*' (Ya), '*sa*' (sa) of the Sanskrit alphabet. ... called the *Ushman* or energy sounds. *Shri* is that which belongs to countability. It diminishes by giving and the wooden trunk of the tree is representative of this consumable form of energy. *Usha* is the *Shakti* that replenishes itself. The sunlight, the flowing water in the river are all its forms and the leaves of the trees naturally belong to this regenerative realm. The *Saraswati* is that energy which increases by giving ... It is this relentless increasing magnitude of *Saraswati* that leads one to the fourth sibilant ha (h), the aspirate, which represents *Brahman*, the Unknown. ... the Banyan

102. (Baumer, 1996); See *Prakriti*, p. 1 to 47.

103. (Malhotra, *Sanskrit Non-Translatables*, 2020); See pgs. 45, 77; Note. 62 on p. 206.

104. (Sheldrake, 2020)

105. (Radhakrishnan, 1989)

106. (Khanna, Natural Philosophy - In Conversation with Ravi Khanna, 2010)

tree or ficus *bengalensis*, is considered to be the abode of *Brahman* as the tree keeps expanding its base. It does this by dropping aerial roots which give it its majestic expanse to the extent that the central trunk is indistinguishable. One such tree is Thimmamma Marimanu in Anantpur district, Andhra Pradesh that is spread over 5.2 acres and propped up by 1500 odd roots.

The plant kingdom automatically embraces the rhythms of the universe and balances all the three levels of *Shakti*-s. It takes from the surroundings, just what it requires, through its intricate network of roots and branches; giving back to nature more than it absorbs. It lives symbiotically with thousands of bacteria, fungi, ants, birds and what have you, seeding the rain with its water evaporation and constantly converting the noxious carbon dioxide of the air to nurturing oxygen.

The karmic cycle closes for the *vriksha* or tree as it gives back to *Purusha* (One)—the flower, fragrance, and fruit without expecting anything in return. (No wonder a *yagna* is not complete without the offerings of *pushpa*, *gandha*, *anna* and *phala*[107]). Following the natural rhythms of ritam the tree completes the circle of life with the ever-increasing possibilities of growing incessantly adding ring after ring to its trunk.[108] (See Fig. 10)

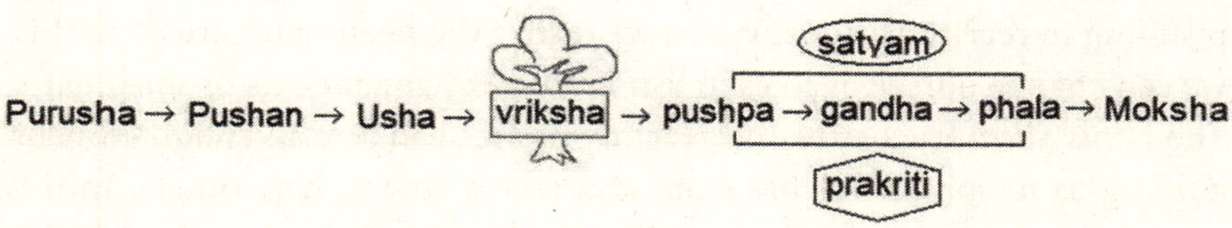

Figure 10: 'Tree': The Returning Forms

The Four Purusharths and Artificial Intelligence

The four bonds of carbon spread their symmetry through transfinite numbers of connections creating this passing play of life on this planet.

107. Both *anna* and *phala* or grain and fruit, are the profuse plant produce both for sharing their abundance and for propagating.

108. (Das, 2001); Also see *shloka*, fourteen and thirty-eight of Medicinal Herbs; Chap. 5 (AaOYaiQa pirvat-)

We have seen how this symmetry occurs as four levels with three steps[109] between them and we have returned to Malhotra's earlier quote on ritam. Learning from the vriksha we understand how the three steps of efforts are required to maintain the momentum of this symmetry in forming the returning path. These are the four purusharth-s that Malhotra refers to, namely, *artha, kama, dharma,* and *Moksha*. (See Fig. 11)[110]

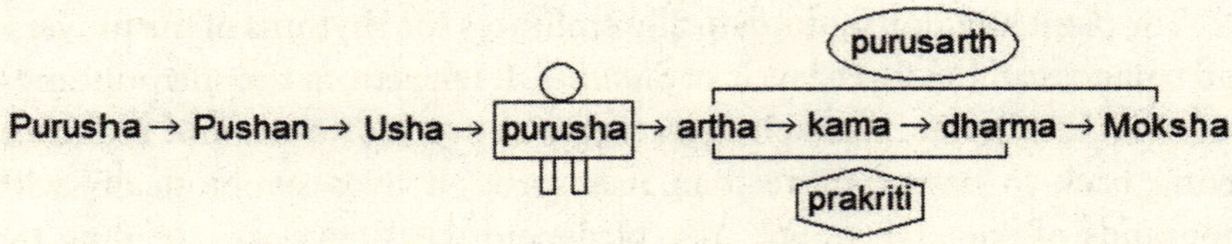

Figure 11: The four purusharth-s

Quoting Veda Vyasa: '…it is through dharma that *artha* and *kama* should be acquired'.

He is indeed correct, for accumulating artha or treasures of the storehouse gives satisfaction only until the next desire or *vikalpa* germinates in the mind. Therefore, this sequence can only give relative happiness. The earthly desires keep building up and start to create a series of vikalpa-s resulting in recriminations. When we realize the fleeting nature of all this, we can change ourselves to establish more permanent goals or *sankalpa*-s. The *Lotus Sutra* teaches us that 'earthly desires can lead to enlightenment' guiding us to spread our branches and take a vow to help others. In this process we become like 'human flowers'[111] following a healthy lifestyle gaining treasures of the body or *kama*. This virtually is a period of great efforts or purusharth pushing us even higher, to a vow to work for the betterment of all of humankind. This is the lofty dharma to truly achieve absolute happiness. And this is the pattern on which Artificial Intelligence should take up the challenge.

We have seen earlier how the four bonds of carbon give us the symmetry of life and then the next layer of similar, but larger, silicon bonds give us semiconductors. Now, Artificial Intelligence based on this spiraling

109. *Rig Veda* talks about the 'Three Steps of Vishnu' - I.154.1 to 3.

110. (Malhotra, *Artificial Intelligence and the Future of Power: 5 Battlegrounds*, 2021) - pp. 327-9

111. See Note 106.

technology is swamping us with applications that could be either good or bad, a future that is strangely reminiscent of the mythical *samudra-manthan.*[112] To win this battle we need a churning of an ocean of ideas based on the four-fold symmetry of the purusharth-s. This positive vortex of efforts should be based on conserving and disseminating scarce resources of both the individual and the Gaia, the Greek goddess of Earth.[113] In the case of the former, it is their time, health, and money, while in the latter it is oceans, forests, and minerals. Artificial Intelligence is at a pivotal stage as is apparent from Rajiv Malhotra's book. Can we harness AI's advanced abilities that are rapidly taking over human brain functions, as neural networks and 'machine learning' capabilities,[114] to usher in a collaborative era of deeper spiritual insight?

To answer this, we need to look at few common features of human and Artificial Intelligence. Both have rhythms that drive data collection and delivery mechanisms. In humans there are two main rhythms driving the brain-body duality. Firstly, the *hridaya* or heart, provides the preliminary pulse for the bodily and brain functions, beginning in the womb as the first beat[115] and ticking away as a bomb with a lifetime countdown of three to four billion. The *antahkarana* or the consciousness is framed at this stage and is the seat of the tender atma. When a child is born, the first cry establishes a second rhythm, that of prana or life-breath, heaving at approximately fifteen to twenty times per minute, on an average, throughout earthly life and summing up to a possible billion breaths till the last.

The AI processor, on the other hand, has a single 'clock' frequency that is generated accurately using precise piezo-electric crystals. The clock drives the entire logic linearly, step by step every cycle. Even the slightest variation in the pulsation could lead to complete malfunctioning of the 'motherboard'. On the contrary, the human rhythms are non-linear in nature and vary

---

112. The *Puranic* myth at the beginning of time when the Gods and demons battle each other, with Mount Meru as the pivot and the serpent *Vishaka* as the rope, churning the primeval ocean of energy. The Gods are victorious for they prepare ahead by convincing the demons to hold the head of the serpent ...

113. James Lovelock (1919), a British environmental scientist and futurist proposed the Gaia Hypothesis suggesting that living organisms on the Earth interact with their surrounding inorganic environment to form a synergetic and self-regulating system that created, and now maintains, the climate and biochemical conditions that make life on Earth possible.

114. (Fierce Electronics, 2020) The article explains the research on clustering of Graphic Processing Units (GPU) by Meta & Nvidia in a collaboration for machine learning applications.

115. The first heartbeat happens approximately six weeks into the development of the foetus.

constantly, adjusting themselves to the external feedback from the senses, and from the innumerable loops of internal chemical triggers.

Vedic wisdom tells us that the heartbeat arises from the *anahat* or a state of pure unperturbed consciousness that we have studied above as '*a*' (A), while the *prana*, according to the *Shiv Sutra* is the duality of in-breath and out-breath denoted respectively by the '*ha*' (h) *bija* or seed sound, and '*sa*' (sa) *bija*. Thus, the simple process of respiration is a subliminal chanting of the mantra *hamsa* where the nasal sound in between the two seed sounds is the *jiva* or awareness.[116] Starting from many cycles per minute the Vedic meditative practices teach us how to pursue slower and more calming frequencies, gradually guiding us towards a state of samadhi or equanimity and inner glow. The AI clock frequencies are taking us in the opposite direction of tinier micro time intervals reaching a phenomenally high count of instructions per second. At present, the count is sitting at 'petaFLOPs' or a one followed by fifteen zeros, instructions per second for some of the fastest supercomputers. This amazing capacity is doing for the human mind what the space program has done for the outreach of the human body. If the carbon-based organic world is a *mayanvi* dream, then the silicon structured AI web is a dream within a dream spinning a second circle of digression for the senses. This is where the case for collaboration converges between Vedic wisdom and AI.

Fundamentally, AI is based on linear logic and materially restricted to the space-time continuum as Malhotra says: 'an algorithm has no self'.[117] But, at the software level, non-linear mathematical algorithms coupled with Augmented Reality (AR) can help us delve deeper into the complexity of the conscious mind. We can thus use this cutting-edge technology to push the limits of our visualization for probing the dimensions beyond space-time. Fractal graphics and neural-network simulation can assist the investigation into the infinite recesses of our brain functions. All this can be done without the ingestion and ill effects of psychotropic substances that have been used for this purpose, by occultists and psychologists alike, over the centuries.

For, it is true that the Absolute Infinite is elusive to our five senses but, it is the purpose of purusharth to pursue it relentlessly. And this is exactly what persons like Georg Cantor have done a century back or the Vedic

---

116. (Singh, 2000) p. 190-1 *prana* and the *hamsa* mantra that we automatically chant 21,600 times daily.

117. (Malhotra, *Artificial Intelligence and the Future of Power: 5 Battlegrounds*, 2021); See p. 215, Chap. 5. *The Battle for the Self* in the section *Algorithm Versus Being.*

rishi did many millennia ago, and through each individual effort helped in raising the collective consciousness. Artificial Intelligence can aid not only in pushing the frontiers of introspection but also in closing the circle between worldly services and the needs of every citizen. Governments and agencies can use AI and its ability to handle large data, for enabling services like health, governance, finance, education and so on for each and every person in their populace in a leap so that no one gets left behind.

In conclusion, we must control AI very sensibly and painstakingly spread a philosophy of humanism so that, in the words of Rajiv Malhotra: 'the people who are anchored in *dharma* have a more cultivated conscience, a deeper and more vibrant awareness of the consequences of their actions, and they are less likely to be swayed by *kama-artha* based temptations'.[118]

In handling AI therefore, we must heed the warning of Rabindranath Tagore that 'a mind all logic is like a knife all blade. It cuts the hand that wields it'.

Artificial Intelligence should be tempered with True Wisdom.

Bibliography

Ahitagni, S. (1918). Rigveda Sarasangreh. Dehradun: Vaidic Jiwan Ashram.

Baumer, E. B. (1996). *Kalatattvakosha* - Vol. III. New Delhi: IGNCA & Motilal Banarsidass.

BBC Ideas. (2019, November 28). *How fractals can help you understand the universe | BBC Ideas*. Retrieved from YouTube: https://www.youtube.com/watch?v=w_MNQBWQ5DI

Bhattacharya, V. (1930). Vedic Interpretation and Tradition. *Sixth All India Oriental Conerence, Patna* (p. Booklet). Shantiniketan, Bengal: Visva-Bharati.

Brittanica. (n.d.). *Great Books of the Western World* - Vol. 28. Brittanica.

Capra, F. (1984). *The Tao of Physics*. Boston, USA: Bantam Books.

Chidbhavananda, S. (1974). The Bhagavad Gita. Tiruchirapalli: Sri Ramakrishna Tapovanam.

Chinmayananda, S. (1950). *Ishavasya Upanishad.* Madras : The Chinmaya Publication Trust.

118. (Malhotra, *Artificial Intelligence and the Future of Power: 5 Battlegrounds*, 2021); p. 329.

Chinmayananda, S. (1950). *Japgayatri - Tune in the Mind.* Bombay: Central Chinmaya Mission Trust.

Chinmayananda, S. (1992). *Aitareya Upaniṣad.* Bombay: Chinmaya Mission Trust.

Critchlow, Keith (2019) *The Hidden Geometry of Flowers - Living Rhythms, Forms and Number.* Edinburgh: Floris Books.

Das, D. R. (2001). *Saddharma Pundrika Sutra.* Patna, Bihar: Bihar - Rashtrabhasha - Parishad.

Desai, S. (2021, December 6). Metaverse as a Destination. *Times of India*, New Delhi, Pg. 8.

Dirac, P. A. (1974). *The Principles of Quantum Mechanics.* London: Oxford University Press.

Fierce Electronics. (2020, June 16). Electronics. Retrieved from What is a neural network accelerator?: https://www.fierceelectronics.com/electronics/what-a-neural-network-accelerator

Fox, D. (2016, February 16). *What sparked the Cambrian explosion?* Retrieved from Nature.com: https://www.nature.com/articles/530268a

Hatfield, G. (2014, January 16). *Stanford Encyclopedia of Philosophy.* Retrieved from René Descartes: https://plato.stanford.edu/entries/descartes/

Howell, E. (2021, June 9). *How many stars are in the Milky Way?* Retrieved from Space.com: https://www.space.com/25959-how-many-stars-are-in-the-milky-way.html

Hugo, T. B. (1987). *Les Miserablis*. New York: New American Library.

Kapoor, D. K. (1996). Vivarta & Parinama - Bhartrihari's Theory of Language. New Delhi: Jawaharlal Nehru University.

Keith, A. B. (1995). *The Aitareya Aranyaka.* Delhi: Eastern Book Linkers.

Khanna, R. (2004). The Metaphysics of the Sanskrit Alphabet. In S. S. Paranjpe, *Shabda: Text and Interpretation of Indian Thought* (Pgs. 40 to 65). New Delhi: Mantra Books.

Khanna, R. (2006). Divinity in Sound. In H. V. Dehejia, *Gods Beyond Temples* (Pgs. 142 to 151). Delhi: Motilal Banarsidass Publishers.

Khanna, R. (2008). The Shanti Path & Cantor's Infinities. *Sutra - Vol.1, No.1,* 107 to 117.

Khanna, R. (2010). Natural Philosophy - In Conversation with Ravi Khanna. In E. -N. Singh, *The Secret Abode of Fireflies - Loving & Losing Spaves of Nature in the City* (p. 44 to 51). New Delhi: Youthreach.

Lauwerier, H. (1991). *Fractals - Images of Chaos.* New York: Penguin Press Science Series.

LeShan, L. (2003). *The Medium, The Mystic and the Physicist.* New York: Helios Press.

Lorenz, E. N. (1963). Deterministic Nonperiodic Flow. *Journal of Atmospheric Sciences,* 130.

Malhotra, R. (2011). *Being Different - An Indian Challenge to Western Universalism.* Noida, India: Harper Collins Publishers India.

Malhotra, R. (2020). *Sanskrit Non-Translatables.* New Delhi: AMARYLLIS - Manjul Publishing House.

Malhotra, R. (2021). *Artificial Intelligence and the Future of Power.* New Delhi: Rupa Publications.

Mancuso, S. (2018). *The Revolutionary Genius of Plants - A New Understanding of Plant Intelligence & Behaviour.* New York: Atria Books (Simon & Schuster).

Mishra, D. V. (1972). *A Critical Study of the Sanskrit Phonetics.* Varanasi: The Chowkhamba Sanskrit Series.

Muller, F. M. (1878). The Hibbert Lectures - On the Origin and Growth of Religion, as illustrated by Religions of India. London: Longmans, Green, and Co.

Nambiar, K. K. (1996). Set Theory, Computer Science, and Vedānta Philosophy. New Delhi: School of Computer and Systems Sciences, Jawaharlal Nehru University.

Penrose, R. (2007). *The Road to Reality—A Complete Guide to the Laws of the Universe.* New York: Vintage Books (Division of Random House Inc.).

Powers, R. (2018). *Overstory (winner of the Pullitzer Prize).* New York: WW Norton & Co.

Radhakrishnan, S. S. (1989). *The Principal Upanishads (Centenary Edition).* Delhi: Oxford University Press.

Rucker, R. (1983). *Infinity and the Mind.* New York: Bantam Books.

Saraswati, S. S. (2006). Tripura Rahasya—The Mystery Beyond the Trinity. Tiruvannamalai, Tamil Nadu: Sri Ramanasraman.

Sarup, L. (1984). *The Nighantu and The Nirukta.* Delhi: Motilal Banarsidass.

Schrödinger, E. (1992). *What is Life? with Mind & Matter.* Cambridge: Cambridge University Press.

Sheldrake, M. (2020). *Entangled Life—How Fungi Make our Worlds, Change our Minds and Shape our Futures.* London: The Bodley Head.

Singh, J. (2000). *Shiva Sutras—The Yoga of Supreme Identity.* Delhi: Motilal Banarsidass Publishers.

Tripathi, S. N. (Ed.). (1965). Tripura Rahasyam (Jnana Khand) (Vol. 15). Varanasi, UP: Varanaseya Sanskrit Vishvavidyalaya.

Vatsyayan, G. E. K. (1992). Kalatattvakosha—*Volume 2.* New Delhi: IGNCA & Motilal Banarsidass Publishers.

Wikipedia. (2021, September 15). *Consorts of Ganesha.* Retrieved from Wikipedia - The Free Encyclopedia: https://en.wikipedia.org/wiki/Consorts_of_Ganesha#:~:text=Ganesha%20was%20depicted%20as%20a,Hindi%20film%20Jai%20Santoshi%20Maa.

Wikipedia. (2021, July 3). *Moore's Law.* Retrieved from Wikipedia: https://en.wikipedia.org/wiki/Moore%27s_law

Wikiquote. (2021, June 29). *William Thompson.* Retrieved from Wikiquote: https://en.wikiquote.org/wiki/William_Thomson

Williams, M. M. (2002). *Sanskrit - English dictionary.* Delhi: Motilal Banarsidass.

NINE

Artificial Intelligence as an Enabler of Western Universalism

Subhodeep Mukhopadhyay and Divya Reddy

Introduction

In a 2021 study, *Re-imagining Algorithmic Fairness in India and Beyond*, by Nithya Sambasivan, staff researcher at People+AI Research (PAIR), and others at Google Research, USA, it was found that Artificial Intelligence (AI) algorithms in India are not neutral, and fail to take into account caste biases and discrimination against minorities. The study, based on thirty-six qualitative interviews of activists and academics, concludes that India is still a long way off from algorithmic fairness. One of the issues studied is the use of safety applications by law enforcement agencies. The authors contend that such applications are inherently unfair as they tend to victimize certain communities. There is a propensity among software users to mark Muslim and Dalit residential areas as unsafe, thereby leading to increased patrolling of those localities. Another issue is neutrality of facial recognition, and here the authors argue that such algorithms tend to be unfairly biased against Dalits, Adivasis and Muslims, since the training data itself is biased. The authors conclude that in order to meaningfully bring about algorithmic fairness in India, stakeholders and policymakers must heed the advice of Dr B.R. Ambedkar, who headed the committee drafting

Independent India's Constitution, that social reform must necessarily precede political reform.[1]

An area where such data biases also come to the forefront is Lesbian, Gay, Bisexual, Transgender, and Queer or Questioning (LGBTQ+) sensitivity, where India has, by definition, not adopted the Western liberal position. For example, in 2018 an AI start-up, working on an automatic system to filter out images depicting nudity and explicit sexual content, tasked Indian taggers to label millions of online photos, which could be used to train AI systems to identify those it deemed 'indecent'. An inspection of the data revealed that the Indian taggers had classified all images of same-sex as indecent. It was therefore concluded that this was a reflection of the Indian mindset towards gay and lesbian relationships, and was significantly different from that in the United States.[2]

Other similar examples too, according to the authors, illustrate the inherent biases in Indian AI models, and thereby expose the underlying societal prejudices of Indian society, especially the majority community. This bias is also reflected in the research infrastructure for AI and other cutting-edge technologies, and experts insist that India needs to award international fellowship opportunities to students from marginalized communities, and create an army of 'Dalit Fields medalists, Muslim neuroscientists and Bhil artificial intelligence researchers.' Only then can India create a robust, as well as inclusive, world-class research infrastructure.[3]

When such issues are debated in the mainstream of Indian academia and media, discussions tend to devolve into shout-fests and polemics. The Left-liberal establishment will lambast the so-called upper caste Hindus, and treat this as one more example of the way in which discriminatory, and oppressive evil practices pervade all aspects of Indian life, invading even purely scientific domains. The Indian Right, on the other hand, will counter these claims by asserting that such studies are ideologically motivated and embody typical Left-liberal views, where Indian minorities and so-called lower castes are always seen as victims at the hands of an oppressive Hindu majority.

---

1. Sambasivan, Arnesen, Hutchinson, Doshi, & Prabhakaran, 2021.

2. *Using A.I. to Find Bias in A.I.* Retrieved 15 July 2021, from *The New York Times:* https://www.nytimes.com/2021/06/30/technology/artificial-intelligence-bias.html

3. *India Needs Muslim Neuroscientists and Dalit Fields Medalists Among its STEM Researchers.* Retrieved 15 July 2021, from The Print: https://theprint.in/opinion/india-needs-dalit-field-medalists-and-muslim-neuroscientists-among-its-stem-researchers/95680/

How is one then to analyze and interpret all this? Are Indian AI systems inherently biased?

In this essay, the authors argue that while it is natural for biases to creep in into data driven AI models, there is an immediate need to first ascertain their existence and analyze their degree of influence in Indian data sets. We should not blindly assume that since racial and gender biases have been evidenced in Western data sets, Indian data sets must therefore naturally have embedded caste, tribal and minority biases, as some recent academic studies and commentaries seem to imply. This is simply a perpetuation of Western claims of Universalism, which unfortunately is a dominant *Weltanschauung*, or view, in India, where the West is the gold standard against which India must measure itself. The authors challenge with evidence, efforts of some inclusive-AI public intellectuals and activists to equate White supremacy, and so-called Hindu supremacy in Indian machine learning data sets. It will be demonstrated through numerous examples, including a detailed case study on the Kumbh Mela on how there is a greater likelihood that data sets on India are, in fact, heavily biased against dharma traditions, causing irreparable harm to the pluralistic nature of Hindu society.

We do not argue that the biases against dharma neutralize those against the lower castes and minorities, nor that one type of bias justifies the other. Rather, we wish to point out that AI biases are diverse, as diverse as human biases, and that the field of identifying and remedying biases is in its nascent stage with a lot more work needed to be done. We wish to shine the spotlight on an area of bias that has not received the attention it deserves in the expanding field of AI bias studies.

Western Universalism and Artificial Intelligence

Bias and discrimination are real-world issues. How the terms are defined depends on the assumed world view. The most dominant one happens to be that of the West, which critically acclaimed author Rajiv Malhotra refers to as Western Universalism (WU). In this Western universalistic meta view, which the Indian establishment and especially its elites too have adopted, India is studied through different binary categories like sacred/secular, Left/Right, monotheism/polytheism, oppressor/oppressed, and majority/minority and so on. Every aspect of Indian society, economics, and polity gets mapped onto these categories.

> The unity of the indigenous culture is broken into parts; these are then mapped onto Western taxonomy, which is presented as more objective or else based on a more correct spirituality. This is nothing less than the systematic dispossession (an epistemic cannibalization, as it were) of the colonized world ... Victims might even get blamed as the source and cause of their own degradation.[4]

Dharma	Western Universalism
Varna and *jati*	Caste system: oppressor/oppressed
Dharma	Religion: monotheism/polytheism
Shruti and *smritis*	Human Rights Abuses: oppressor/oppressed
Agama and *tantra*	Rituals and superstitions: perpetrator/victim

The above elucidates a few instances of how dharmic ideas get mapped onto Western Universalism binary categories.

As stated, the basic premise of the hypotheses and position statements make clear that the authors use a Western universalistic framing to define bias, discrimination, and proposed solutions. Western Universalism continues to be used as the template for mapping and defining all cultures and we thus need to be cognizant of its distorted interpretations of Indian traditions. Indian society, and especially Hinduism, is perceived as primitive and undesirable, and so the West must sanitize it and civilize the natives. The latest avatar of this civilizing mission adopted by think tanks, scholars, and activists involves 'human rights' intervention and empowering of subalterns in India. Indian society is analyzed based on Western social science and anthropological models assumed to be universal and context-free, and Western societal solutions of emancipation are recommended as remedies.

A crucial point is that dharma traditions like Hinduism, Jainism, and Buddhism are not premised on a single absolutist version of history or an immutable holy book documenting one-time divine revelations. They are instead, based on the inner experiences of *rishis* who have attained higher states of consciousness. While this allows dharmic systems the flexibility to re-contextualize themselves according to time and location, it also

4. Malhotra, 2013, pp. 309-10.

makes them vulnerable to fragmentation on account of different views of what constitutes truth. Artificial Intelligence has the potential to greatly aggravate such distinctions, and fan the flames of bigotry.

> This disadvantage turns into vulnerability in the face of AI, because algorithms can be trained by their owners depending on the social-political preferences they wish to proliferate ...this can challenge the masses and AI can be used to create a wedge among the followers of Hindu Dharma by training the AI algorithms using different texts and interpretations.[5]

Western Universalism facilitates the digestion of Vedic civilization into Western civilization, by allowing the West to absorb what is good and useful and labeling it universal, or western, knowledge. At the same time, ideas found difficult to digest or culturally uncomfortable, are rejected. This entire process of digestion is accompanied by a vilification of the target culture, in this case Hinduism, and negative stereotypes like caste, Sati, dowry, infanticide, patriarchy and minority-ism get amplified significantly. Digestion compromises, and even leads, to the atrophying of certain dharmic elements, especially when the Western substitute becomes acceptable usage, despite not accurately reflecting the original Indian idea. This problem is especially pronounced in Sanskrit because the very form, sound, and manifestation of the language carries effects that are inseparable from their conceptual meanings. Cultural digestion, often hiding behind the façade of modernity, thus compromises the non-translatable nature of Sanskrit, and consequently experiential knowledge is sidelined, nuances are lost, and first-person empiricism of dharma is relegated to obscurity.[6]

Artificial Intelligence models built on a Western universalistic paradigm are inherently problematic. They have the potential to vastly amplify this distortion of dharma and accelerate the demise of Sanskrit and *sanskriti* as a legitimate knowledge system and world-view. They not only pose a cultural threat to Hinduism but a national security threat as well, as they can potentially exploit fault lines in the guise of human-rights intervention and foment divisiveness.

---

5. Malhotra, 2021b.

6. *Prefaces*. Retrieved 15 July 2021, from *Sanskrit Non-Translatables: The Importance of Sanskritizing English* https://sanskritnontranslatables.com/prefaces/

Biases in Artificial Intelligence

Intentional, as well unintentional, biases of people that control AI systems can enter in several ways. An important bias could be in the objective of the AI system determined by the client, whether an individual, a government, a private company, or Non-governmental Organization (NGO), which in turn are determined by a combination of factors like their strategic aims, political or cultural affiliation and so on. The other kind of bias could be in the data itself, used for training and validation of the model. There is no pre-defined golden standard to be adhered to, and the choice of goals as well the data sets are arbitrarily made by people in control of the Machine Learning Process (MLP).[7] It must be noted that psychologists have identified more than one hundred cognitive biases which can very well seep into machine learning algorithms.[8] Given the ubiquitous nature AI models today in varied, and often critical, applications, algorithmic and data biases inherent in the models tend to get amplified at scale. The problem of biases in machine learning algorithms has been established and many such instances are well-documented.

A criminal justice algorithm used in Broward County, southeast Florida, turned out to be racially prejudiced against African-Americans in forecasting who would re-offend. It not only mislabeled Black defendants as 'high risk' at nearly twice the rate as Whites, but also mislabeled Whites as low risk more often than Black defendants.[9] A 2019 study published in the academic journal *Science* found that an algorithm widely used in American hospitals to allocate health care to patients had been systematically discriminating against the Blacks. Not only were Blacks less likely to be referred to the personalized-care programs, they also had to be sicker than Whites before being referred for additional help.[10]

A Massachusetts Institute of Technology (MIT) study of three commercial gender classification algorithms found these systems were prejudicial against darker skin types and females, and performed worst

---

7. Malhotra, 2021a, pp. 52-4.

8. *The Cognitive Biases Tricking Your Brain.* Retrieved 15 July 2021, from *The Atlantic:* https://www.theatlantic.com/magazine/archive/2018/09/cognitive-bias/565775/

9. *Machine Bias.* Retrieved 15 July 2021, from ProPublica: https://www.propublica.org/article/machine-bias-risk-assessments-in-criminal-sentencing

10. *Millions of Black People Affected by Racial Bias in Health-care Algorithms.* Retrieved 15 July 2021, from *Nature:* https://www.nature.com/articles/d41586-019-03228-6

for darker females.[11] Amazon had to scrap an AI-based recruiting system when it was discovered that the system was biased against women. The system, billed as the 'holy grail' of recruitment would penalize résumés that included the word 'women's', as in 'women's chess club captain', and favored words like 'executed' or 'captured', more commonly found on male engineers' résumés.[12] Research has shown that Natural Language Processing (NLP) models trained on Wikipedia dataset or Google News, exhibit gender stereotypes. The classic example is the visual recognition of two individuals wearing white coats: the system will tend to identify the male as a doctor and the female as a nurse.[13]

The above examples of discrimination against Blacks and women, while morally reprehensible, are essentially Western problems. They embody peculiarly Western issues and are a product of American and Eurocentric historical experiences, which have little overlap with Eastern history. This is not to say that discrimination and biases do not exist in India. They exist the same way as in other parts of the world. The relevant point is that the Indian historical experience is distinct from the West, and hence problems that exist in India are a product of its own cultural trajectory. However, the Western Universalist claim is that problems they face as a society are normative, so solutions which work for them must necessarily be universal.

> The profound assumption is that the shape and direction of world history is leading to a single Western goal – be it salvation or scientific secular progress. All peoples and cultures are forced into the various schemes put forward to bring this about. Indeed, modern laws, regulations, conventions and common practices are formed with this in mind (whether consciously or not).[14]

This assumption of universality is problematic. For example, there is no reason to assume that just because Blacks were victims of racism (as well as biased AI systems) in the US, there must be similar institutionalized racism

---

11. Buolamwini & Gebru, 2018, p. 12.

12. *Amazon Scraps Secret AI Recruiting Tool That Showed Bias Against Women.* Retrieved 15 July 2021, from *Reuters*: https://www.reuters.com/article/us-amazon-com-jobs-automation-insight/amazon-scraps-secret-ai-recruiting-tool-that-showed-bias-against-women-idUSKCN1MK08G

13. *Man is to Doctor as Woman is to Nurse: the Gender Bias of Word Embeddings.* Retrieved 15 July 2021, from Towards Data Science: https://towardsdatascience.com/gender-bias-word-embeddings-76d9806a0e17

14. Malhotra, 2013, p. 309.

in India with its own version of black and whites. However, as elucidated in the following section that is exactly what the West and Westernized Indians is doing, and efforts are now being made to 'uncover' such biases in Indian AI systems.

Are Indian Artificial Intelligence Systems Biased?

There are numerous instances where the West has deconstructed Indian society and retrofitted them onto their own framework of desirable/undesirable and good/bad, and proposed sanctions and resolutions. For example, the 1990s US-operated and funded Afro-Dalit Project came up with an innovative framing where inter-*jati/varna* interactions and the Dalit movement in India was analyzed through the American cultural and historical lenses of racism, slavery, and Black/White relationship. Consequently, the Dalits became the 'blacks' and non-Dalits were painted as the Indian 'whites', a different racial group. The project attempted to empower Dalits using the same model used for Black emancipation in the US. While no one denies the discrimination against Dalits in certain parts of India or the historical discrimination against Blacks in US, the project chose to ignore the glaring differences between the two experiences.[15] The movement took on a life of its own and lives on as Dalit Lives Matter movement, modeled on the Black Lives Matter (BLM) movement. In this regard, the American academician and Black rights activist, Angela Davidson says:

> As Dalit activists and intellectuals have pointed out, the history of making connections between our two communities stretches back to the 19th century when most U.S. black people were enslaved. We deeply appreciate the solidarity that has been generated on so many occasions by Dalit activists… Therefore, we stand with those who are issuing a global cry for an end to racism and who not only say black lives matter but also Dalit lives matter and Muslim lives matter.[16]

---

15. *Introduction*. Retrieved 15 July 2021, from *Breaking India: Western Interventions in Dravidian and Dalit Fault Lines* https://breakingindia.com/introduction

16. *Angela Davis Speaks up About #DalitLivesMatter.* Retrieved 15 July 2021, from International Dalit Solidarity Network: https://idsn.org/angela-davis-speaks-up-about-dalitlivesmatter/

The aforementioned positions are now increasingly becoming part of the discourse on AI, and AI-enabled technologies. Given that many Indians, especially the English-speaking elite have accepted this Western lens, we are seeing increasing research on AI and how it purportedly increases caste biases, promotes Brahminical patriarchy, and encourages Hindutva. As per a 2018 report by the news channel *NDTV*, the Foundation for Human Horizon-USA had planned an event in partnership with the United Nations Department of Economic and Social Affairs, on the occasion of the 127th birth anniversary of Dr B.R. Ambedkar. The event was expected to be attended by AI experts from IBM, Google, Facebook, and Microsoft amongst others, to discuss how it could be used to eliminate the caste system and reduce inequality in India by the year 2030.

> AI if used properly can be main driver to reduce inequalities as it has (the) ability to create and protect much-needed safe zone ie, the AI predication of caste violence by zipcode, or caste group can provide tools to develop preventive measures to stop caste violence *similar to the western world* where they are using 'crime maps' or 'diseases map'[17] (emphasis added).

There is no further information whether the event actually took place, but what it does illustrate is the continuous effort to find parallels between Western evils and problems in Indian society, and then adopting Western solutions in Indian contexts and positioning them as universal.

Unlike the West, there is no *actual* evidence to suggest that data sets used in Indian AI models are biased. The predictions of various predictive AI models, whether deployed in law enforcement or other governmental departments, have so far not warranted any scrutiny or detailed examination of data sets for implicit biases. Had there been even an inkling of data models promoting discrimination against minority or marginalized communities, it would have elicited a hue and cry by the Indian media, social activists, and the judiciary. Their absolute silence in this regard is a telling testimony to the robustness and fairness of these AI systems.

However, many activists and academicians continue to write on how potential data bias in India could lead to social fragmentation and entrenchment of discriminatory practices. In a 2019 expert commentary

---

17. *Ambedkar Followers Believe Artificial Intelligence Can Eliminate Caste System.* Retrieved 15 July 2021, from *NDTV:* https://www.ndtv.com/india-news/ambedkar-followers-believe-artificial-intelligence-can-eliminate-caste-system-1820739

published by Observer Research Foundation, the author, a prominent academic and writer on society and technology presents a number of hypothetical scenarios:[18]

- Muslims being denied personal loans despite having good financial background;
- Dalits getting a longer sentence for the same crime than non-Dalit co-conspirators;
- Women's résumés being rejected by job search websites, despite better qualifications than fellow male applicants; and
- Certain communities or people with certain sexual orientation being denied housing

The author suggests that the above scenarios based on religious, caste, gender, or sexual discrimination will become increasingly common unless systematic efforts are put in place to guard against algorithmic biases in decision-making systems in lending, law enforcement, recruitment, and judiciary. In other words, judgment has already been passed and the Hindu majority convicted, before any crime has been committed!

Another well-known academician and founding director of a think tank promoting inclusiveness, writes that women's participation in the labor force in India is only twenty-seven percent and declining, and data sets used for machine learning are therefore 'likely to have a marked gender bias'. In some states, the percentage of incarcerated Muslims is almost thrice the overall Muslim population percentage, and thus any law enforcement AI model built on this kind of data is likely to be prejudiced against Muslims. She concludes the section by stating:

> … the recently set-up national AI task force is comprised of (sic) mostly Hindu men – only two women are on the task force, and no Muslims or Christians. A recent article in the New York Times talked about AI's 'white guy problem'; will India suffer from a 'Hindu Male Bias'?[19]

---

18. *India Needs to Bring an Algorithm Transparency Bill to Combat Bias.* Retrieved 15 July 2021, from Observer Research Foundation: https://www.orfonline.org/expert-speak/india-needs-to-bring-an-algorithm-transparency-bill-to-combat-bias-55253/

19. *Artificial Intelligence Apps Risk Entrenching India's Socio-economic Inequities.* Retrieved 15 July 2021, from *The Indian Express:* https://indianexpress.com/article/opinion/artificial-intelligence-apps-risk-entrenching-indias-socio-economic-inequities-5094831/

These examples show that the positions of academicians and activists on biases in AI in an Indian context, are largely based on assumptions and informed by their ideological leanings, rather than having any basis in facts. It also highlights the larger issue of Western Universalism that we alluded to earlier – of analyzing Indian society using Western anthropological categories. According to this lens, India is a synthetic mishmash of various subaltern and minority groups in continuous tension with a dictatorial state ruled by an imagined racist, casteist, patriarchal, misogynist, and anti-LGBTQ+ Hindu majority. Hence, it is imperative that caste, gender, minority, LGBTQ+ and other biases in Indian data sets and algorithms be unearthed to bring the racist majority to task. It is interesting to note the way in which the author attempts to create an association between White supremacy and Hinduism.

While we are yet to see evidence of Hindu supremacy in India, the issue of White supremacy driven biases in machine learning in the West is very real and pervasive; it appears in every step of the value chain including definition of data sets, data collection mechanism and data use. A well-known African-Canadian algorithmic bias activist, argues with numerous examples of how data is merely a 'subjective interpretation of someone's reality' and how White supremacy has been accepted as the norm by data scientists.[20] It is interesting to note that the origin of AI as a discipline can be traced to the ambition of the US military elites and the Pentagon (the headquarters of the United State Department of Defense) of the 1960s that wanted to bring order and control to the battlefield using advanced computing capabilities.[21] The first successful AI program deemed capable of solving 'universal' problems, was based on a US military framework, and validated through experiments on all White, economically privileged males.[22] Over the next few decades, things should have changed for the better, yet as numerous studies have shown, the problems of data biases continue to persist in some form or the other.

> AI's celebrated computing systems developed in a society premised on white supremacy and have worked to refuel its myths. Each of AI's

---

20. *How Our Data Encodes Systematic Racism.* Retrieved 15 July 2021, from *Technology Review:* https://www.technologyreview.com/2020/12/10/1013617/racism-data-science-artificial-intelligence-ai-opinion/

21. Katz, 2020, p. 21.

22. Katz, 2020, p. 30.

> iterations has produced racialized, gendered, and classed models of the self, delivered with imperialist rhetorics of colonization and conquest.[23]

A case study illustrates how Artificial Intelligence becomes an enabler of Western Universalism. The Kumbh Mela held in India is a classic example of how AI and WU can come together seamlessly, to the detriment of dharma at large, and Hinduism, in particular.

Kumbh Mela = Western Universalism x Artificial Intelligence

Held every twelve years, the Kumbh Mela is the world's largest and oldest dharmic gathering, mentioned in several early *Puranas*, attracting tens of millions of people from all corners of India, from all strata of society, and all kinds of traditions, ethnicities, and languages. The Kumbh supports as many people as New York, London and Paris combined.[24] The mela is a testament to India's diversity; it showcases the underlying philosophical unity of different traditions and brings to the forefront dharmic values like mutual respect, integral unity, sacrality, and embodied knowing. It demonstrates that even on very large scales, diversity can be self-organized and not anarchic, and the event has been managed very efficiently since time immemorial. There is no central organizing body, or an 'event manager' to send out invitations, draw up a schedule to plan the day's activities for the large gathering, nobody in charge to promote it, nor is there any centralized registration system to gain entrance.

The mela belongs to the public domain, and nobody has official authority or ownership of the event. Numerous groups from all over the country and including the rest of the world erect their own mini-townships and millions go as individuals to participate in the festivities. A team of British psychology experts studied the mela extensively for three years and concluded that the Kumbh could hold the secret to how very large communities could coexist in harmony. The researchers also found that unlike Western societies where a distinct division exists between, say,

23. Katz, 2020, p. 7.

24. *Harvard and the Kumbh Mela.* Retrieved 15 July 2021, from *Mint:* https://www.livemint.com/Opinion/rSz6ZMkjSrBpsDLxScyIsK/Harvard-and-the-Kumbh-Mela.html

immigrants and non-immigrants, the participants at the mela were very comfortable in the midst of diversity.[25]

International Media Frenzy and Academic Obsession

In fact, the interest of international media as well as academia borders on obsession. Nothing is too sacred or out of bounds for the global press that extensively covers every single aspect of the gathering. Several leading foreign media channels are found stationed at the mela days before the festivities begin, so as to capture everything starting from the preparations, the participants, and the final event. The big draw, undoubtedly, is the Naga sadhus, revered by Hindus for their great *tapas* or penance, and renunciation. For the Western media, however, what could be more exotic, outrageous, and bizarre and of course, news-worthy than naked men dancing to the frenzied beat of drums? A former *BBC* India correspondent and Padma Bhushan awardee writes:

> Most spectacular of all are the naked sadhus or holy men, ... dancing to the frenzied beat of drums and leaping in the air as they charge in to the river to bathe. Then there are the sadhus to be seen on any day performing amazing acts of asceticism. One sadhu I saw had held his arm up so long that it was withered and his nails curved round like talons, another was standing on one leg, and a third lying on a bed of thorns.[26]

Academic institutions are not far behind in their relentless fascination for the greatest show on earth, almost like a 'vast biblical scene'.[27] Leading institutions such as Harvard University have devised projects to study the chaotic, diverse, decentralized yet successful model of the mela. One such project is *Mapping the Kumbh Mela*, an interdisciplinary project involving various departments of Harvard, from urban planning to public health to religious studies. The project proposal highlighted how 'multiple and

25. *Harmony Lessons of Hindu Festival.* Retrieved 15 July 2021, from BBC News: http://news.bbc.co.uk/2/hi/uk_news/scotland/edinburgh_and_east/6322593.stm

26. *Kumbh Mela Festival.* Retrieved 15 July 2021, from *BBC* News: https://www.bbc.com/news/world-asia-india-20778818

27. *The Greatest Show on Earth.* Retrieved 15 July 2021, from University of St Andrews News: https://news.st-andrews.ac.uk/archive/the-greatest-show-on-earth-2/

conflicting systems, problems, and challenges converge at the Kumbh Mela' and thus warranted an interdisciplinary study to understand existing indigenous systems and to help develop better models of management.[28] Various departments of Harvard including urban planning, religious studies, public health school, and business school, collaborated to study the mela in a cross-disciplinary fashion. An important Harvard project was to support the Kumbh administration to build data sets to assess the health care systems and potential for outbreaks over the course of the Kumbh.[29]

The Indian government has always welcomed the idea of foreign institutions studying the mela, and also proposed collaborative research with several of them. Invitations were sent to twelve prominent academic institutes including Harvard, Cambridge, Oxford, and Stanford to study different aspects of the 2019 Kumbh Mela. This would ostensibly act as a 'third-party evaluation' of the preparations and provide independent feedback to the government. The collaborative research would delve into the history and mythological significance of the Kumbh, its impact on the economy, and gender issues. Based on the findings, the government could then adopt new and improved strategies for the upcoming Kumbh Mela.[30]

In all of this, the West has been very clear about its intent. While Western academia intends to map out and understand every aspect of the mela, the international media is present to simply peddle Oriental exotica to a starved Western populace looking for the next bit of sensationalism. What is shocking, however, is the reaction of the Indian state, akin to a guinea pig laying out the proverbial red carpet for the scientist who will study it and perform all sorts of experiments.

The Wonder That is Kumbh!

Beyond the popular curiosity and wonderment at this massive diverse gala, at a deeper level the Kumbh Mela highlights an important civilizational

---

28. *Kumbh Mela: Mapping the Ephemeral Mega-City.* Retrieved 15 July 2021, from Harvard University: https://mittalsouthasiainstitute.harvard.edu/wp-content/uploads/2013/05/Kumbh-GSD-Proposal.pdf

29. *Harvard Video Proves Their Infiltration of Kumbh Mela: Rajiv Malhotra.* Retrieved 15 July 2021, from Rajiv Malhotra Official, YouTube: https://www.youtube.com/watch?v=EMznloyYysU

30. *UP Government Invites Top Varsities for Kumbh Research.* Retrieved 15 July 2021, from *The Economic Times:* https://economictimes.indiatimes.com/news/politics-and-nation/up-government-invites-top-varsities-for-kumbh-research/articleshow/66111831.cms

difference between the West and dharma traditions: their attitude towards order, chaos, and complexity.

Eastern societies in general and Indians, in particular, are comfortable with chaos, uncertainty, unpredictability, and diversity, while the West views them as a profound threat that needs to be eradicated either by containment or complete assimilation. When it comes to checklists and Standard Operating Procedures, the West has distinct cultural advantages. On the other hand, while deciphering complex relationships and moving parts, Asian counterparts perform better and are able to transcend binary epistemic categories like left/right or God/Satan. This has a profound impact on how the West perceives and deciphers complex relationships. A 2005 study by Michigan University shows that Asians and White North Americans indeed see the world differently. When White Americans are shown a photograph, for example, they tend to pay more attention to what is in the foreground, whereas Asians tend to study the background as well, taking in the whole scene. The research highlighted how cultural differences extend to low level perceptual processes such as how we control our eyes, and thus, what we see literally depends on where we come from.[31] Artificial Intelligence-based visual inspection systems have a high probability of embedding these kinds of deep-seated worldviews. Sophisticated computer-vision machine learning algorithms rely on a large corpus of labeled images to get trained. However, the process of labeling of images is a manual process requiring human intervention, and thus has the potential to perpetuate these deep-seated biases.

Another Western cultural trait that drives their fascination for the Kumbh Mela is the view that anything chaotic, decentralized, diverse, and unpredictable is inherently dysfunctional, and needs an intervention to eliminate chaos and set things in order. Thus, we find articles published by the foreign media with titles like *Kumbh Mela: Case Study in Chaos Attracts Harvard Business School.*[32] A neuroscientist who studied Kumbh writes about the West's pre-conceived notions 'that the Mela seems designed to increase stress in every way—it is very noisy day and night, very unhealthy, and very packed'.[33] The Western perceptions of aesthetics and morality

---

31. *University of Michigan Vision Study Says Asians, Whites See World Differently.* Retrieved 15 July 2021, from Diverse Issues in Higher Education: https://diverseeducation.com/article/4582/

32. *Kumbh Mela: Case Study In Chaos Attracts Harvard Business School.* Retrieved 15 July 2021, from *International Business Times:* https://www.ibtimes.com/kumbh-mela-case-study-chaos-attracts-harvard-business-school-1076944

33. *The World's Largest Festival.* Retrieved 15 July 2021, from World Peace Through Technology:

are also closely associated with these ideas of order and chaos. There is an implicit assumption that what is 'beautiful' (in their own, peculiar, and culturally constructed sense) is also 'good' and 'true'. Likewise, what is 'ugly' is also 'bad' and 'wrong'. Often, judgment about one of the values implicates the other two. In fact, this can be traced to two distinct value systems driving the West.

> Biblical theology and Greek influence were fused to undergird the racial stereotyping of dark-skinned peoples. Greek norms of beauty and aesthetics combined with biblical concerns about purity and exclusive lineage became the basis for evaluating other cultures, which were often depicted as ugly, savage, and sexually promiscuous – with their deities and symbols viewed as asymmetrical, shadowy, threatening, and grotesque.[34]

Thus, we see the covert, as well as overt, Western (and westernized Indian) disdain for the Naga sadhus who are pejoratively referred to as the 'naked' sadhus, simply because they keep their bodies unclad. They are often compared to the Western nudists known for sensual self-indulgence, thereby trivializing the higher spiritual goals of the fiercely dignified and austere sadhus. For the West, the Naga sadhus, among a myriad other Hindu aesthetics, are a symbol of 'uncivilized ugly barbarians', consequently 'bad' and 'wrong'. Now imagine an AI-based image recognition system built on data where the images of Naga sadhus are labeled as 'ugly', 'uncivilized', 'bad', 'naked' or 'barbaric'. It is quite possible, that in the light of any untoward incident, the Naga sadhu community faces a high risk of false implications.[35]

Kumbh Big Data and Artificial Intelligence

Once the Indian government granted access to the Maha Kumbh Mela, foreign teams were visibly enthusiastic. They employed every available technology — from DSLR cameras to high resolution satellites that capture

---

https://wptt.org/2013/01/15/the-worlds-largest-festival/

34. Malhotra, 2013, p. 204.

35. There are many examples of how Hindu gurus were persecuted for crimes they did not commit simply because of their cultural affiliation. See *Persecution of Hindu Gurus Who Challenge Hinduphobia*. Retrieved 15 July 2021, from Rajiv Malhotra Official, YouTube: https://www.youtube.com/watch?v=dvcJI5yAd6M

aerial photographs and handheld cameras mounted on kites, to capture the minutest detail of the mela, including private footage of scores of devotees, grossly violating all norms of data privacy.[36] In fact, the principal investigator of Harvard's Kumbh Mela project made a telling remark on how the 2013 Kumbh was the first 'Big Data Kumbh', with cell phone usage ubiquitous in India, and with the millions of cellphones at the Kumbh Mela acting as mobile sensors. The research team, along with the help of local cellular providers and government authorities could amass, arguably, the biggest ever telecom data set.[37] With so much data available, the potential is limitless: Researchers now have the ability to slice and dice the Kumbh and Hinduism on the basis of factors like caste, place of origin, family details, food habits, gender, and age and so on. The data will be trained on Western social theories using a subaltern lens in order to identify human rights, public safety, and environmental impact issues. When correlated with private health data and mobile usage data, any number of studies can be visualized.

They may conclude, for example that there is a protein deficiency in the diet of certain lower castes visiting the Kumbh, so non-vegetarian food, rich in protein must be made available to them within the Mela premises.[38] In fact, a renowned professor of Hinduism studies lamented the fact that she missed seeing feminist NGOs at the mela.[39] It won't be long before case studies will be published in Western journals on (the Kumbh Mela being a ruse for) sexual exploitation, tantric sex orgies, 'naked' sadhus exploiting sadhvis, source for waterborne diseases and myriad other 'observations'. The Kumbh Mela may become another classic case of a White man's civilizing mission. As is always the trajectory of Western interventions, once the valuable lessons and elements, in this instance, of the mela are extracted and digested into the Western framework, what will be left is a case for ridicule and treated as problematic. Driven by the West's penchant

---

36. *Mapping a Megacity's Metabolism.* Retrieved 15 July 2021, from *The Harvard Gazette:* https://news.harvard.edu/gazette/story/2013/02/mapping-a-megacitys-metabolism/

37. *Studying India's Maha Kumbh Mela Festival.* Retrieved 15 July 2021, from *Harvard Business Review:* https://hbr.org/2013/01/a-closer-look-at-one-of-indias.html

38. For example, a 2015 NPR report claimed that India's vegetarian upper-caste elites were denying tribal children access to protein-rich non-vegetarian food. See: *Egg War: Why India's Vegetarian Elite Are Accused Of Keeping Kids Hungry.* Retrieved 15 July 2021, from NPR: https://www.npr.org/sections/thesalt/2015/07/14/422592127/egg-wars-india-s-vegetarian-elite-are-accused-of-keeping-kids-hungry

39. *Rajiv Malhotra Newsletter: Issue 03 - June 2016.* Retrieved 15 July 2021, from rajivmalhotra.com: https://rajivmalhotra.com/wp-content/uploads/2017/06/RM_Newsletter_June-2016.Final_.pdf

for eliminating chaos and setting things in order, they are likely to develop AI systems that could potentially help transform the decentralized model into a centralized one. It is also not unlikely that once they own all the data, they may soon become the de facto owners of the Kumbh driving the ('uncivilized', 'ugly' and 'bad') Akhada Parishad Naga Sadhus into oblivion.

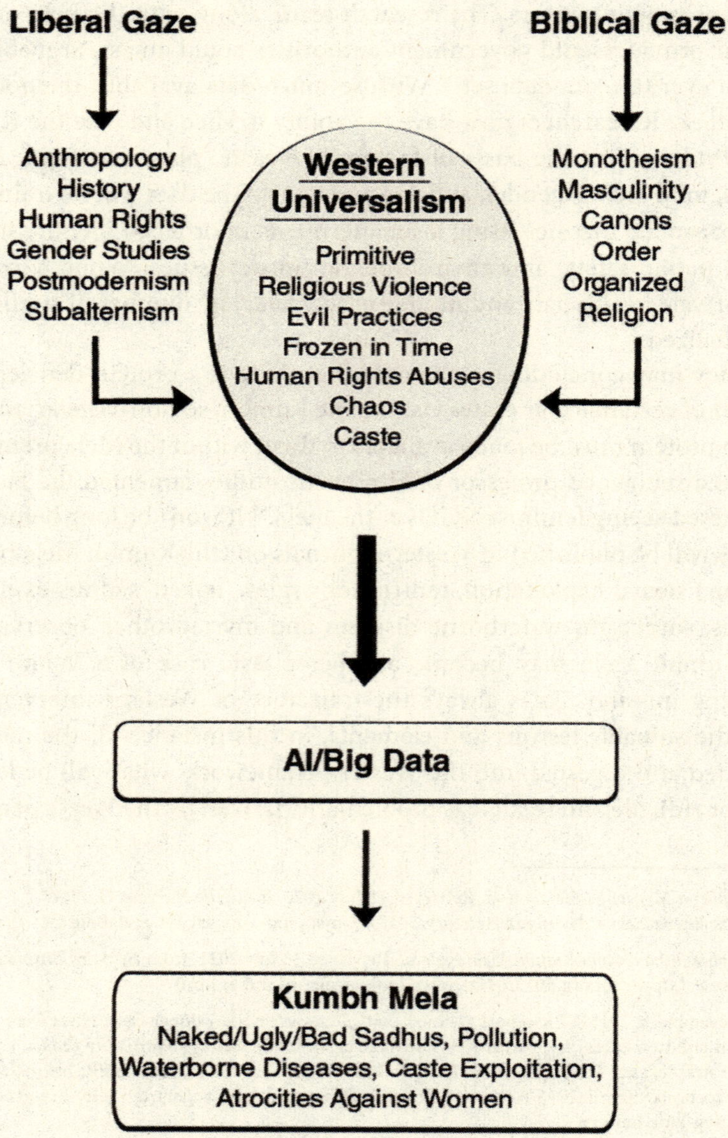

Figure: 1

The Kumbh Mela has already entered the watchlist of the World Health Organization, which predicts that given the millions of people in such close proximity, the potential for disease outbreaks is higher. Therefore, they have taken upon themselves the responsibility to help India oversee the safety of the event, despite the safe and successful track record of the Kumbh Mela for centuries. In fact, there have already been attempts to map the problems of Hajj, a mass Muslim pilgrimage to Mecca, to the Kumbh Mela, despite the stark fundamental differences between the two events.[40]

The Kumbh Mela is a classic example and representation of everything the dharma traditions epitomize: unity in diversity, ability to perform amidst chaos, highly efficient and localized decentralized models, adaptability and flexibility, reverence for the environment and so much more. In fact, it is safe to say that the Kumbh data gives a template to decipher how dharma traditions have thrived for millennia. It only makes sense for Indians to guard and control the Kumbh data more than ever. In an age where 'data is the new oil' and when 'there is no such thing as too much data', it is worth pondering what would happen if the West gained access and control of the Kumbh data. They can build sophisticated models to identify factors that impact the robustness and resilience of Hinduism, and then use those very factors to attack and dismantle Hinduism. Experts and public intellectuals like Rajiv Malhotra have been warning the Indian government to not allow foreign institutions unfettered access to precious social, economic, and genetic Kumbh data, yet the Central as well as state governments do not seem to appreciate the clear and present danger.[41]

Artificial Intelligence and Hinduism

When the Japanese Buddhist robot priest Mindar was deployed at Japan's four-hundred-year-old Kodaiji temple in Kyoto, speculation was rife in AI circles on how AI had now taken over religion too, a domain deemed to be at a crossroads with technology. The chief priest of the temple pointed out that with the phenomenal growth of AI it was only logical for the Buddha to transform into a robot, since it would be immortal and constantly update

40. *The Shortest Route to God.* Retrieved 15 July 2021, from *Slate:* https://slate.com/technology/2014/06/dangers-of-the-hajj-kumbh-mela-and-other-religious-gatherings-fire-mers-disease-drownings-stampedes.html

41. Malhotra, 2021a, pp. 308-10.

its knowledge and evolve.[42] However, 'Mindar' isn't the first religious priest; a sutra-chanting doe-eyed robot named 'Pepper' has been in use in Japan for performing funerals.[43] Inspired by the Japanese Buddhist robotic priest, American theologians and social scientists are clamoring for robotic Christian priests to tackle the issue of male patriarchy and toxic masculinity in the Catholic Church ecosystem, already reeling under numerous sexual abuse scandals. Indian public intellectuals, not wanting to be left behind, wondered if Indians could replicate the Japanese robo-priest by training it with a few basic mantras. However, the bigger challenge they foresaw was the limited acceptability of such AI enabled robo-priests given that it would be difficult to ascertain its caste.[44]

This is precisely the problem in the mainstream discourse which inevitably gravitates to caste, minority, patriarchy and all sorts of Western Universalism categories. Given this pervasive presence of WU, and the Hindu inferiority complex to accept whatever the West does as the gold standard, it is quite possible that in the near future we may have a thriving market for robotic priests. Such robots would not only help eliminate the mythical '*Brahminical patriarchy*' that social justice warriors fear deeply, but perhaps also do away with the Brahmins completely. Why have Brahmins at all when a robot can officiate ceremonies better, faster, and more efficiently?

These examples highlight a major problem of Western Universalism. From the dharmic perspective, enlightenment is not dependent on scriptural authority, or any holy book. Rishis in the dharma traditions, who can belong to any varna and jati, (collapsed wrongly into the idea of caste) do not gain spiritual authority by merely mastering the scriptures passed down by any prophet, but rather by attaining higher states of consciousness adhering to rigorous and well-defined inner processes using a combination of mantras, sadhana or yoga – a concept referred to as 'embodied knowing'.[45] Mantras, an important part of this process, are

42. *Buddhist Temple in Japan Puts Faith in Robot Priest.* Retrieved 15 July 2021, from *The Straits Times:* https://www.straitstimes.com/asia/east-asia/buddhist-temple-in-japan-puts-faith-in-robot-priest

43. *Buddhism, Robots and Artificial Intelligence, the New Frontier.* Retrieved 15 July 2021, from *The Washington Post:* https://www.washingtonpost.com/technology/2019/08/22/introducing-mindar-robotic-priest-that-some-are-calling-frankenstein-monster/

44. *The Enlightened One.* Retrieved 15 July 2021, from *The Indian Express:* https://indianexpress.com/article/opinion/editorials/artificial-intelligence-android-priest-japan-the-enlightened-one-kannon-religion-5911242/

45. Malhotra, 2013, p. 70.

believed to have a profound and transformative impact on the doer due to the well-documented vibrational aspect of Sanskrit sounds, and so cannot be considered the equivalent of church sermons. The continued success of dharma traditions has been the ability to produce living spiritual masters across the spectrum of space and time so that they may serve specific communities with customized teachings. Thus, the very idea of training Hindu robo-priests on a mantra data set is ludicrous. While it may be able to mechanically officiate a marriage or a cremation, it will not help one in their journey towards enlightenment or realizing the Truth, a core tenet of almost all Hindu traditions, and a concept alien to Judeo-Christianity. However, the discourse on AI ethics does not consider an automated *yajna* or robotic rishi to be problematic at all. Given the foundational differences between dharma and the Abrahamic traditions, any discussion on the impact of AI and dharma using Western categories is counter-productive to the integrity and sustenance of dharma.

Finally, let us examine a pervasive method whereby Hinduphobic biases potentially can, and in fact do, easily creep into the mainstream discourse – and that is through the use of Wikipedia as a data set for the interpretation of dharma traditions. While the popular belief is that Wikipedia is neutral and universal, the reality is vastly different. There is an increasing consensus that not only does Wikipedia passively reflect biases, it also amplifies and reinforces them. For example, of the first authors of academic works cited on the page for political science in late 2020, only four percent were women. Nearly half of the political scientists with a Wikipedia biography were found to be American, while several countries did not have even a single political scientist with a Wikipedia biography.[46] In other words, there is a pronounced Western Universalist bias in how Wikipedia data sets are constructed, given that Wikipedia's editors have a hierarchy of privileges. Many entries on Hinduism are openly prejudicial, as they rely on Indological studies rooted in colonial era bigotry. Machine learning algorithms relying on such data sets, therefore carry the same biases as Wikipedia. Hinduism studies today is based on frameworks established by scholars, many of whom were non-practitioners and also had vested interests and motives. Consequently, experts from within the Hindu fold find such Indological studies highly biased and problematic,

---

46. *Wikipedia's Political Science Coverage is Biased. I tried to fix it.* Retrieved 15 July 2021, from *The Washington Post:* https://www.washingtonpost.com/politics/2021/02/24/wikipedias-political-science-coverage-is-biased-i-tried-fix-it/

and there are many movements to decolonize this field. 'Thus, whether you use Wikipedia or any Indological work for training an algorithm, the effect can be biased. This can range from outright nonsensical and blatant falsehoods to more subtle and nuanced prejudices'.[47]

We hope that with the fair representation of dharma in the space of AI and ethics, these issues can efficiently be addressed for a more inclusive and well-rounded discussion.

Conclusion

Artificial Intelligence, like all other technologies, depends on the objectives and methodology of its use to obtain the desired outcome. India, as a society, is already weighed down with social constructs imported from the West, and in an age where software systems are hailed for neutrality, precision and efficient decision-making capabilities, AI systems become a convenient framework to legitimize Western Universalist constructs. For instance, a hypothetical AI-enabled social justice system might insist on more diverse 'caste representation' in the Sabarimala pilgrimage (a pilgrimage to a temple in Kerala dedicated to Lord Ayyappa) under the guise of social inclusiveness and in line with an imagined diversity standard. Social scientists can mine socio-economic data of certain demographic groups and assert that Indian Christian converts have a better standard of living, and then Church-based AI systems trained on such data can 'predict' how conversion to Christianity would benefit Hindus. In fact, given the deep-seated biases embedded in Western AI models today, and India's penchant for imitating the West, it is quite possible that Indians start imbibing well-documented Western evils like racism, gender discrimination, unbridled consumerism, and ecological indifference. Adopting a 'them-and-us psychology' premised on Abrahamic ideas like 'chosen people', will only result in social conflict and prove devastating to India's civilizational unity and growth.

Yet, Indians continue to engage with Western corporations and share valuable sensitive data. Recently, the Indian government collaborated with Microsoft under its initiative 'AI for Good' to tackle 'human-rights' issues in India. Beneath all the 'AI for good' rhetoric, of course lies the unstated, but self-evident, agenda on how AI can become an effective tool

47. Malhotra, 2021b, p. 4.

for propagating Western Universalism, especially in a country like India where the educated elites have a habit of importing the latest Western lenses as a way to identify with Westernization.[48] As we progress in the realm of technological advancement, Western Universalism embedded in AI models will only get amplified leaving little room for any course correction, unless we proactively take charge of our data and also start creating in parallel, data sets modeled on dharmic categories.

Bibliography

Buolamwini, J., & Gebru, T. (2018). Gender Shades: Intersectional Accuracy Disparities in Commercial Gender Classification. *Proceedings of Machine Learning Research, 81*, 1-15. Retrieved from http://proceedings.mlr.press/v81/buolamwini18a/buolamwini18a.pdf

Katz, Y. (2020). *Artificial Whiteness – Politics and Ideology in Artificial Intelligence.* New York: Columbia University Press.

Malhotra, R. (2013). *Being Different: An Indian Challenge To Western Universalism.* New Delhi: HarperCollins.

Malhotra, R. (2021a). *Artificial Intelligence and the Future of Power: 5 Battlegrounds.* New Delhi: Rupa Publications India.

Malhotra, R. (2021b, 8 April). A Dharma Perspective on Artificial Intelligence. *AI and Faith, April 2021 Newsletter.* Retrieved 10 July 2021, from https://www.aiandpower.com/wp-content/uploads/2021/04/AI-and-Faith-April-2021-Newsletter.pdf

Sambasivan, N., Arnesen, E., Hutchinson, B., Doshi, T., & Prabhakaran, V. (2021). Re-imagining Algorithmic Fairness in India and Beyond. *Proceedings of the 2021 ACM Conference on Fairness, Accountability, and Transparency,* 315-328. doi:https://doi.org/10.1145/3442188.3445896

48. Malhotra, 2021a, p. 364.

About the Contributors

Rajiv Malhotra: Rajiv Malhotra was trained initially as a physicist, and then as a computer scientist specializing in Artificial Intelligence in the 1970s. After a successful corporate career in the US, he became an entrepreneur and founded and ran several IT companies in twenty countries. He exited all for-profit activities in the early 1990s. As the founder of his non-profit Infinity Foundation (in Princeton, USA), he has, on a full-time basis, been researching civilizations from a historical, social sciences and mind sciences perspective. He has authored several bestselling books including his recent works *AI and the Battle for Future, Sanskrit Non-Translatables* and *Snakes in the Ganga.*

Lt. Gen. P.J.S. Pannu: Lt. Gen. P.J.S. Pannu, PVSM, AVSM, VSM is former deputy chief of Indian Integrated Defence Staff, who commanded 14 corps (XIV Corps), including in the highest active war zone in the world. He was also the head of the Infantry and of the Maratha Light Infantry Regiment. He has been responsible for initiating the raising of Indian Defence Cyber and Space Agencies as also creating the Special Forces Division. He is a frontline combat officer who has served mostly on the Line of Control facing Pakistan, Line of Actual Control facing China and counter insurgency in the Northeast and Kashmir valley. He is a technology enthusiast and is pursuing a PhD on Indigenization of the Defence Industry. He has had three tenures at the Indian Army's Military Operations Directorate at various levels. He was also responsible for developing doctrines and strategies for the defence forces. He is distinguished fellow of the United Service Institution of India, the oldest think tank of India. He has served as chief of operations in two UN missions in Mozambique and Sudan. He has participated in a number of multinational military exercises in India and abroad.

Velina Tchakarova: Velina Tchakarova is the founder of a geopolitical consulting company FACE in Vienna, Austria, and former director of the Austrian Institute for European and Security Policy. She is an instructor at the Real World Risk Institute led by bestselling author Nassim Taleb and a member of the Strategy and Security Policy Advisory Board of the Scientific Commission at the Federal Ministry of Defense in Austria. She holds an MA in political science and political science of South Asia from the University in Heidelberg, Germany and a BA in international relations from the University of World and National Economy in Sofia, Bulgaria. Currently, she is completing a PhD dissertation at the University of Vienna.

Ruchir Sharma: Ruchir Sharma is an award-winning international civil servant and public policy reformer, who has worked on defense, intelligence, police, and constitutional reform in post-socialist and post-conflict countries in the Balkans, environmental advocacy at the United Nations, the concept of neutrality in foreign policy, and the roots of modern terrorism and extremism. He is also an international affairs commentator in the media, having been quoted in *The New York Times*, and contributing to the *Huffington Post*, *FirstPost*, *Swarajya*, and *Russia Insider*, with a keen interest in European and Indian history and politics, international terrorism, and the BRICS (Brazil-Russia-India-China-South Africa).

Ishwara Bhat A.: Ishwara Bhat is an entrepreneur and consultant in Artificial Intelligence. He is a co-founder of Manomaya AI Systems which is into behavioral AI products and services. He has five patents filed in AI-related to human behavioral sciences. He also consults and architects AI applications in engineering domains. He has worked on autonomous driving vision systems where he led several critical parts of the AI system.

Other than this, over a career spanning nearly two and a half decades, he led many systems programs in global companies Honeywell, Bosch and Infosys. He led the development of products ranging from sensors, control networks, wireless systems and distributed server technologies. He has expertise in a variety of industry verticals: semiconductors, oil and gas, power, smart cities and smart buildings. He has global product leadership experience from all major economies and continents.

Dr Mrittunjoy Guha Majumdar: Dr Mrittunjoy Guha Majumdar is a postdoctoral fellow at Harvard University, working in statistical thermodynamics. He has been a senior postdoctoral researcher at the Centre for Excellence in Quantum Technology, Indian Institute of Science, Bengaluru and a postdoctoral associate of Prof. Brian Josephson (Nobel Laureate, 1973) at Cambridge University. He completed his PhD from Cambridge University in 2019, at the age of twenty-five. Lately, he has been working in the area of hyperentanglement, particularly around quantum-walk-driven hyperentanglement as well as hyper-conditional gates, with possible applications for cluster states and quantum networks. He has previously worked in IIT Guwahati, PRL Ahmedabad, IISER Kolkata, USIC-DU as well as SSPL (Government of India) in research stints. He has taught at Cambridge University and Delhi University as well as worked on science popularization, with a recent talk on Quantum Mechanics aired on *Doordarshan*. He has been involved in science policy, having worked with Cambridge University Science Policy and Exchange and the Government of India (on competency-based learning of science in India). He was showcased by UNESCO in 2018 in its international convention on higher education and also led the drafting of the position paper on youth advocacy and leadership in scientific, social and cultural realms in 2022. He initiated and convenes Mandala, a wing of Vijnana Bharati, under the guidance of Shri Jayant Sahasrabuddheji. He was a 35 under 35 UK India Young Leader 2018 and a four-time elected student leader of Cambridge University. Dr Majumdar is a fellow of the Infinity Foundation and has organized a number of interactions and events for the Foundation.

Ravi Khanna: Ravi Khanna is a businessman and a Vedic scholar. He pursued B.Sc. Physics (Hons) at St. Stephen's College, Delhi. He completed his B.S. and M.S. in Electrical Engineering from Madison, University of Wisconsin, USA with specialization in Solid State Physics. Having returned to India in 1978, while conducting the family business, he has been carrying on an intense self-study in Metaphysics and the *Upanishads*. From 1995 he took to consolidating his studies in Vedas and Science under the guidance of Prof. Dr Kapil Kapoor, JNU, New Delhi. He has published various articles on the *Upanishads*, *Shiv Sutras* and *Lotus Sutra* and has researched some of their deeper connections with consciousness and cosmology in terms of Western science.

Subhodeep Mukhopadhyay: Subhodeep Mukhopadhyay is a civilization studies researcher whose writings on culture, economics and philosophy have appeared in newspapers, magazines and academic journals. His scholarly contributions have provided insights on the social impact of technology and on *dharma*-religion encounters. He is editor of the Intellectual Kshatriya research platform and serves as a Trustee for Infinity Foundation India. Subhodeep is a student of Sanskrit and Vedanta in the traditional mode and a recipient of the Foundation for Indian Civilization Studies award 2017. He is a B.Tech in Computer Engineering, MBA (Finance) and MA in Journalism and Mass Communication. For more information, please visit his website: www.subhodeepmukhopadhyay.com

Divya Reddy: Divya Reddy is an engineer and a post-graduate in management who joined Infinity Foundation India (IFI) as a researcher and host of the 'Youth Asks Series'. At IFI, she is actively involved in consolidating the youth to carry forward the vision and mission of the organization. Her research interests encompass studying ancient Indian history, science, technology, philosophy, and its relevance in the contemporary world. Her writings have appeared on the Intellectual Kshatriya platform of Infinity Foundation.

Acknowledgments

This book is the result of important support from several individuals throughout its development. We would like to begin by thanking the authors for their valuable time and dedication to this project. Each one of them deserves special credit for their in-depth research, attention to detail, and for their selfless effort in ensuring that the essays are of the highest academic standards while also catering to the non-academic segment.

T.N. Sudarshan and Manogna Sastry were responsible for the internal review, editing, and co-ordination with the authors to ensure smooth and efficient completion of the book. They also took overall ownership for the quality of the manuscript till it was turned over to the publisher. Shalini Puthiyedham helped with internal review and provided some valuable feedback. Sanjana Roy Choudhury edited all the essays on a tight schedule with meticulous attention to detail. Mini Narayanan and Prachi Kishore from the BluOne Ink Team helped with detailed reviewing and print cycle of the book.

It is thanks to the combined efforts of the wonderful team at Infinity Foundation India that the book became possible after it was first conceptualized post the response received for *AI and The Future of Power*, the game changing book of Infinity Foundation's mentor, Sri Rajiv Malhotra.

We would like to thank all our donors, supporters, and well-wishers for helping us achieve important milestones in the Dharmakshetra. In particular, the following have helped in important ways: Sashi Kejriwal, Mahesh Krishnamurthy, Laxman Prajapat, Hariharan Raghavan, Shasta Foundation, Prakash Agrawal, Prakash Bhalerao, Vijay Bist, Arjun Bhagat, Sanjay Tripathi, Devendra Singh, Seema Singh, Professor R. Vaidyanathan, Rakesh Mehrotra, Shilpa Memani, Daksh Lohia, and Ratan Sharda.

Index

C

D

N